CLASSIC RAILWAY
JOURNEYS OF THE WORLD

CLASSIC RAILWAY
JOURNEYS OF THE WORLD

AN ILLUSTRATED ATLAS OF BEST-LOVED STEAM
AND RAIL ROUTES AROUND THE GLOBE

Max Wade-Matthews

LORENZ BOOKS

This edition is published by Lorenz Books, an imprint of Anness Publishing Ltd,
Blaby Road, Wigston, Leicestershire LE18 4SE
Email: info@anness.com

Web: www.lorenzbooks.com; www.annesspublishing.com

If you like the images in this book and would like to investigate using them for publishing,
promotions or advertising, please visit our website www.practicalpictures.com for more information.

Publisher: Joanna Lorenz
Projet Editor: Joanne Rippin
Designer: Michael Morey
Cover images: 92½

ETHICAL TRADING POLICY
Because of our ongoing ecological investment programme, you, as our customer, can have the pleasure and
reassurance of knowing that a tree is being cultivated on your behalf to naturally replace the materials used to
make the book you are holding. For further information about this scheme, go to
www.annesspublishing.com/trees

A CIP catalogue record for this book is available from the British Library.

A full list of contributors appears on page 254

Previously published as *The World's Great Railway Journeys*

PUBLISHER'S NOTE
Although the advice and information in this book are believed to be accurate and true at the time of going to press,
neither the authors nor the publisher can accept any legal responsibility or liability for any errors or omissions that
may have been made.

● ABOVE
Several interurban cars gather at East Troy, Wisconsin, USA.

● HALF TITLE PAGE
Boone & Scenic Valley's Mikado takes on water on a hot June day, Iowa, USA.

● FRONTISPIECE
**Part of the coastal section of the London Paddington to Penzance line,
England.**

● TITLE PAGE
A black-liveried Baldwin 2-8-0 runs over the viaduct at Alausi.

CONTENTS

● **ABOVE**
No. 4498 Sir Nigel Gresley travelling under a bridge near Ais Gill.

Introduction

If asked what makes a great railway journey, some will say the distance, some the countryside, some the scenery, others will delight in the locomotive that pulls the train, while for others it is the people they meet on the way. All these factors and more have a part to play in the journeys described in this book, which range from the 16 km (10 mile) journey from Leicester to Loughborough that set Thomas Cook on his career, to the journey of the Red Arrow, which travels half-way around the world from Brussels to Hong Kong.

Some of these journeys have been made recently, others are historical accounts of routes that are no longer possible. While it is accepted that the character of a railway journey will change over time, the historical accounts included here are unique snapshots of a railway's life, taken at the height of its popularity or success.

Divided into two sections – Great Journeys of the West, and Great Journeys of the East – the journeys are arranged geographically, from North America to the South Pacific, covering vast stretches of terrain, immense cultural differences and irreconcilable political extremes. What binds them together is the spirit of the railway, a pioneering adventurousness that exists as much now as when those first tracks were laid down all over the world.

● **OPPOSITE**
An InterCity Express heads south on England's
West Coast main line.

● **ABOVE**
Journey's end. Passengers disembark and head for
the exit at a typical English city station.

Great Journeys of the West

This section of the book will take the reader from the thrilling 3,200 km (2,000 mile) trip from Chicago to Oakland in North America to the 27 km (17 mile) jaunt back in time between Bedford and Bletchley in rural Bedfordshire, England. We will ascend the high mountains of Peru and Switzerland; and descend under the English Channel as we travel through one of the wonders of the modern world – the Channel Tunnel.

Rail journeys for pleasure began in the late nineteenth century with growing prosperity and the adoption of the workers' holiday. In many parts of Europe and America are to be found towns that came into prominence in the latter half of the nineteenth century for the simple reason that they had the good fortune to find themselves connected to the growing railway network. Many of the journeys detailed in this section are still in operation; others, however, are now part of history and can only be travelled in the pages of a book such as this.

● OPPOSITE
A summer view of the train from the Look-out in
Agawa Canyon, Ontario, Canada.

● ABOVE
Superliners in Amtrak's Chicago's coach yard.

TORONTO TO VANCOUVER

Only one transcontinental train journey for passengers is still operating across Canada, over a length of 4,467 km (2,776 miles). This is from Toronto to Vancouver by the Canadian National route under the auspices of the VIA Rail Corporation.

The train runs three times a week as the Canadian, a name taken over from Canadian Pacific, which inaugurated it in 1954 with the first streamlined sleeper train in Canada. Three days and three nights are spent by the Canadian on its journey, which is a mixture of tour land-cruise and point-to-point transportation. Passengers in the former category pay quite large sums for superior accommodation and brilliantly restored public rooms and diner.

Although transcontinental trains used to run from Montreal, the starting-point

for the journey today is Toronto, and the route lies by way of Capreol (close to Sudbury, Ontario), then across hundreds of kilometres of pre-Cambrian shield to Sioux Lookout, later winding through the Manitoba Lake District to Winnipeg, 1,958 km (1,217 miles) from Toronto. After a stop of one hour, the Canadian heads west across rolling prairies to Saskatoon, Saskatchewan, and Edmonton, Alberta, before climbing into

● **TOP**
An exterior view of Vancouver's Pacific Central railway station.

● **ABOVE LEFT**
An interior view of one of the Canadian's domed park cars. From these seats, passengers can drink in the full beauty of the diverse Canadian countryside.

● **LEFT**
VIA's Canadian on the tracks of the Canadian Pacific between Montreal and Vancouver.

the foothills of the Rocky Mountains.

Jasper is high amid these mountains,
and here the train halts for 70 minutes
while some of the cars are attached to the
Skeena, which has come from Edmonton
on its way to the Pacific at Prince Rupert.
The main part of the Canadian carries on
through the Rockies, going over Yellow
Head Pass and down to Kamloops. The
final part of the journey is beside the
Fraser River (with the tracks of the
Canadian Pacific Railway on the opposite
bank) down to Vancouver, which is
reached at 08.30 Pacific Time on the
third morning after leaving Toronto.
Inevitably some of the best scenery is
passed at night, but the high points of the
Rockies are viewed in daylight. At one
time, Canada had three transcontinental

routes, which it could not support
economically. These came down to two
when Canadian National was formed
from earlier private systems (Grand
Trunk, Canadian Northern and Grand
Trunk Western). As recently as 1967
there were four transcontinental trains
each day, all from Montreal.

While air competition hurt these
trains, the greatest damage was done by
the completion of the Trans-Canada
highway in 1968, leading to the
reduction in service to just one train
thrice weekly. However, thanks to
support from tour operators in the USA
and particularly Britain and Germany, the
Canadian now seems profitable in its new
dual role as tour train and short-haul
passenger service. For tour passengers,
meals in the refurbished diner, use of the
vista domes, lounges and sleeping cars
newly equipped with showers, are
included in the fare.

● **ABOVE LEFT**
The Canadian leaves Montreal's Windsor
Station on the first part of its journey across
the Canadian continent.

● **LEFT**
The Canadian winds its way through a
background of autumnal colour.

INFORMATION BOX	
Termini	Toronto and Vancouver
Country	Canada
Distance	4,467 km (2,776 miles)
Date of opening	1885

Sault Sainte Marie to Hearst

Running from south to north across Ontario, the Algoma Central & Hudson Bay Railway (ACR) is a private company dating from 1899. The starting-point is Sault Sainte Marie (known as the Soo) at the eastern end of Lake Superior, the world's largest lake. Its main line, 476 km (296 miles) long, ends at Hearst, still more than 240 km (150 miles) from the sub-Arctic bay. It passes through mountains that are the highest in Canada

● **RIGHT**
Part of the train trip is by the shore of the mighty Montreal River.

INFORMATION BOX

Termini	Sault Sainte Marie and Hearst
Country	Canada
Distance	476 km (296 miles)
Date of opening	1899

east of the Rockies. The daily passenger-train threads its way through a landscape of canyons, forests, lakes and fast-flowing rivers. On spring, summer and autumn weekends, this is the longest and busiest passenger-train on the North American continent.

The great train runs as an excursion because so many people want to visit Agawa Canyon in the heart of Algoma Country. While about three cars continue to Hearst, another 18 to 20, including the restaurant cars and one diesel

locomotive, are uncoupled and stay on the floor of the canyon for about two hours. Hikers and picnickers can enjoy the area until the southbound train from Hearst arrives to join up the heavy load, hook on the waiting diesel and run back to the Soo, 183 km (114 miles) to the south. Originally the railway was built for iron-ore traffic coming from the Helen Mine near Michipicetin, to which a branch was extended, while the main route to Hearst sought to carry general freight, especially lumber.

● **LEFT**
During the autumn, Algoma Central County is ablaze with colour. Here is an autumnal shot of the Agawa Canyon train tour crossing the Montreal River by a trestle bridge.

● **RIGHT**

● **RIGHT**
The train snakes
through the
autumnal beauty of
the Agawa Canyon.

● **BELOW**
● **BELOW**
As well as travelling in the public coaches,
passengers can also hire their own car. Here is
one of the private cars – "Michipicoton" –
which was built by Pullman of Chicago in 1910.

● **BELOW RIGHT**
The train also runs in
winter, the warmth of
the coaches keeping
the ice and sub-zero
temperatures at bay.
Here we see it making
its way through the
deep snow.

spectacular trestle affords stupendous
views. There is a twisting climb to
Hubert, 461 m (1,512 ft) above sea level
and the summit of the line.

While the section to Agawa Canyon
carries holidaymakers *en masse*, the
northern part of the line numbers big
game hunters and fishermen among its
customers. In the autumn, when foliage
colours are fantastic, and moose and deer
are "in season", the train, which stops on
flag request along the way, is called the
Moose Meat Special.

The Algoma Central possesses 25
diesel locomotives painted in maroon,
cream and grey, while the passenger cars
are in a very attractive maroon.

Although it is allied to the Algoma
Steel Corporation, the railway is a
separate entity and enjoys steady
profitability. A large proportion of
Algoma Central's profit comes from its
well-advertised passenger service. It is
not unusual for 1,200 to 1,500
passengers to ride to Agawa Canyon on a
summer Sunday, paying about $30
Canadian (£14) each for the excursion.

It helps that there are no roads
competing with the railway, except at
Hawk Junction, 265 km (165 miles)
from the Soo. The line's isolation is
interrupted at two points: Franz, where
there is a junction with Canadian
Pacific's main line (now freight only), and
Oba, where the Canadian National
crosses it. Both are hamlets, and only at
Oba, a flag stop, can a change be made
for passengers when VIA's Canadian
comes through three times a week.

Great rivers are crossed on fine trestle
bridges, including those over the Goulais,
South and North Chippewa, and the
Batchewana. The biggest of these crosses
the Montreal River at Milepost 93. This

VANCOUVER TO SQUAMISH

The route from North Vancouver to
Squamish is on the British Columbia
Railway (known as BC Rail or BCR),
which is primarily a freight railway. The
section travelled is, at 61 km (38 miles),
only a small fraction of the company's
network, which totals over 2,172 km
(1,350 miles). Passenger services are
limited to a daily service each way
between North Vancouver, Lillooet and
Prince George. The train named the
Cariboo Prospector, takes 13 ½ hours to
travel 745 km (463 miles). In addition,
there is a school train between Seton
Portage and Lillooet. In the summer
months, there are two tourist-oriented
services: a weekday service north from
Whistler and the Royal Hudson service
described here.

The BCR, which was called the Pacific
Great Eastern Railway until 1972,
connects to the Canadian National railway
(CN) and so to the rest of the Canadian
rail network at North Vancouver Junction.
There is also a connection to the
Vancouver Wharves Railway, which, as its
name implies, serves the port area.

The section of line from Squamish to
Vancouver only opened in 1956, quite a

● **LEFT**
The Royal Hudson
train, soon after
departure from
North Vancouver,
seen from Prospect
Point. Lions Gate
Bridge is just out of
sight to the right.

● **LEFT**
BCR diesels 4642+762+4615 at the north end
of Squamish yard waiting to depart on a
northbound freight. No. 4642 is a 4400 HP
General Electric DASH 9 built in 1995; 762 is a
3000 HP General Motors SD40 of 1980; 4615
is a General Electric 4000 HP DASH 8 of 1990.

INFORMATION BOX

Termini	Vancouver and Squamish
Country	Canada
Distance	61 km (38 miles)
Date of opening	1956

● **LEFT**
Shannon Falls seen from the water, a couple of miles south of Squamish.

construction of a 132 km (82 mile) electrified branch (the Tumbler subdivision) in 1983.

The Royal Hudson runs Wednesdays to Sundays from June to September and takes two hours for the northbound trip. The train is named after the class of steam locomotive used to haul it, a type which were built by the Montreal Locomotive Works in 1939 for the Canadian Pacific Railway. Hudson is the name for the locomotive's wheel arrangement, 4-6-4. The Royal prefix comes from the occasion when one of the class (No. 2850) was used to haul the royal train during a visit of King George VI and Queen Elizabeth to Canada in 1939. Upon withdrawal, 2860 became the property of the British Columbia

while after the railway reached Squamish from the north. This was because the railway's main purpose was to link the logging and mining areas with the sea, and there are port facilities at Squamish for large bulk carriers. The BCR has expanded relatively recently, with the

● **BELOW**
Royal Hudson No. 2860 passing Porteau Cove in June 1996. The road, known as the Sea to Sky Highway, runs close to the line for most of the way from Horseshoe Bay to Squamish and provides several excellent photographic opportunities.

Government, who currently lease it to
BCR. In addition, BCR leases the 2-8-0
3716, built by MLW in 1912 for
Canadian Pacific, as a reserve for these
trains. Locomotive No. 2860 is
resplendent in polished maroon and
black, with a polished, unpainted metal-
clad boiler and firebox, and royal crowns
on each side above the cylinders.

The journey starts from BCR's North
Vancouver station (depot). Adjacent to
the station is the small shed used to store
and maintain the steam locomotives.
Across the tracks, there are extensive
freight-yards and a diesel locomotive
depot. The train is made up of 12
coaches, mostly ex-CN stock of 1954,
painted Tuscan Red. In the middle is an
open-sided observation coach named
Britannia, which was built in 1920.
In June 1996 the weather was too
chilly for all but the hardiest of
passengers! The last vehicle is a parlour
car, called Mount Cascade, which can be
used on payment of around twice the
normal fare.

The train leaves the station slowly,
heads west and passes the freight-yards.
At the end of these, it passes under the
approaches to Lions Gate Bridge. This
was reputedly built with money from the
Guinness brewing family to help in
opening up the north shore, where they
owned land. An excellent photographic
location is the viewing area at Prospect
Point on the Stanley Park Drive on the
opposite bank, close to the bridge. The
line keeps a short way from the waters of
English Bay as it passes through
residential areas and skirts Ambleside
Beach. It then passes through the
1,280 m (4,200 ft) Horseshoe Bay
tunnel, cutting off the "corner". Leaving
the tunnel, the train heads north for the
remainder of the journey. Just visible is
the Horseshoe Bay ferry terminal, used
by car ferries to Vancouver Island. Soon
after this, the railway comes back down
to the water's edge and rarely leaves it
before reaching Squamish. Across the
Sound there are views of great forests and
snow-capped peaks.

The line, while curving considerably,
is largely flat with only short gradients.
The highest point is in Horseshoe Bay
tunnel, 51 m (167 ft) above sea level,
around 16 km (10 miles) out. Between
North Vancouver and Squamish, there
are passing-points at Brunswick, Porteau
and Britannia.

● **LEFT**
A BCR track patrol vehicle passing Porteau Cove. This precedes the Royal Hudson by around five minutes to ensure that the line is free from such obstructions as fallen rocks.

downtown area, away from the main line. Squamish is home to the BCR workshops and main locomotive depot, and has a large area of sidings. It is also the home of the West Coast Railway Heritage Museum, which is by the north exit to the yards, a couple of kilometres from where the Royal Hudson stops. For those interested, there is a bookable add-on coach excursion to visit the museum during the Royal Hudson's layover.

At Porteau, the railway skirts a small bay in which some old ships have been scuttled to provide interest for divers. Porteau is also one of the best photographic locations. Eight kilometres (5 miles) further on, at Britannia Beach, there is the British Columbia Museum of Mining, at what was the largest copper producer in the British Empire. The scar on the scenery caused by the mine is visible from a considerable distance.

At Squamish, the Royal Hudson is reversed on to a siding adjacent to the

The town of Squamish, population around 12,000, is not a tourist destination. However, it is a regional centre with a wide range of small shops and pleasant restaurants. The town is overshadowed by towering, rocky hills, those to the east being part of Garibaldi Provincial Park, the 816 m (2,677 ft) Mount Garibaldi being around 19 km (12 miles) to the north. The valley of the Cheakamus River, which drains into Howe Sound at Squamish, heads north to Whistler amid increasingly mountainous scenery.

● **ABOVE RIGHT**
BCR Budd diesel railcar BC-33, built in 1957, at BCR's North Vancouver station soon after arrival on the southbound Cariboo Prospector.

● **RIGHT**
The lighthouse at the confluence of Howe Sound and English Bay, with the skyline of downtown Vancouver in the background.

WHITEHORSE TO SKAGWAY

The White Pass and Yukon Railway has had a chequered history. That history, however, is an integral part of the story of this exciting land, just as much as that of the great Canadian Pacific, and riding this down-to-earth line is one of northern Canada's great experiences.

The 117 km (72 mile) narrow-gauge railway connects Yukon's capital, Whitehorse, to the historic port of Skagway and the coastal shipping that calls there. In doing so the line passes through the territory of Yukon, British Columbia and Alaska. It was constructed to transport thousands of gold seekers and their supplies from Skagway through the coastal mountains to the beginning of the river route to the Klondike gold fields. Work began in May 1898, and the railway's last spike was driven at Carcross on 29 July 1900, the conclusion of 26 months of blasting, chipping, shovelling and hardship suffered by construction crews whose number fluctuated from 700 to 2,000. A narrow, moss-filled

INFORMATION BOX

Termini	Whitehorse and Skagway
Country	Canada
Distance	177 km (110 miles)
Date of opening	1900

● **ABOVE LEFT**
A photograph of the interior of the passengers' parlour car.

● **LEFT**
A view of the line stretching into the horizon.

● **BELOW LEFT**
A train passing through woodland on the descent to Skagway.

ledge beside the track, marked by a stone inscription, is a mute reminder of the trudging steps of the thousands of men and women who succumbed to the lure of gold.

When the gold rush died away, the Yukon population dwindled; and during the dark days of the 1930s, the trains operated only once a week, but the steam locomotives and the rotary ploughs kept the line open. Afterwards the line was used by tourists as well as for the transportation of ore; when some of the vintage parlour cars of 1883 were still in use. They made strange bedfellows with the heavy steel mineral wagons and multiple diesel locomotives that formed the rest of the trains. Then it became a goods-only line for a period. Today, only

the route between Skagway and the half-way point of Bennet is used by tourists, mainly those from cruise ships.

Probably no tunnel in the world was built under greater difficulties than the one that penetrates a perpendicular barrier of rock, which juts out of the mountains like a giant flying buttress some 16 km (10 miles) north of Skagway. A short distance from the summit of the pass, a deep canyon is spanned by a steel cantilever bridge, 66 m (219 ft) from the creek's bed. Below, in Dead Horse Gulch, winds the old White Pass Trail, worn into the native rock by thousands of Sourdough boots. To improve the grade and curvature of the railway, both bridge and tunnel were replaced in 1969, but the originals still stand. From sea level at Skagway, the line climbs to the summit of the pass, 879 m (2,883 ft), in 34 km (21 miles). The highest point of the line is Log Cabin, BC, which is at an altitude of 889 m (2,917 ft).

From terminal to terminal, the journey takes about eight hours, and the views of the mountains and lakes are superb. Just 64 km (40 miles) from Skagway is a frame building called the Bennet Eating House, where trains from both directions used to meet. Here passengers descend to sit down to a lunch, included in the ticket, of stew, beans, sourdough bread and apple pie.

THE SAN FRANCISCO MUNI

● RIGHT
A Muni herald.

San Francisco is one of America's most scenic and most compact cities, and it is famous for its eclectic flavour and wonderful weather. The San Francisco Municipal Railway – better known as just the Muni – operates the city transit system, an integrated network of buses, electric buses (trolley coach), light rail, light-rail subway (Muni Metro) and the world-famous cable-cars. The Muni is one of the best ways to experience the city, and most of San Francisco is within a four-block walk of a transit line.

The Muni's cable-car routes are the most interesting rides in the city. The cable-car originated in San Francisco as a way of moving people by rail over its

● ABOVE RIGHT
Muni PCC 1056 is painted in the scheme used by streetcars in Kansas City, Missouri. Like all the cars in regular service on the F-Market line, this PCC came from Philadelphia, Pennsylvania.

exceptionally steep hills. There were many different routes operated by several companies. While other American cities also operated cable-cars, including New York City, Chicago and Seattle, today only San Francisco's remain. The three cable-car routes are a big tourist attraction, and at the peak tourist season it is not unusual to wait an hour or so to ride. The Powell & Hyde line is the most interesting line and the most popular. Both the Powell & Hyde and Powell & Mason routes begin at the corner of Market and Powell Streets near the downtown area. The Powell & Hyde line runs to Fishermans Wharf, passing through Chinatown and over both Russian Hill and Nob Hill. The best time to ride the cable-cars is on an early weekday morning in the winter. While you'll need a warm jacket, you might find yourself the only rider on the car! A vastly more attractive prospect than fighting the summer noontime hoards. The cable-cars are a very pleasant way to view the city, and are fun to ride.

The Muni operates six light-rail lines, five of which use modern equipment and feed into the Muni Metro subway downtown. The remaining route is the F-Market line, which runs from the Transbay bus terminal downtown along Market Street to Castro using historic PCC (President Conference Committee)

● RIGHT
A Boeing-Vertol LRV pops out of the Muni Metro on to Duboce Street. This J-Church car will take the turn on to Church. N-Judah cars also use this portal, but continue due west on Duboce up into the Sunset Tunnel and then to the Pacific Ocean.

INFORMATION BOX	
Terminus	San Francisco
Country	USA
Distance	48 km (30 miles)
Date of opening	1873

● **LEFT**
San Francisco's extraordinarily steep hills are the reason for the cable-cars: no conventional form of transport could negotiate these grades successfully. A Powell & Mason car rolls past the San Francisco Academy of Art on Powell Street in downtown San Francisco.

● **ABOVE**
Interior of a rebuilt PCC used on the F-Market line.

● **BELOW**
The San Francisco skyline at sunrise.

30th Street. Some cars turn back here, while others continue to Balboa Park via San José Avenue on a new line opened in the early 1990s. At present the Muni has a fleet of ageing Boeing-Vertol light-rail vehicles – an unsuccessful design used only in San Francisco and Boston – but it has a fleet of new Breda LRVs on order.

cars. In the early 1990s the Muni acquired secondhand PCCs from Philadelphia, had them rebuilt and painted each one differently. Each car wears the colour scheme of an American city transit system that once ran PCCs. One car is painted for Boston, another for Kansas City, etc. These cars entered regular revenue service on the F-Market route in 1995. The differently coloured cars make quite a spectacle coming up the street and are well worth riding.

Of the five light-rail lines operating into the Muni Metro, the J-Church line is the most interesting. It leaves the subway at Duboce and Church Streets, then follows Church for several blocks before winding up a steep grade on a private right of way through Dolores Park, which offers a spectacular view of the San Francisco skyline. The line rejoins Church after cresting the hill and runs to

CHICAGO TO SEATTLE
THE EMPIRE BUILDER

James J. Hill was a giant of American railroading. Small in stature, one-eyed and bearded, he was described by the legendary Lucius Beebe as piratical. By 1901 he was in control of three railroads, which served the then wilderness of the Pacific Northwest: the Great Northern, the Northern Pacific and the Burlington. These became known as the Hill Railroads. His crack train was the Oriental Limited, which ran from

Chicago and the Twin Cities (Minneapolis-St Paul) to Seattle, where his own steamships linked the Pacific North-west to Japan and China. Much later, in 1929, when the Asiatic connection had faded, a splendid transcontinental train was named for him as the Empire Builder.

The Great Northern Railway worked as a separate entity to the Northern Pacific Railway, which also served Seattle

from the Twin Cities. But by 1971, with the coming of the quasi-nationalized Federal Corporation AMTRAK, only the Great Northern route – closest to the Canadian border – carried a passenger-train. This is still called the Empire Builder and is arguably the finest transcontinental ride in the States.

Since 1980, the train has been composed of the latest "superliner" equipment with day coaches, diner, sightseeing lounge and sleeping cars, all 5.2 m (17 ft) above track level. The first 687 km (427 miles) from Chicago to St Paul are over the Burlington. From St

● **RIGHT**
A view from the
Empire Builder as it
heads through
Flathead River
Indian Reservation,
Montana.

● **OPPOSITE
FAR LEFT**
Amtrak's eastbound
Empire Builder
passes through
Grizzley, Montana,
against a backdrop
of the Rocky
Mountains.

● **OPPOSITE
LEFT**
An Amtrak
Superliner coach,
part of the Empire
Builder at Chicago
Union Station.

● **BELOW**
Amtrak's eastbound Empire Builder
approaches its station stop at Columbus,
Wisconsin.

Paul it is 2,888 km (1,795 miles) to
Seattle, making a total journey of 3,575
km (2,222 miles).

From the start at Chicago's Union
Station there is a smart run to
Milwaukee, beer capital of America.
Then the train follows the Mississippi
River almost all the way to the Twin
Cities, with enchanting daylight views of
the great river on its upper reaches. The
really wide open spaces begin soon after
Minneapolis. In the small hours of the
first night, there is a stop at Fargo, the
town where the firm of Wells-Fargo –
the forerunner of today's American
Express – was founded. Next morning
the train passes Rugby, a flag-stop, where
there is an obelisk outside the station
marking the exact centre of the North
American continent.

After passing over yet more plains,
through Glasgow and Havre, the train
reaches Browning, Montana, where the
Rocky Mountains begin in dramatic style.

As the train climbs, passengers see to the
north a 2,500 m (8,000 ft) mountain
known as Triple Peak Divide, from which
the melting snows run off to three oceans
– the Atlantic, Pacific and Arctic. The
Empire Builder proceeds through the
scenic wonderland of Glacier National
Park, crossing the Continental Divide at
Marais Pass, which, at 1,596 m (5,236 ft),
is the lowest summit of any rail route

through the Rockies. James Hill sent a
surveyor called John Paul Stevens to find
out if this legendary low pass really
existed. Travelling alone, the first white
man to enter the region, he found it in
bitter winter weather. A statue of Stevens
may be seen on the right-hand side of the
train going west.

There are more mountains and river
scenery to Spokane, "Capital of the
Inland Empire", where the Portland,
Oregon, portion is detached. On the way
to Seattle, the main train passes through
the 12.5 km (7 3/4 mile) long bore of
Cascade Tunnel – the longest in the
Western Hemisphere – which was
opened in 1929. Breakfasting passengers
experience the train winding down from
Washington's Cascade Mountains and are
often treated to views of elk and deer on
the final stretch towards Seattle.

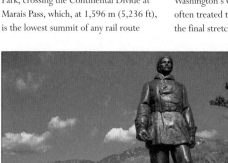

● **LEFT**
Marais Summit on the
former Great
Northern main-line in
northern Montana
hosts Amtrak's Empire
Builder and 30 to 40
daily Burlington
Northern Santa Fe
freight-trains. The
larger-than-life statue
is of John P. Stevens,
the man who surveyed
the line in the late
19th century.

PUEBLO TO DURANGO
THE SAN JUAN EXPRESS

● **BELOW**
A 16mm "fisheye" view of C&T Class K36
No. 487 with passenger-train behind at
Chama, New Mexico.

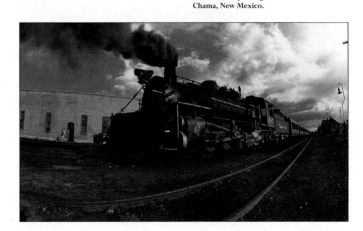

The Denver and Rio Grande Railroad
had the largest 36 in gauge system in the
United States and even operated a
sleeping-car and dining-car train over a
534 km (332 mile) route as the San Juan
Express. This ran until the beginning of
the 1950s from Pueblo, Colorado, via
Alamosa, Colorado, and through
northern New Mexico to Durango,
south-western Colorado.

Some of this track remains and is
operated by steam-trains over two
sections – the 72 km (45 mile) Durango
to Silverton, and the 103 km (64 mile)
Antonito to Chama, New Mexico. The
former line was run for many years as a
tourist route by the Rio Grande before
passing into private hands, and has
become the foremost preserved line in
America, with patronage from the public
increasing year by year. The Antonito to

Chama line is a joint undertaking of the
states of New Mexico and Colorado,
leased to Kyle Railways.

A useful fleet of 2-8-2 locomotives
survived the sad time when diesel engines

replaced steam all over the nation, and
nine splendid steam engines in sound
order work the lines. The coaching stock
on the Durango-Silverton line is partly
original, while the Chama-Antonito line

● **RIGHT**
C&T Class K36 No.
484 descends the
4:100 gradient on
Cumbres Pass.

● **OPPOSITE
BOTTOM**
C&T K36 No. 484
near the summit of
Cumbres Pass
during a September
thunder shower.

● **BELOW
RIGHT**
A C&T passenger-
train at the summit
of Cumbres Pass.

level. From the train windows in this area, one can look down to see a cattle drive, with horsemen and countless steers, moving through a valley, looking no bigger than ants.

Durango is over 1,800 m (6,000 ft) up, and the line to Silverton climbs all the way through the San Juan mountains, at its most spectacular in the Animas Canyon, to reach nearly 2,750 m (9,000 ft) at the chilly old silver-mining town (which is how Silverton got its name). The train journey to Silverton takes about 3 1/2 hours through the wilderness. The train waits at Silverton for 2 1/4 hours before returning downhill to Durango in about 15 minutes faster.

On the Cumbres and Toltec trip, some 6 1/2 hours are spent travelling one way, including a picnic lunch stop at Osier near the summit. Both for this open-air venue and for travel in gondola cars, passengers must wrap up warmly, even in summer. The westbound train is called Colorado Limited, and the eastbound is called New Mexico Express. Return trips are made by buses the same day or the next day by train.

uses converted boxcars. As many as three trains each way daily are run on the Silverton line in peak season, with one a day at other times of the year, apart from around Thanksgiving in November to the New Year when there is no service, apart from one holiday train, until the spring snow melts. There is a daily train over the Chama-Antonito line from mid-May to mid-October.

This is high-country railroading. The Chama-Antonito line, whose proper title is the Cumbres and Toltec Scenic Railroad, climbs over the Cumbres Pass to reach 3,055 m (10,022 ft) above sea

INFORMATION BOX

THE SAN JUAN EXPRESS

Termini	Pueblo and Durango
Country	USA
Distance	534 km (332 miles)
Date of opening	1876

MANITOU SPRINGS TO PIKE'S PEAK

In 1806, Army Lieutenant Zebulan M. Pike, a United States military surveyor, came across a dramatic Rocky Mountain peak in what was then unknown Colorado Territory. He never climbed it but "established" the height at 5,500 m (18,000 ft). Ten years later an army team did climb to the summit, which was found to be 4,300 m (14,110 ft). Seventy-five years later, a steam railway wound its way up with the aid of a cog.

Cog railways were an American invention, the first being the White Mountain Line up to the summit of Mount Washington in New Hampshire – a mere 2,134 m (7,000 ft), but the windiest place on earth. The Swiss engineer Niklaus Riggenbach was an apprentice during the construction in 1866. All trains up this pioneer cog line are still steam powered.

On the Pike's Peak climb, a steam locomotive pushed a car upwards, and remained in operation from the 1891 opening until final retirement in September 1958. From 1938 onwards, though, some of the climbs were shared with a curious petrol-powered (gasoline-powered) railcar, which only carried 24

INFORMATION BOX

Termini	Manitou Springs and Pike's Peak
Country	USA
Distance	14.3 km (8.9 miles)
Date of opening	1891

passengers compared to 50 aboard the steam car. Since 1964, Swiss-built diesel-electric units (each carrying 80 passengers) have been in use, at first two of them, but later joined by two more from the Winterthur builders. In 1973, the Swiss works produced two diesel-electric sets – the first articulated ones to be used on a cog railway. They carry 216 passengers, and the volume of traffic on a clear summer's day is shown by the fact that sometimes as many as 16 trains are run. The round trip is just under four hours and trains operate, subject to visibility, from May to October.

The Manitou and Pike's Peak Railway is standard gauge, starting from the resort town of Manitou Springs, at the mouth of Englemann Canyon, through which the cog railway begins its journey. The old Colorado Midland railway used to bring passengers close to the cog line's depot, but today they come by bus. In early days, there was also an interurban tramway from Colorado Springs.

Passengers bound for the summit see the retired old Baldwin Tank No. 5. All

● **LEFT**
Swiss units at Manitou Springs, the bottom
terminus of the railway.

4,300 m (14,110 ft) above sea level. This
is a desolate spot with limited shelter, and
it is the highest point reached by rail on
the North American continent. Exactly
14.3 km (8.9 miles) from the Manitou
Springs depot, the views on a clear day are
described by the cog company as "showing
the grandest scenery on the Globe".

The stopover is usually 40 minutes, by
which time the chilled and breathless
passengers, satiated with views that take
in Denver, 113 km (70 miles) away, and
most of the 30 Colorado Rockies' peaks,
which are higher than Pike's, must return
to the train. In August 1911, a man and
his wife failed to return, having taken a
short walk, inadequately clad. They were
found frozen to death.

the other steam engines have been saved
and dispersed to museums. At 2,003 m
(6,571 ft), the start is already quite high,
but on its way through the canyon the
gradient increases to 1:4, and at the first
station, Minnehaha, the line reaches
2,540 m (8,332 ft). Then comes Son-of-
a-Gun Hill, also at 1:4, to Halfway
House. Passing through Lion Gulch on
easier gradients, the railway attains the
3,048 m (10,000 ft) mark at Mountain
View, where a dramatic panorama unfolds.

The climb continues, twisting and
turning, past Grecian Bend, Big Hill and
Windy Point to reach Summit House,

● **ABOVE**
A train waits at the
summit of Pike's
Peak. Train services
operate from May
(depending on snow
conditions) to late
October.

● **LEFT**
Pike's Peak summit
terminus, which is
4,300 m (14,110 ft)
above sea level.

St Albans, Vermont, to Washington DC
The Vermonter

Vermont is among the most beautiful and pastoral regions in the eastern United States. It is bordered on the east by New Hampshire and on the west by New York State. It is known for its dairy farms, its maple syrup and its ski resorts. Following the discontinuance of the nocturnal Montrealer in 1995, a train that had run between Washington DC and Montreal, Quebec, Amtrak began operating a daylight train between Washington and St Albans, Vermont. Appropriately named the Vermonter, the train is funded by the state, and it is one of the most popular new trains in the north-eastern United States. It features a distinctive baggage car carrying the name of the train, and stops at rural towns in Massachusetts, New Hampshire and Vermont. Without the train, these communities would have no public transport.

Between St Albans, Vermont, and Palmer, Massachusetts, the Vermonter operates over the New England Central, a short-line railroad run by RailTex, a large short-line operator based in Texas. The New England Central began operations in February 1995, only a few months before the Vermonter, on trackage that

● **LEFT**
On a cold winter's day, the Vermonter crosses the Quaboag River on the old Boston & Albany line. The Vermonter uses a short stretch of the old B&A between Palmer and Springfield, Massachusetts. A specially painted baggage car makes Amtrak's Vermonter particularly distinctive.

● **ABOVE**
The Vermonter pauses at Amherst, Massachusetts, on a sunny Sunday afternoon.

● **BELOW**
The southbound Vermonter approaches the short, narrow tunnel at Bellows Falls, Vermont.

was formerly operated by the Canadian National through its Central Vermont subsidiary. The Vermonter has the distinction of being one of the few daily Amtrak trains to operate over a short-line freight railroad (as opposed to a larger Class I railroad), and one of the few Amtrak trains to operate in "dark territory" – a section of track not protected by automatic block signals. This is not to say operations are casual or haphazard: a strict system of track occupancy authority is in place. The Vermonter safely shares the tracks with New England Central's couple of daily freights.

South of Palmer, the Vermonter operates to Springfield over Conrail's busy Boston Line – a route used by several

INFORMATION BOX	
The Vermonter	
Termini	St Albans, Vermont, and Washington DC
Country	USA
Distance	975 km (606 miles)
Date of opening	1995

● RIGHT
The Vermonter,
Amtrak train No. 56,
runs swiftly along
the Connecticut
River backwater
near Vernon,
Vermont.

● BELOW LEFT
On New Year's Day
1997, the
southbound
Vermonter crosses
the high bridge at
Millers Falls,
Massachusetts.

● BELOW
RIGHT
On a crisp clear
October afternoon,
the Vermonter
approaches
Amherst,
Massachusetts.

other Amtrak trains. From Springfield to New Haven, it uses the Springfield Branch of the North-east Corridor, and then follows the main stem of the Corridor – Amtrak's most travelled route – all the way to Washington. However, the most interesting section of the trip is the New England Central portion. The train stops in Amherst, Massachusetts, a small college town, and once the home of the famous poet Emily Dickinson. In Vermont, the train serves Brattleboro, Bellows Falls, Windsor, White River Junction, Randolph, Montpelier, Waterbury, Essex

Junction and St Albans. Bellows Falls is the site of a short tunnel, which passes directly below the town centre.

In the summer and early autumn, the Bellows Falls station is shared with the privately operated Green Mountain passenger-train which carries sightseers on a round trip to Chester, Vermont. Between Bellows Falls and Windsor, the tracks cross over the Connecticut River into New Hampshire, and the train stops at Claremont – currently the only point in the Granite State served by a passenger-train. From the train, passengers can see

Mt Ascutney, one of the tallest mountains in Vermont, and wooden-covered bridges, for which the region is famous.

The northbound train, No. 56, departs Washington in the early morning and arrives in St Albans in the evening, while the southbound train, No. 55, features the same schedule but in reverse. It arrives in Washington about the same time as its counterpart arrives in St Albans. The Vermonter requires reservations. Amtrak revises its schedules every six months, and prospective passengers should consult the carrier before riding.

BOSTON TO CHICAGO
LAKE SHORE LIMITED

The Western Railroad of Massachusetts – one of the first mountain railroads in the world – crossed the Berkshire Hills to connect Boston with the Erie Canal at Albany, New York. The line was surveyed by American railroad pioneer George Washington Whistler in the 1830s and completed in the early 1840s. To maintain a reasonable ascending grade on the east slope of the Berkshires, Whistler followed the course of the west branch of the Westfield River, crossing the river several times using large stone-arched bridges. Although the ruling westbound grade was kept to 1.67 per cent, on its completion it was one of the longest adhesion grades in the world. Especially powerful locomotives were required to bring trains through the hills.

In 1867 the Western Railroad merged with the Boston & Worcester to form the Boston & Albany, and in 1900 the New York Central leased the route. Ownership of the line has since changed several times, but to local residents it is known as simply the "B&A". Today, Whistler's railroad makes up the most scenic portion of the route traversed by the Boston

● **LEFT**
Amtrak's Lake Shore Limited climbs Springfield Hill against the dramatic backdrop of a brooding, stormy November sky.

● **BELOW LEFT**
One of George Washington Whistler's famous stone-arch bridges over the Westfield River, near Middlefield. This is one of several bridges abandoned in 1912 when the railroad was realigned.

section of Amtrak's Lake Shore Limited, trains 448 and 449. This train operates daily between Chicago Union Station and South Station in Boston, Massachusetts. Between Chicago, Illinois, and Rensselaer, New York, the Boston section is combined with the New York section.

Bound for Boston the Lake Shore leaves Rensselaer around lunch-time for a relaxing run over the Berkshires. To climb out of the Hudson River valley, the train uses a section of track to a junction at Post Road, which was abandoned in the early 1970s after Penn Central (then the owner of B&A) discontinued the passenger service. Since all freight traffic

INFORMATION BOX

LAKE SHORE LTD

Termini	Boston and Chicago
Country	USA
Distance	1,636 km (1,017 miles)
Date of opening	1840s

● **LEFT**
Amtrak No. 448 exits from the east portal of the State Line tunnel on a clear summer morning. This famous short, curved tunnel is located only about a mile from the New York-Massachusetts state line.

uses the Castleton Cutoff west of Post Road to Selkirk, the old passenger line to Albany was deemed redundant. However, after Amtrak reintroduced a passenger service, the old track was put back. East of Chatham, New York, the tracks pass over the New York State Thruway, and a short while later through the famous

direction on both tracks. On the east slope, near the village of Middlefield, several of Whistler's stone arches are visible through the trees on the north side of the tracks. These bridges were abandoned in 1912, when the railroad was realigned to reduce the gradient. At Chester, the remains of an engine facility, complete with roundhouse and cooling tower, can be seen on the south side of the tracks. The westbound run out of Boston is less revealing because, except in the long days of summer, the train unfortunately runs through the most interesting scenery at night.

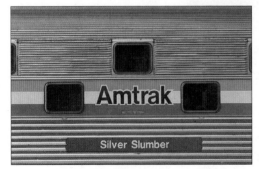

State Line tunnel – so named because it is located near the New York-Massachusetts state line. This is a twin-bore tunnel, although at present only the south bore is used. The north bore was abandoned in the late 1980s.

East of the station stop at Pittsfield, Massachusetts, the track begins the climb up to Washington Summit, elevation 445 m (1,459 ft) above sea level – the highest point on the old B&A. It is not unusual for the Lake Shore to overtake a slow-moving eastbound freight climbing the grade. The railroad is bi-directional double track over Washington Mountain, so trains may safely operate in either

● **ABOVE**
An Amtrak Heritage sleeping car, typical of those used on the Lake Shore Limited.

● **RIGHT**
Amtrak No. 448 winds down the grade on the east slope of Washington Hill, east of Middlefield, Massachusetts.

CHICAGO TO OAKLAND
THE CALIFORNIA ZEPHYR

Connecting Chicago and Oakland, California, is one of Amtrak's most popular western trains, the California Zephyr. On the way it traverses some of the most spectacular scenery in the West, from the towering Colorado Front Range to the California coast. It runs up around the "Big Ten curves" west of Denver, crests the divide via the famous Moffat Tunnel, runs through the deep rugged Gore and Glenwood Canyons, across the Utah Desert and over Soldier Summit to Salt Lake City. Then it passes through the Nevada deserts, over California's Donner Pass, across the Central valley and along the Carquinez Straits to Oakland.

While some routes may have a scenic highlight, the route of the California Zephyr is defined by the scenic splendour it passes through; it has not one highlight but rather a continual succession of great vistas. Among the best are those found when climbing high above the Plains up into the Front Range, where the city of

Denver is seen in the distance against a seemingly infinite horizon. However, the most spectacular view is on the west slope of Donner Pass. After crossing the Smart Ridge, which separates the Yuba River Basin from that of the American

River, the railroad follows the American River Canyon; while the river drops deep into the cavernous ravine, the railroad rides high on the north side, along the right of way laid out in the 1860s by the Central Pacific's chief supporter and

● **ABOVE LEFT**
Amtrak No. 5 crosses Yuba Pass after a winter storm. The City of San Francisco was snowbound at Yuba Pass for three days in the early 1950s.

● **LEFT**
The westbound California Zephyr crosses Smart Ridge, leaving the Yuba River Basin and entering the American River Basin, west of Donner Pass.

great visionary genius, Theodore Judah.
At American, just east of the village of
Alta, California, the tracks ride the very
edge of the canyon, 610 m (2,000 ft)
above the river. From this spot on a clear
night, the lights of Sacramento nearly
113 km (70 miles) away can be seen.

Although the original California
Zephyr began operations in 1949, this
train was discontinued in 1970. The
present-day California Zephyr uses much
of the original route, except that it goes
over Donner Pass rather than via Feather
River Canyon. Amtrak's reincarnated
California Zephyr began operation in the
mid-1970s, but did not start operation,

via the Denver and Rio Grande Western
line over the Front Range, until 1983. It
runs with Amtrak's typical western
equipment: the high-level Superliners,
which may be hauled by its ubiquitous
Electro Motive F40s (200-400 series), the
boxy General Electric P32 "Pepsi Cans"
(500 series) and the aesthetically
controversial streamlined General Electric
Genesis diesels (series 1-99 and 800s).

● **ABOVE**
Cosmic sunrise over Donner Lake in June
1990. Amtrak runs high above this serene
mountain lake on the right of way located by
Theodore Judah in the 1860s.

● **BELOW**
Amtrak No. 5 passes through the Colorado
Rockies on the Dotsero Cutoff – a line that
was finally completed in the 1930s to connect
the Denver & Salt Lake with the Denver & Rio
Grande Western.

INFORMATION BOX

THE CALIFORNIA ZEPHYR

Termini	Chicago and Oakland
Country	USA
Distance	3,218 km (2,000 miles)
Date of opening	1949

SEATTLE TO LOS ANGELES
THE COAST STARLIGHT

The Coast Starlight, connecting Seattle with Los Angeles, is Amtrak's premier West Coast train. It offers first-class accommodations and features splendid scenery all along its route. On the way it traverses several mountain ranges, including the Oregon Cascades and California's Coast Range, and south of San Luis Obispo, California, it runs along the Pacific Ocean for many miles. Amtrak advertises the Coast Starlight as "superior service": first-class passengers are treated in comfort to complimentary wine tasting and champagne.

South of Eugene, Oregon, at the village of Oakridge the Starlight begins its ascent of the Oregon Cascades. Southern Pacific completed its Cascade Route in the mid-1920s, when it opened its Natron Cutoff between Black Butte and Eugene. Today this is among the most impressively engineered lines in the West. A few miles out of Oakridge the tracks wind over a tall trestle at Heather, amid tall evergreen trees. The tracks twist their way up the mountain and pass through a series of long snowsheds and tunnels.

● **LEFT**
Amtrak No. 11, the Los Angeles-bound Coast Starlight, rolls down the Embarcedero at Jack London Square in Oakland, California. Two General Electric P32 diesel-electric locomotives, which are nicknamed "Pepsi Cans", lead the train.

● **BELOW LEFT**
Amtrak No. 11 climbs up through Cruzatte, Oregon – high in the Cascades – on its way to California from Seattle and Portland.

INFORMATION BOX

THE COAST STARLIGHT

Termini	Seattle and Los Angeles
Country	USA
Distance	2,235 km (1,389 miles)
Date of opening	1894

Near Cruzatte, the tracks pass from a tunnel into a snowshed, then out across a tall curved trestle over the cascading Noisy Creek, into another snowshed, then through a long curving tunnel. As breathtaking as the scenery is in the summer, it is downright awesome in the winter, when the trees are heavily laden with pristine snow, and the snowsheds protect the tracks from avalanche. Unfortunately, the southbound Starlight usually crosses the Cascades at night in the winter, although the northbound makes a daylight run.

Amtrak does not serve San Francisco directly, but instead provides a bus service from its new Emeryville Station. Passengers wishing to ride into San Francisco by rail can change for a Cal Train "commute" at San José. In Oakland, the Starlight runs down the Embarcedero through Jack London Square, where the train stops at Amtrak's new Oakland station. The street here is a memorable experience. There are few places where Amtrak's high-level Superliner cars share the right of way with automobile traffic! To reach San Luis Obispo from the agricultural Salinas

valley, the Starlight crosses the Cuesta Grade, a steep, tortuous 22.5 km (14 mile) stretch of railroad that winds its way through some of California's prettiest scenery: rolling grassy hills punctuated by perfectly placed oak trees. The grass is iridescent green for a few weeks in March and April, and golden brown for the rest of the year.

The ride along the coast brings the Starlight through Vandenberg Air Force Base, land otherwise restricted to militia. You will not find many photographs of the train in this isolated spot. North of

● **ABOVE LEFT**
Coast Starlight advertisement at the new Amtrak station in Oakland, California.

● **ABOVE RIGHT**
On a misty June day, the Seattle-bound Coast Starlight descends Southern Pacific's Cascade Line near Fields, Oregon.

Santa Barbara, the tracks pass over a tremendous trestle at Gaviota and along several popular beaches. The southern end point is Los Angeles Union passenger terminal, one of the last great American passenger terminals. It was completed in 1939 and blends Spanish-Moorish architecture with 20th-century Art Deco motifs.

● **ABOVE**
Amtrak's Coast Starlight has just passed through Tunnel 5¹/₂ in the Salinas valley. Before the tunnel was drilled the railroad ran around the mountain on a circuitous alignment (visible to the left of the tunnel).

● **LEFT**
The Pacific Ocean glints in the morning sun.

BELLOWS FALLS TO CHESTER, VERMONT
THE GREEN MOUNTAIN FLYER

The Rutland Railway once connected
Bellows Falls, Rutland and Burlington,
Vermont, with Ogdensburg, New York; it
also had a line running south from
Rutland to Bennington, Vermont, and on
to Chatham, New York. The Rutland
discontinued all operations in the early
1960s and portions of the line were
abandoned.

Today the Green Mountain Railroad
operates a segment of the former
Rutland Railway, and a very short portion
of the former Boston & Maine Railroad
in south-central Vermont between North
Walpole, New Hampshire (directly across
the Connecticut River from Bellows Falls,
Vermont), and Rutland, Vermont. This
colourful short-line railroad maintains
the spirit of the old Rutland Railway by
using Rutland's shield and green and

● **LEFT**
The Green Mountain
Flyer departs
Chester, Vermont,
bound for Bellows
Falls.

● **LEFT**
The Green Mountain Railroad logo is
reminiscent of the old Rutland herald.

● **BELOW**
On a brilliant autumn morning, Green
Mountain Alco RS-1 405 leads the Green
Mountain Flyer at Brockway Mills, Vermont.

● **RIGHT**
When the passenger-train is running heavy, it rates one of the powerful Green Mountain's GP9 locomotives.

● **BELOW RIGHT**
At the end of the day, the Green Mountain Flyer rests at Bellows Falls, Vermont.

yellow colour scheme on its rolling stock. From late spring through early autumn Green Mountain operates a tourist train called the Green Mountain Flyer.

The train runs twice a day on Tuesday through Sunday (daily in foliage season) between the Amtrak station in Bellows Falls (also serves the daily Vermonter) and Chester. The train runs with vintage passenger-cars including two historical former Rutland cars, still bearing the name of their former owner.

The Flyer is reminiscent of a typical backwoods branch-line passenger-train of an earlier period, giving passengers a refreshing change from the modern Amtrak trains that are most prevalent in the United States today. Green Mountain operates several Electro Motive GP9

diesel-electric locomotives, which it purchased secondhand from other railroads, as well as a vintage Alco RS-1 diesel-electric, which dates from the mid-1940s and was once owned by the Rutland. Often Green Mountain operates the Flyer with the RS-1, and the train appears even more the way a traditional Rutland passenger-train might have looked 50 years ago.

The scenery along the line is outstanding. Passengers may board the Flyer at either end of the line, and both Bellows Falls and Chester feature splendid stations. Leaving Bellows Falls,

the railroad briefly follows the Connecticut River and then winds its way inland. At Brockway Mills the tracks cross a deep gorge on a high-deck bridge. Along the way several of Vermont's quaint covered bridges and a number of old rustic barns are visible. Vermont is most enjoyable in the early autumn when the days are crisp and clear and the foliage turns to brilliant colours, and there is no better way to view the scenery than to ride the Green Mountain Flyer. Special trains are run on October weekends, the peak period for autumnal colours, all the way to Ludlow, Vermont.

INFORMATION BOX

THE GREEN MOUNTAIN FLYER

Termini	Bellows Falls and Chester, Vermont
Country	USA
Distance	21 km (13 miles)
Date opened for passenger traffic	1984

CHICAGO METRA'S "RACE TRACK"

Chicago's Metra operates a comprehensive network of suburban commuter lines with more than a dozen routes over half a dozen different railroads. Its busiest route is the former Chicago, Burlington & Quincy line to Aurora – a suburb about 56 km (35 miles) west of the the downtown area.

The route, known colloquially as the "Race Track", is owned by Burlington Northern Santa Fe. It carries approximately 50,000 weekday Metra

● **RIGHT**
An express makes a station stop at Stone Avenue, La Grange.

INFORMATION BOX	
Termini	Chicago and Aurora, Illinois
Country	USA
Distance	61 km (38 miles)
Date of opening	1853

passengers on more than 80 daily commuter trains, handles several daily Amtrak long-distance passenger-trains, including the Southwest Chief and the California Zephyr, and carries between 40 and 60 daily freight-trains operated by host railroad Burlington Northern Santa Fe, plus those by Canadian National and Southern Pacific/Union Pacific.

The combination of heavy passenger-traffic and heavy freight-traffic makes this triple-track main-line one of the busiest in the United States, and one of the most

interesting to watch and ride. Aurora-bound trains serve Chicago Union Station, one of four large passenger terminals in Chicago. The operation of the triple track is handled by Centralized Traffic Control, allowing trains to use all three tracks in both directions.

In the evening rush hour, when the bulk of passengers are leaving the city, local and express-trains depart Chicago Union every few minutes. Local trains normally use the outside track on the north side, while the express-trains use

● **LEFT**
An F40M "Winnebago" races westbound at Stone Avenue. These locomotives are unique to Chicago.

the centre track and inbound trains the outside track on the south side. To avoid interference during the peak passenger times, freight-trains are either held in yards in either Chicago or Eola, or west of Aurora.

Metra normally uses bi-level "gallery cars" hauled by Electro Motive Division F40s or F40Ms. The F40s are America's most common passenger locomotives, while the F40Ms – nicknamed "Winnebagos", after the popular motor

home – are unique to Chicago Metra. All Metra trains are operated in a push-pull fashion, with the locomotive facing westward. Eastbound trains are operated from a control cab in the leading passenger car. Running time between Chicago and Aurora varies from 1 hour and 20 minutes on a local run to just 52 minutes on an express train.

One way to enjoy the action on the "Race Track" is to ride a midday Metra train from Union Station to one of the

suburban stops – Hollywood (Brookfield Zoo) and Stone Avenue, La Grange, are recommended – and spend the afternoon watching the railroad. On a typical weekday, there will be plenty of freight- and passenger-trains. At weekends Metra service is limited. Other interesting Metra routes include: Metra Electric to University Park – the former Illinois Central electric lines; Rock Island District to Joliet, Illinois; and any of the three former Chicago & North Western routes.

MILWAUKEE TO EAST TROY

Beginning in the 1890s, interurban electric railways were in use across the United States. Employing relatively lightweight construction, they often operated along country roads and in city streets. A great many interurbans operated in the Midwest, connecting such large cities as Chicago and Milwaukee with rural outlying towns. In addition to their passenger operations, many interurbans carried freight, using small electric locomotives. However, the interurban era was short-lived. The advent of the automobile put a swift end to many of these marginally profitable lines, and most were abandoned in the 1920s and 1930s.

The Milwaukee Electric Railway & Light Company, which operated a 320 km (199 mile) long interurban electric empire in south-eastern Wisconsin,

● **ABOVE**
The East Troy Electric Railroad serves several industries in East Troy by means of the Trent Spur. An excursion using open-bench car 21 celebrates the inauguration of electric service in 1996.

● **LEFT**
The East Troy Electric Railroad herald.

● **BELOW**
A car rolls through Beulah on its way from East Troy to the Elegant Farmer.

● RIGHT
One of East Troy's most popular cars is Duluth-Superior Transit "Gate car" No. 253, a typical American streetcar. The interior of the car has been meticulously restored.

● BELOW LEFT
Former Milwaukee Electric Railway & Light Company steeple-cab L9, and former Chicago, South Shore & South Bend interurban coach No. 1130 in front of the old substation, now a museum, at East Troy, Wisconsin.

● BELOW RIGHT
One of East Troy's interurban cars rolls through the Army Lake Road crossing near Mukwonago, Wisconsin. Much of this rural line follows the highway on the 8 km (5 mile) run between East Troy and Mukwonago.

● BOTTOM
A former Chicago, South Shore & South Bend interurban takes the siding at Beulah for two eastbound cars heading for the Elegant Farmer. This old interurban route is single track with passing sidings at several locations to allow "meets" between passing trains.

opened its line to rural East Troy, Wisconsin, in 1907. While Milwaukee Electric abandoned passenger service to East Troy in 1939, this line survived for many years as an electric freight line. The village of East Troy maintained the line to serve local industries. Today it is one of the last electrified remnants of the interurban era. It is operated by the East Troy Electric Railroad and provides weekend passenger excursions in conjunction with the Wisconsin Trolley Museum between May and September, using traditional interurban equipment. It is still a freight-hauler too, although in the 1990s it has only carried 20–30 cars per year.

Passengers may board at either East Troy or the Elegant Farmer, near Mukwonago, Wisconsin. The 16 km (10 mile) round trip runs along a county highway through pastoral farming country and takes a little more than an hour. East Troy operates a fleet of vintage electric

interurban equipment, including cars that operated on the Chicago, South Shore & South Bend. It also operates streetcars from several North American cities, including Duluth, Minnesota and Philadelphia. The pride of its fleet is car No. 21, a single-truck open-bench

streetcar replica, typical of street railway operations at the turn of the century. At East Troy an old electric substation is part of the museum and the car-barn is just a block away. Adjacent to the museum is J. Lauber's Ice Cream Parlor, where one can order traditional ice cream sodas.

INFORMATION BOX	
Termini	Milwaukee and East Troy, Wisconsin
Country	USA
Distance	8 km (5 miles)
Date of opening	1907

BOONE SCENIC RAILROAD

Iowa, located in the central portion of the United States, is largely an agricultural state. Near the centre of Iowa is Boone, once an important railroad town on the Chicago & North Western's busy main line between Chicago, Illinois, and Council Bluffs, Iowa. This was once a crew change and an important freight switching yard. Sadly there has been no regular passenger-service on this important main line in many years.

Amtrak crosses Iowa on the old Chicago, Burlington & Quincy (now operated by Burlington Northern Santa Fe) many miles to the south. A few miles west of Boone is the gigantic Kate Shelley High Bridge – named after a young woman who risked her life to warn a train of a washed-out bridge – which spans the valley of the Des Moines River. Today the Kate Shelley bridge handles 40–60 daily freight-trains operated by the Union Pacific Railroad (UP acquired the Chicago & North Western in 1995).

On the west side of Boone is the Boone & Scenic Valley Railway, a popular tourist line that operates steam, diesel and electric trains seasonally along the

● **ABOVE**
Every morning before it hauls passengers, Boone & Scenic Valley's steam-engine runs light (without cars) to the tall trestle in order to blow down its boiler – a procedure intended to remove mineral impurities.

● **LEFT**
Charles City & Western interurban car No. 50 is reminiscent of the sort of electric equipment that once ran on the Fort Dodge, Des Moines & Southern through Boone. The Boone & Scenic Valley runs the vintage electric at weekends in the summer.

● **OPPOSITE**
Boone & Scenic valley's Mikado takes on water between runs on a hot June day. Boone is proud of its railroad heritage and every year hosts "Pufferbilly Days" in September.

● **ABOVE LEFT**
Boone & Scenic Valley's Chinese-built 2-8-2 Mikado type marches into Boone, Iowa.

● **ABOVE RIGHT**
An eastbound Union Pacific coal-train crosses the Kate Shelley High Bridge. Although the big bridge has two tracks, it can only support the weight of one train at a time.

INFORMATION BOX

Terminus	Boone
Country	USA
Distance	11 km (7 miles)
Date of opening	1906

right of way of the Fort Dodge, Des Moines & Southern, known as the Fort Dodge Line – the largest of the Iowa interurbans. Iowa was once criss-crossed by lightweight electric interurban lines that carried freight and passengers. While most of these lines have been abandoned, a few segments remain in place, primarily as freight operations. This particular line operated under wire until the mid-1950s, when it was converted to diesel operation. In later years it was taken over by the Chicago & North Western and operated as a freight-only branch line. Several years ago, Boone & Scenic Valley acquired the picturesque route from the

C&NW and began operating passenger excursions. Since that time, Boone Scenic has re-electrified a short section of its line into town and operates an interurban car reminiscent of those that traditionally operated here.

In the summer the main attraction is Boone's steam-train, hauled by the brightly painted Chinese 2-8-2 Mikado type locomotive No. JS8419. This locomotive was ordered new by the railroad from the Datong works in 1988, and it was delivered in 1989 for the specific purpose of hauling passengers. The steam-train operates along the right of way of the old interurban north-west out of Boone, along the bucolic valley of the Des Moines River. The engineering highlight of the trip is Boone Scenic's high bridge, a 48 m (156 ft) tall trestle, which crosses a creek that feeds into the Des Moines River. Trains cross the bridge very slowly to allow passengers to admire the view.

During the summer the railroad operates three steam trips at weekends and one round trip on weekdays. Diesel-powered trips are offered at other times. For an extra fare, passengers can ride in the elevated cupola of a traditional American caboose. The electric portion of the line is also generally operated during summer weekends.

LOS MOCHIS TO CHIHUAHUA
THE COPPER CANYON

● BELOW
Here we see the train to Chihuahua starting its
journey to Los Mochis.

In 1961, with the opening of the newest
transcontinental railway in North
America, the tremendous spectacle of
canyons deeper and longer than Arizona's
Grand Canyon was made available to
travellers. However, they could only see it
by rail, for there were no roads and
certainly no airfields amid the wild Sierra
Madre mountains of Mexico.

The Chihuahua Pacifico Railway is a
success. In its 36 years of existence, it has
carried millions of passengers – many of
them from overseas. It runs for 655 km
(407 miles) from Los Mochis on
Mexico's west coast tidewater to the city
of Chihuahua, passing through 87 tunnels
and across 36 bridges. At one stage, it has
to negotiate a triple loop to gain altitude.
The summit is attained at kilometre post
583, some 2,502 m (8,209 ft) above sea
level, near the halt of Divisadero where
the Barranca (meaning copper) Canyon
divides from the almost equally awesome
Ulrique Canyon.

Originally planned at the end of the
last century as a freight route for Texas
and central America to serve the deep-
water Pacific ports of Mexico, the railway
took some 60 years to complete. Only

surveyors and missionaries had ever been
to these remote canyons, populated by a
tribe of Tarahumara Indians who lived in
caves in the canyon walls. The
Tarahumara retain their traditions, and
are mostly unable to speak Spanish,
although they have a school at Creel, a
logging township on the railway where a
few basic roads exist. Travellers by train
may see some of the more venturesome
Tarahumaras selling souvenirs at stalls

beside the tracks at Divisadero, where all
trains stop for 20 minutes to allow
passengers to enjoy the wonderful views.

Two passenger-trains run each way
daily, providing what is reckoned by
experts to be among the world's five top
scenic train rides. They are usually well
patronized, and both make early morning
starts to provide a daylight ride over the
full length of the line. Foreign visitors to
Mexico are often in a majority in the first

INFORMATION BOX	
THE COPPER CANYON	
Termini	Los Mochis and Chihuahua
Country	Mexico
Distance	655 km (407 miles)
Date of opening	1961

● LEFT
The arrival, from the Pacific, of El Tarahumara
at Divisadero station. The train is named after
the indigenous people of the canyons.

class, where meals are served. There are also freight services, usually one by day and one by night, serving the deep-water port of Topolobampo, some 20 km (12¹/₂ miles) beyond the growing city of Los Mochis.

Once a week, a set of special cars called the Sierra Madre Express are attached to the Mexican trains coming down from Nogales and are coupled to the first Chihuahua-Pacifico train over the Copper Canyon line. This takes place

at Sufragio, the junction of the new line with the Ferrocarril Pacifico. Usually two sleepers, a lounge, restaurant and dome car (all restored from US equipment of the 1950s) constitute the Sierra Madre Express, all of which make a very heavy load to haul up from sea level to 2,500 m (8,000 ft). Detached at Divisadero, these American cars lay over in the sidings, passengers sleeping aboard. They will have begun their "train cruise" in Arizona, and the special fares are high.

● **TOP LEFT**
The Rio Chinipas bridge is the highest on the line.

● **TOP RIGHT**
A parked US cruise train at Divisadero station.

● **ABOVE RIGHT**
Trains at Divisadero, Copper Canyon. On the left is the lounge car Arizona, which is part of the Sierra Madre train.

● **RIGHT**
The Copper Canyon. This is one and a half times deeper and longer than Colorado's Grand Canyon.

SANTOS TO SÃO PAULO

The São Paulo Railway in Brazil was described as Britain's most successful transportation investment abroad. Incorporated in 1856 as the San (this was a wrong interpretation, which the company retained all its working life) Paulo Railway, it was built to link the port of Santos with the healthy uplands of Brazil, mainly – in early days – for the coffee growers. It contributed greatly to the growth of São Paulo, now one of the biggest cities in the world and one of South America's most industrialized urban areas.

This unique line is a 5 ft 3 in gauge railway that is literally hoisted up the Serra do Mar, a mountain precipice, by an endless rope. It was always a full-scale main line with excellent rolling stock, first-class steam locomotives, restaurant cars and an efficient working practice. The whole journey was only 80 km (50 miles) in length, 19 km (12 miles)

through swamps at the coastal end and 53 km (33 miles) along a plain at the top, with 8 km (5 miles) of steep rope haulage in between. The best trains took just two hours for the journey, including up to 45 minutes "on the rope" if more than six coaches had to be hoisted (these were done three at a time). When diesel units were introduced after World War II, times were cut since the whole unit could

be hoisted in one go. The 99-year lease ran out in 1955, when the name of the railway, now under Brazilian ownership, was changed to Estrada de Ferro Santos a Jundia. The railway had been profitable from the start and the take-over was cordial, with huge amounts paid to shareholders at the end. But since then circumstances have changed, with the construction of a Canadian-financed

● **ABOVE**
Santos railway station where the journey begins.

● **LEFT**
One of the 0-4-0 tram-like steam brake-vans on the Santos a Jundia section of the line. As can be seen the engines produce a lot of smoke, so much so that they sometimes appear to be on fire.

● **RIGHT**
The journey starts at
the beautiful seaside
resort of Santos.
Travellers must
often be loath to
leave the sandy
beach.

● **BELOW LEFT**
São Paulo's Estación
de la Luz (Station of
Light). This 1936
scene shows the
train to Santos
about to depart. The
locomotive would
run the first 53 km
(33 miles) to the
start of the incline.

● **BELOW
RIGHT**
Three coaches of a
Santos-São Paulo
train going up an
incline with a
breaking locomotive
attached.

highway, the Anchieta, which sweeps up
the escarpment to São Paulo, and on
which cars and buses make the trip in
under 90 minutes. There are now only
two passenger-trains each way daily, all
second-class, taking 115 minutes. They
are still patronized because the fare is low
compared to the buses. The ownership is
now with Rede Ferroviaria Federal, São
Paulo, a government department. After
1927, five new inclined planes were built
on a gentler gradient (about 1:11), which
speeded ascent and descent. Ropes are
renewed every two years and re-spliced
every six months. A trained gang re-
splices a rope in 40 minutes. None has
ever broken. The height above sea level at
the top of the incline is 792 m (2,598 ft).
The beautiful roofed Estación de la Luz
(Station of Light) in São Paulo is still
there as a reminder of the days of great
prosperity and 12 per cent dividends.

INFORMATION BOX	
SAN PAULO RAILWAY	
Termini	Santos and São Paulo
Country	Brazil
Distance	80 km (50 miles)
Date of opening	1856

SANTA ROSA DE LOS ANDES TO LAS CUEVAS, ARGENTINA

Although the Trans-Andine railway was projected in 1854, work did not begin until 1887, and the line was not finally opened until 1910. Built to provide a rail link over the Andes between Chile and Argentina, the line now terminates at the border between the two countries.

The first section of this metre-gauge line, which goes 34 km (21 miles) from Santa Rosa de Los Andes to Rio Blanco, rises some 640 m (2,100 ft). On this stretch the trains average about 29 kph (18 mph). The second section of the trip, from Rio Blanco to the frontier, about two-fifths of the way through the 3,028 m (9,934 ft) long Uspallata tunnel, is just under 36.5 km (23 miles) long and rises 1,730 m (5,676 ft). In this 71 km (44 mile) stretch of line, there are six rack sections and no less than 26 tunnels with a total length of 3,183 m (10,443 ft) – not counting the Uspallata. The electric trains average about 18 kph (11 mph) on this stretch. The Uspallata

INFORMATION BOX

Termini	Santa Rosa de Los Andes and Las Cuevas
Countries	Chile and Argentina
Distance	71 km (44 miles)
Date of opening	1910

tunnel, between the peaks of the 7,040 m (23,097 ft) Aconcagua and the 6,187 m (20,298 ft) Tupungato , lies at an altitude of 3,200 m (10,500 ft).

One of the locomotives used on the line was a Shay type, built by Lima in 1904. It was carried on two four-wheeled bogies with the tender on another four-wheeled bogie. This engine took light trains up the rack grades and

worked the section between Portillo and the Summit tunnel. There were also two 2-6-2T rack and adhesion engines, made by Borsig of Berlin. A 0-8-0+0-6-0T Meyer is kept at Los Andes mainly for use in snow clearance.

The main problems encountered on the route were, in winter, snow, which can reach as much as 6.4 m (21 ft) deep, and, in summer, rock falls and avalanches. Indeed, owing to the many landslides that have occurred over the years, the rail route over the Andes has now been closed for good – there is neither money nor incentive to restore it, especially as a road now crosses its path and, ironically, uses the rail tunnel beneath the great statue of Christ.

When the Trans-Andine train did run, it was at Las Cuevas, 3 km (2 miles)

into Argentina, that the Chilean crew with their Swiss-built Brown-Boveri electric locomotive would hand over the train to their Argentine colleagues with their Czech-built cog-wheel diesel unit. Once the start of a 1,088 km (676 mile)

journey to Argentina's Santiago Alameda station, the line is now mainly only used during the winter sports season, when the resort of Portillo, altitude 2,743 m (9,000 ft), suddenly comes to life with the influx of winter sports enthusiasts.

● **ABOVE LEFT**
A spacious Chilean State Railways restaurant car.

● **ABOVE RIGHT**
A main-line express, the "Trans-Andino Combinación" near Llay Llay, en route to Los Andes.

● **LEFT**
The Laguna del Inca (Inca Lake), which is seen as the train progresses on its journey.

● **LEFT**
A Swedish-built electric locomotive shunts coaches for the "Trans-Andino Combinación" at Llay Llay.

Asunción to Encarnación

It has truly been said that a Paraguayan train journey is one of the most high-rated rail experiences in the world. Although Paraguay has other railways, only one, the Ferrocarril Presidente Carlos Antonio López, carries passengers. One of the abiding memories of a trip on the line is the firework display that comes from its fleet of 100 per cent wood-burning locomotives. This is a truly unforgettable experience.

The first section of the line, from Asunción to Paruguar, was opened in 1861. In 1889 it was acquired by the London-based, British-controlled Paraguay Central Railway. The line, which reached Encarnación in 1911, was nationalized in 1961. Originally built to the 5 ft 6 in gauge, in 1911 it was reduced so that it could be connected to

- **LEFT**
A train for Encarnación waits to leave the grand station in Asunción.

- **BELOW**
A North British, 2-6-0, No. 103, at Parguar Station.

- **OPPOSITE BOTTOM LEFT**
Train no. 286 passes through the streets of Asunción. This picture was taken just before the train was hit by a bus! Thankfully there were no casualties.

- **OPPOSITE BOTTOM RIGHT**
Engine No. 51, one of the original North British-built Moguls of 1910, at San Salvador at the head of an overnight train from Encarnación to Asunción.

One of the North
British-built wood
burners surrounded
by wood at Colonel
Belgrado.

● BELOW
A steam tram built by Borsig of Berlin for
working around the docks of Buenos Aires.
After a long life in the Argentinian capital, this
veteran was pensioned off to the sugar fields
of neighbouring Paraguay, and during its
workaday chores it regularly sallies forth on to
the international main line linking Asunción
to Encarnación.

Argentina's standard gauge. Although the
railway is run down and the line in poor
condition, a trip over the line should be
very high on the list of any South
American traveller.

The 376 km (234 mile) journey, which
lasts from 14 to 18 hours, commences at
Asunción's multi-colonnaded colonial-
style station and heads in a south-easterly
direction across undulating countryside to
Villarica. Thereafter the landscape
changes to flat pampas and swampland for
the rest of the journey to Encarnación.
Here the through train to Argentina leaves
the station to proceed down the length of
a street towards the ferry terminal at Paca
Cua. The coaches are then lowered on to

the train ferry by a steam-operated winch
and cable. The ferry, which can carry six
coaches at a time, crosses the Parana·
River to Posadas, Argentina.

The twice-weekly train is usually
hauled by one of the country's British-
built locomotives, from the North British
of Glasgow or the Yorkshire Engineering
Company's Meadow Hall works in
Sheffield. There are still Edwardian
2-6-0s in service. This sole passenger
line in the country, where passenger
comfort is an unheard-of concept, is
operated with only nine passenger-cars.
There used to be a sleeping car, but it
was withdrawn in 1972. The restaurant
car, which used to be fitted to the train,
has also been out of use for some years,
so that during the journey food has to be
purchased from itinerant vendors along
the track.

The future of this unique railway is in
doubt. The new road bridge over the
Parana River at Encarnación now brings
road and rail traffic directly from

Argentina, rendering the ferry defunct.
At present, all services are suspended,
ostensibly for track up-grading, and it is
hoped that the railway will eventually
work again. This must be open to
question, however, as traffic has dwindled
progressively over recent years. At
present the locomotive fleet of vintage
rolling stock remains intact, as it waits for
a tomorrow that may never come.

INFORMATION BOX	
Termini	Asunción and Encarnación
Country	Paraguay
Distance	376 km (234 miles)
Date of opening	1861

JULIACA TO CUZCO
THE HIGHEST RAILWAY IN THE WORLD

Crossing the Andes meant constructing the highest railway in the world. Because of its altitude, the Peruvian Central Railway presented civil engineers with major problems, for, in a confined space and short distances, they had to build railways over passes that exceeded Mont Blanc in altitude. The solutions they adopted were tight curves, zigzags and rack sections.

Operating the lines was also fraught with difficulties: steep gradients, lack of local sources of fuel, heavy wear and tear on locomotives and rolling stock, and frequent landslides and washouts. Even the change from steam to diesel was, initially, a step backwards, because diesel units were prone to power loss in the rare atmosphere, and there were cases of trains being unable to take the gradients.

The three lines of the the Southern Railway of Peru serve the *altiplano*, a windswept plain 3,901 m (12,798 ft) above sea level. Of standard gauge, they run to Mollendo on the Peruvian coast through the country's second city, Arequipa, to the town of Juliaca on the altiplano. Here the line divides. A short section continues to Lake Titicana and around its shores to the port of Puno, while a 339 km (211 mile) line from Juliaca runs north to Cuzco, the ancient Inca capital, crossing a summit of 4,314 m (14,153 ft) at La Raya.

A glance at the map of Peru shows that the route of the Central Railway forms a lop-sided T, with Lima at its base, running up to La Oroya at the junction of the cross-piece. The main line runs from

INFORMATION BOX	
THE HIGHEST RAILWAY IN THE WORLD	
Termini	Juliaca and Cuzco
Country	Peru
Distance	339 km (211 miles)
Date of opening	1908

● LEFT
A Hunslett 2-8-0 No. 108 at an isolated mountain stop on the Huancayo to Huancavelica line.

Lima through La Oroya to Huancavelica, its terminal, on the right. To the left, a privately owned railway runs from La Oroya to Cerro de Pasco, site of Peru's copper mines. The Southern and Central Railway systems are unconnected.

The Central Railway is regarded as one of the wonders of the Americas, and the engineering of the route involved immense problems. The deep Rimac valley between Lima and La Oroya, the only feasible route to the central region of the country, narrows to a maximum width of about 198 m (650 ft). Within its limits, the engineers had to find a way of climbing nearly 3,960 m (12,992 ft) within a distance of less than 76 km (47 miles). The twists and turns that the railway needs to gain height have made the railway considerably longer at 117 km (73 miles).

To keep the gradient down to 1:23, the line has to utilize the whole width of the valley, crossing frequently from one side to the other. Even this would be impossible without the use of the famous zigzags to gain height. Between Chosica and Ticlio, the highest point of the line at 4,783 m (15,692 ft), there are six double and one single zigzags, 66 tunnels, including the 1,177 m (3,861 ft) long

Galera, and 59 bridges, including that over the Verrugas, which, at 175 m (574 ft) long, when built in 1890, was the third longest in the world.

Construction of the line, which began in 1870, presented problems in addition to the geographical ones. A mysterious disease killed off thousands of workers in 1877, and Peru went bankrupt, which effectively held up completion until 1929. The chief reason for the Central

Railway has been freight-carrying, particularly since 1897 when the La Oroya copper mine opened. However, the incredible journey still remains attainable to travellers. Except for those unfortunates who suffer from altitude-sickness and have to be given oxygen by the white-coated attendants on the train, all will marvel at the ingenuity of the men who built this railway amid some of the most rugged landscapes on earth.

GUAYAQUIL TO QUITO

The chief component of the Ecuadorian State Railway is the Guayaquil to Quito line (misleadingly nicknamed the "Good and the Quick"), which connects the two major cities of the country; the former on the coast, the latter high up in the Andian mountains.

Construction work began in 1871, but it was not until 1908 that the contractors completed the rare 3 ft 6 in gauge line. To traverse the 463 km (288 miles) and 3,609 m (11,840 ft) altitude, tight curves and zigzags were incorporated. It has never been a commercial success and its resulting

● **LEFT**
Passengers board a first-class train on the Ibarra to San Lorenzo line.

● **LEFT**
Travellers on the *tren mixto* (mixed train) ready to leave Sibambe.

INFORMATION BOX

Termini	Guayaquil and Quito
Country	Ecuador
Distance	463 km (288 miles)
Date of opening	1908

● **BELOW**
A small Baldwin 2-6-0 No. 7 passes through Milagro non-stop on market day.

near-bankruptcy has given it a poor reputation for chaotic administration, breakdowns and derailments. Its lines are antique, and the fact that the railway is continuing to operate tends to raise more amazement than the fact that it was ever built. But for anyone interested in travelling on impossible railway lines, who is not put off by an uncomfortable ride punctuated by possible disasters, the G&Q must be a prized experience. It has sometimes been called "the world's mightiest roller coaster".

Guayaquil, Ecuador's second city, has its railway station at Duran, a long way out of town and on the opposite side of the Gyayas River estuary. The spectacular line to Quito begins its zigzagging course within a narrow gorge before climbing the famous Mariz del Diablo (Devil's Nose), a perpendicular ridge rising to a height of 3,230 m (10,597 ft). Another

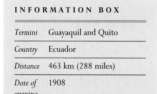

engineering challenge, this almost insurmountable obstacle was finally conquered by the construction of a series of switchbacks on a 5¹/₂ per cent grade. First one way and then the other, the train zigzags higher and higher to gain an altitude of 3,609 m (11,840 ft) at Urbino, a small town lying near the foot of the 6,705 m (21,997 ft) volcano of Chimborazo.

The northbound line from Quito runs to San Lorenzo on the coast. At least the line does, if not many services use it. It is erratic, to say the least, and a bus – sometimes – now takes over from the trains if the passenger load warrants it or if there's not enough freight for a *tren mixto*. Even today the *Thomas Cook Overseas Timetable* finds itself unable to prise proper timings of the service out of the administration.

The train, when it decides to put in an appearance, is a little monster called an *autocarril*. Basically this is a vehicle that was born as a British Leyland lorry and ended its life on flanged wheels and a fixed course. Although the ticket stipulates a reserved seat, there are in fact no seats to reserve.

On one occasion the River Mira cut the line in two by sweeping away the bridge. This meant that for a while the passengers had to alight and cross the river on a temporary rope structure, four at a time. A few kilometres on, along ill-laid and worn track, the train comes to a waterfall that descends directly on to the track to drench passengers who have failed to close their windows.

The total curvature of this line is no less than 16,200 degrees – the equivalent of more than 45 complete circles. The entire line is adhesion-worked and accounts for no less than 40 per cent of the country's total rail length.

● **ABOVE**
Looking down Devil's Nose as the train enters Sibambe.

● **LEFT**
A large Baldwin 2-8-0 No. 44 leaves Bucay on a *tren mixto* (mixed train), which has plenty of room on top.

DUBLIN TO CORK

The principal railway route in the Republic of Ireland is that which joins the country's two main cities, Dublin and Cork. It was built by the Great Southern & Western Railway and, like so many of the major trunk lines in the British Isles, it was a product of the railway mania of the 1840s.

Even by the standards of the time, the project was an ambitious one. At 265 km (165 miles), this line was longer than any comparable scheme in Britain. Given the much less favourable economic conditions in Ireland at the time – construction of the route was undertaken during the dark years of the Great Famine – the fact that the line was completed on schedule was a remarkable achievement. The line opened to a temporary station on the outskirts of Cork in October 1849, five years after the passing of the Act of Parliament authorizing the railway.

INFORMATION BOX

Termini	Dublin and Cork
Country	Ireland
Distance	265 km (165 miles)
Date of opening	1849

● **ABOVE**
The Dublin to Cork express speeds its passengers between two of Ireland's largest cities.

● **ABOVE LEFT**
The CIE logo used from the 1960s.

● **LEFT**
The train leaves the town and heads out into the beautiful Irish countryside.

BELOW
On leaving the capital, passengers will see
many of Dublin's Metropolitan Dart trains.

BELOW
Ireland's efficient train service helps make the
country a favourite destination for holidaymakers keen to leave the car at home.

The line starts from Heuston
(formerly Kingsbridge) station in Dublin.
The magnificent building that fronts the
station, containing offices and the board
room used by the three organizations that
have run the line over the decades, was
designed by the architect Sancton Wood
and opened in 1844. This is in marked
contrast to the rather dingy train shed,
which lurks behind the frontage and,
rather pointedly, is not physically
connected to it.

The route is relatively level except for
short sharp gradients at either end.
Leaving Dublin, trains are soon speeding
across the Curragh of Kildare where
thoroughbreds can be seen exercising on
the gallops alongside the track. After
passing through Portarlington,
Ballybrophy and Thurles, trains reach
Limerick Junction where, until track
changes were made in 1967, every train
serving the station since its opening in
1848 had to reverse to get into its
platforms. Here the line from Limerick
to Rosslare crosses the Cork line on the
level, the only such occurrence that is
met in Ireland today.

At Mallow the route that serves
County Kerry branches off, and the
tracks for Cork cross the River
Blackwater on a viaduct that replaced the
original one, destroyed in the Troubles of
the 1920s – one of the few notable
engineering feats of the line.

ABOVE
A remarkable survivor from the dawn of the
railway age in Ireland is preserved under cover
in Cork station. This is 2-2-2 locomotive
No. 36, built by Bury, Curtis & Kennedy in
Liverpool for the commencement of services
on the Dublin to Cork line in the 1840s. It
remained in service, covering about half a
million miles in its time, until 1875. It was not
scrapped but remained at Inchicore works in
Dublin until the 1950s, when it was renovated
and put on display in Cork.

Approaching Cork the line plunges
into one of the longest railway tunnels in
Ireland at over 1,189 m (3,901 ft) in
length. The tunnel virtually brings a train
to the platforms of Cork station. The stiff
gradient through the tunnel provided a
daunting start for Dublin-bound trains in
the days of steam. The line continues
through the curving platforms of the
station to the final terminus at Cobh.
Cobh was known as Queenstown, and
was once a stopping-point for the great
Atlantic liners; it was also the last port of
call for the ill-fated *Titanic* in 1912.

Now a frequent service of fast express
trains runs throughout the day. The trains
are powered by the latest General Motors
diesels, and they generally operate at
speeds approaching 160 kph (100 mph).
There is, however, a reminder of the
line's earliest days in the foyer of the
station at Cork in the form of a steam
locomotive No. 36. A 2-2-2. This train
was built by Bury, Curtis & Kennedy
Company in Manchester for the opening
of the line in the 1840s, and is a
remarkable survivor from the dawn of
the Railway Age in Ireland.

DROMOD TO BELTURBET

Ireland was sadly lacking in deposits of coal and iron ore, the raw materials that fuelled the Industrial Revolution in the 19th century. One place where both these elements could be found was at Arigna in County Roscommon. Though the surrounding districts in the county of Leitrim were thinly populated and consisted of poor boggy land often inundated by the area's many lakes and streams, the prospective mineral wealth of Arigna led to plans being made in the 1880s for a narrow-gauge railway to connect Belturbet, County Cavan, in the north to Dromod, on the main Dublin to Sligo railway, in the south. A branch was planned from Ballinamore, midway along the route, to Arigna.

Most journeys along the line began at Dromod, where the narrow-gauge station adjoined the main-line one. The mixed train consisting of a tail of wagons and a carriage with a veranda and open platform at either end – shades of the

● **LEFT**
4-4-0 tank No. 2, originally named Kathleen, one of the locomotives built for the opening of Cavan & Leitrim Railway in 1887 simmers in the shed yard at Ballinamore in the late 1950s. When the line closed, No. 2 was preserved and now resides in the Ulster Folk & Transport Museum at Cultra near Belfast.

● **ABOVE**
At Belturbet the C&L shared a platform and station with the standard-gauge Great Northern branch. Trains on Ireland's two gauges are seen in this April 1956 view.

● **LEFT**
This Cavan to Leitrim train is being hauled by a 0-4-4 tank complete with cow-catcher.

● **OPPOSITE BOTTOM**
The deplorable state into which the locomotives had been allowed to fall is graphically illustrated in this view of Ballinamore shed in March 1959, just before the line finally closed.

INFORMATION BOX

Termini	Dromod and Belturbet
Country	Ireland
Distance	53 km (33 miles)
Date of opening	1887

● **LEFT**
One of the locomotives transferred to the C&L from the Cork, Blackrock & Passage line, when this closed in the 1930s, is seen here at Ballyconnell.

● **BELOW**
The view from the train on the roadside tramway to Arigna, which religiously followed the undulations and curves of the road for most of the way.

Wild West – threaded north through an area of small lakes and boggy land, with sharp curves and stiff gradients impeding progress. At the main stations, passengers were left to drum their fingers as the engine rambled off to shunt the goods yard. After 26 km (16 miles) the line's hub and headquarters at Ballinamore was reached. Here the main line was met by the branch from Arigna. For much of its 23 km (14 miles), the line, always known as the tramway, ran alongside the public road. It criss-crossed the road on ungated level crossings and stopped at road side halts distinguished only by name boards poking out of the hedges, and at one point passed over Ireland's longest river, the Shannon, here little more than a mountain stream.

From Ballinamore, the main line turned east to Belturbet, where the 3 ft gauge shared a station with a branch of the great Northern Railway. Just outside the station, another of the great rivers of Ireland, this time the Erne, was bridged by a fine stone viaduct.

In later years there was just one train conveying passengers on this section. The journey from Dromod took three hours for the distance of 53 km (33 miles). This was a line on which passengers would not have wanted to be in a hurry!

It was the carriage of Arigna's poor-quality coal that kept the Cavan & Leitrim in business up to 1959. Taken over by the Great Southern railway in 1925, as other narrow-gauge lines in the Irish Free State closed from the 1930s to the 1950s, their locomotives were transferred to the Cavan & Leitrim to cope with the sometimes hectic coal traffic. By the end, it was a veritable working museum and attracted rail fans from far and wide.

The memory of the gallant little line survived undimmed, and in the 1990s a new Cavan & Leitrim Railway Company was formed. Based at the southern terminus at Dromod, preservationists have re-laid part of the track and ultimately hope to run trains some 8 km (5 miles) to the next town of Molhill. This recreation of the railway, which has already brought the sight of a working 3 ft gauge locomotive back to County Leitrim, will rely on tourists and railway enthusiasts, not coal, for its revenues.

LONDONDERRY TO BURTONPORT

At its peak in the 1920s there were over 800 km (500 miles) of narrow-gauge railway open for service to the public in Ireland. The epic of these 3 ft gauge lines was the run from Derry to Burtonport on the tracks of the Londonderry & Lough Swilly Railway Company (L&LSR) in north-west Donegal.

The L&LSR began life as a standard-gauge line but converted its existing route from Derry to Buncrana to 3 ft gauge when a new narrow-gauge line from Derry to Letterkenny was opened in 1883. At this time the British Government was engaged in a policy of attempting to open up some of the more impoverished and remote districts in the west of Ireland by subsidizing the construction of railways in areas where they were of doubtful commercial viability. This was seen by some cynics as an effort to kill with kindness the agitation for Home Rule in Ireland.

Whatever the political motivation, it is hard to believe that serious investors could have been persuaded to put up the money for the extension of the L&LSR's Letterkenny line, which was promoted in 1898. It was to run through some of the

● LEFT
The line from Burtonport was built and, in theory at least, worked by a separate company, the Letterkenny & Burtonport Extension Railway. This was an attempt by the government to distance its enormous investment in the line from the other activities of the L&LSR. Among the first locomotives acquired for the new line were a quartet of 4-6-0 tanks. No. 4, seen here in Londonderry, retained the initials of the L&BER to the end.

bleakest and poorest land in all of Ireland, and to terminate at the fishing harbour of Burtonport on the west coast of County Donegal. A separate company, the Letterkenny & Burtonport Extension railway, was formed to build the 80 km (50 mile) link, which opened in 1903 at

● ABOVE
The final engines supplied to the L&LSR were also unique and magnificent machines. Nos. 5 and 6 were 4-8-4 tanks built by Hudswell Clarke of Leeds, the only locomotives of this configuration to run on any gauge in the British Isles. They weighed 51 tons and had a tractive effort greater than many standard-gauge engines in use in Ireland at the time of their introduction in 1912.

● LEFT
4-6-0T No. 3 arriving at Letterkenny with a goods train from Derry, June 1950. The buses shown in the photo were operated by the L&LSR and continued in service decades after the trains ceased to run.

INFORMATION BOX	
Termini	Londonderry and Burtonport
Country	Ireland
Distance	119 km (74 miles)
Date of opening	1883

4-8-0 No. 12 waits to head a train back to
Derry from Burtonport in June 1937. The
bleak rocky landscape seen in the picture is
typical of the area served by the line.

a cost to the public purse of some
£300,000. The line avoided most of the
tiny habitations it was supposed to serve
– allegedly to enable locals to find some
employment in ferrying goods and
passengers from these villages to their
distant stations.

The 119 km (74 mile) journey from
Londonderry to Burtonport took around
five hours in carriages that were unheated
in winter. It had been a difficult line to
construct, with whole sections of the
formation sinking into the boggy ground
before the track could be laid. Its main
engineering feature was the 347 m
(1,138 ft) long Owencarrow viaduct,
which was so exposed to gales howling in
from the Atlantic that in both 1906 and
1925 trains were blown off it. The 1925
accident resulted in the deaths of four
passengers. To work the line, two 4-8-0
tender engines were supplied by
Hudswell Clarke in 1905, by far the
largest narrow-gauge locomotives ever to
run in Ireland, and the only machines of
this type ever to operate in the British
Isles on any gauge.

The partition of Ireland severely
affected the fortunes of the L&LSR. The
city of Derry was in Northern Ireland,
while its natural economic hinterland in
County Donegal was now across an
international boundary in another
country. Fuel shortages occasioned by
World War II postponed the inevitable
for a few years, but the line beyond
Letterkenny finally closed completely in
1947, ending this heroic chapter in the
history of Ireland's minor railway.

● ABOVE
The Burtonport line soon spawned the largest locomotives ever to run on the
narrow gauge in the British Isles. Nos. 11 and 12 were 4-8-0 tender engines,
introduced in 1905, which looked more like the sort of engines found in India or in
southern Africa. No. 12 is seen near Derry with a Burtonport train in the 1920s.

● RIGHT
The line to Letterkenny and Burtonport left
the Derry to Buncrana at Tooban Junction,
an isolated spot near the shores of Lough
Swilly. 4-6-2 tank No. 10 is seen at the
junction on a special train in June 1953.

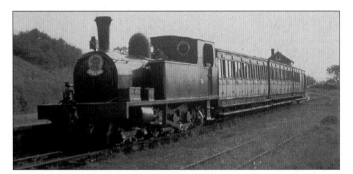

LEICESTER TO LOUGHBOROUGH

In May 1840 the Midland Counties Railway came to Leicester. On the fourth of the month, crowds were assembled at the town's new Campbell Street station as four first- and six second-class carriages, hauled by Leopard, arrived from Nottingham. After a short stop for the officials of the railway who lived in Leicester to take their places, the train pulled out of the station *en route* to Derby, where they dined at the King's Head before returning to Leicester.

The next day the station and all the surrounding area was crowded with spectators to witness the public opening. In spite of the cold, more and more people were arriving as the time of departure of the first train drew near. At seven-thirty the train, with its 50 passengers for Nottingham and Derby, started on its epic journey, reaching Syston, a distance of 9.5 km (6 miles), in 12 minutes.

The train reached Loughborough at eight o'clock where, once again, vast crowds were waiting to see the train, which arrived in Nottingham at nine o'clock. The following week the line was

● **RIGHT**
Built in 1894, two years after Thomas Cook's death, this terracotta building, Franco-Flemish in style, was the firm's Leicester office. At second-floor level, on four bronzed relief panels, are depicted four of the major events in Cook's career.

● **BELOW RIGHT**
The first of the panels shows the train involved in the 1841 excursion. Note that the passengers are travelling in what were affectionately known as "tubs".

● **LEFT**
The statue of Thomas Cook, the father of tourism, outside Leicester's London Road station. The work was commissioned by Leicester City Council in 1992 to mark the centenary of Cook's death.

● **BELOW**
Thomas Cook's grave in Leicester's Welford Road Cemetery.

● **LEFT**
The entrance to Campbell Street station, Leicester, as it appeared in December 1843 to mark the arrival of Queen Victoria. The station, built in 1841, was replaced by the present London Road station in 1892.

INFORMATION BOX

Termini	Leicester and Loughborough
Country	England
Distance	16 km (10 miles)
First advertised rail excursion	5 July 1841

● **LEFT**
A view of Loughborough Midland station.

● **BELOW**
A Class 43 leaving Loughborough on the Midland Main Line. It was on this line that Thomas Cook's historic first railway excursion took place.

extended to Sheffield, a journey of 70 miles which took just over four hours.

In July 1841 Thomas Cook organized his first conducted tour. This was the first advertised excursion train in England – if not the world. With the co-operation of John Fox Bell, Secretary of the Midland Counties Railway, Cook arranged a special train to take people from Leicester to the quarterly temperance meeting at Loughborough. Bell not only agreed to the special train, but also gave Cook a contribution towards the preliminary expenses and agreed to a

half-price third-class fare of one shilling. On the morning of Monday 5 July, 570 people got into the nine open carriages, which had been provided for them. These carriages, called "tubs", were seatless open trucks in which the passengers stood unsheltered from the weather. As well as the crowds of people at Campbell Street station to witness the departure, all the bridges along the route

were lined with hundreds of people eagerly waiting for a look at the train.

Thus began, in the heart of the English Midlands, the company whose name has become synonymous with travel. By 1865 Cook's business had grown so big that he was organizing tours to the Continent and the USA and had had to relocate his head office from Leicester to London.

FORT WILLIAM TO MALLAIG

The start of this, arguably the most scenic rail journey in Britain, is Fort William, a town that nestles under the lofty peak of Ben Nevis. At 1,343 m (4,406 ft), this is Britain's highest mountain.

Soon after leaving the station, the train crosses the River Lochy, and then, at Banavie, the swing bridge over the 97 km (60 mile) long Caledonian Canal. Started by Thomas Telford in 1803, the canal traverses the Great Glen from Fort William to Inverness.

At Corpach, there is a pulp-paper mill, which is of note inasmuch as it is mainly responsible for the line remaining open. The West Highland line was used to deliver timber and then collect the finished product from the factory. After skirting the northern shore of Loch Eil, still with Ben Nevis in view, one soon arrives at Locheilside at the western end of the loch. This station, like others on the route, is still painted in the blue of the original Highland line. Having

● **LEFT**
An LNER on the West Highland line between Fort William and Mallaig.
● **BOTTOM**
The George Stephenson leaves Banavirwith on the 11.05 from Fort William to Mallaig.

lake in Britain. Another 4.8 km (3 miles) brings the train to its destination, the small fishing port of Mallaig. During the summer, some trains are still steam-hauled by the locomotive *The Jacobite.*

In the 1970s and 1980s, the pleasure of the journey was enhanced if passengers, on payment of a supplementary fare, travelled in the observation saloon, where there was a running commentary on the various points of interest on the route. These wooden-bodied Gresley observation cars were the last two in service on British Rail. Although extremely popular, they were withdrawn when the turntable at Mallaig was dismantled, making it impossible for them to be turned. However, one car was fully restored and returned to service on the Great Central Railway in Leicestershire in 2007; it is now in regular public use on the Great Central Railway, and other carriages await restoration.

travelled another 3 km (2 miles) through a narrow glen, the train reaches the Glenfinnan viaduct. It was near here that the Young Pretender, Bonnie Prince Charlie, unfurled his standard in 1745.

Built by Robert "Concrete Bob" MacAlpine, the 21 arches stand 30 m (100 ft) above the ground, the concrete structure curves in a crescent across the Finnan valley. During its construction a cart-horse and its driver were killed when the horse stumbled as it backed to tip its load into one of the shafts. The result was that cart, horse and driver were entombed in the wet concrete. A plaque recording the fatality can be seen on the viaduct.

After leaving Glenfinnan, the train travels through a wooded glen and emerge on the shores of Loch Eilt. From Lochailort station, there is a series of

short tunnels before a viaduct takes the train across Glen Mamie, after which it soon meets the Atlantic at Loch nan Uamh (Loch of the Cave). There are then a few more short tunnels before reaching Arisaig, from where the island of Eigg can be seen.

The line now turns north and at Morar crosses the River Morar. The river, which flows from Loch Morar, is 310 m (1,017 ft) deep, and as such the deepest

INFORMATION BOX	
Termini	Fort William and Mallaig
Country	Scotland
Distance	67 km (41¾ miles)
Date of opening	1901

EDINBURGH TO WICK/THURSO

Soon after leaving Edinburgh, the Forth and Clyde canal is crossed and the train eases slowly round a sharp right-handed curve to Larbert and Stirling, whose large station, still with semaphore signals, was built by the Caledonian Railway. The ground now becomes undulating, and there are distant mountains to be seen. Soon after leaving Stirling, the River Forth is crossed and an 8 km (5 mile) climb at 1:100 begins.

After leaving Perth, 111 km (69 miles) from Edinburgh, the most spectacular part of the run to Inverness begins. After the long climb to the summit of the line at Druimuachdar, 452 m (1,483 ft) above sea level, there is a lengthy undulating section through verdant farming country and woodland.

● LEFT
Named after Scotland's largest lake, Loch Lomond, locomotive No. 37412 speeds its passengers through the Scottish lowlands *en route* to Inverness.

● BELOW
The Loch Lomond snakes its way past one of the lochs on its way to the Scottish Highland city of Inverness.

INFORMATION BOX

Termini	Edinburgh, Wick and Thurso
Country	Scotland
Distance	Wick 540 km (335 miles), Thurso 529 km (329 miles)
Date of opening	1871

Blair Atholl, approached over a castellated bridge, was important in the days of steam traction because banking locomotives were shedded at a small depot still visible to the left of the line. The 29 km (18 mile) length of the line, which raises the railway 315 m (1,033 ft) to the highest rail summit in the UK apart from Snowdon, imposed a great strain on locomotive crews and on the

steam-raising capacity of boilers. Even now, although the HST makes light of the climb, heavy trains hauled by diesel locomotives struggle in bad weather.

The Highland originally reached Inverness down the Spey valley through the Boat of Garten, a junction with the Great North of Scotland Railway, and Grantown on Spey. This 97 km (60 mile) route was shortened by 42 km (26 miles) by constructing a line from Aviemore through what was then wild country over the Slochd Pass, 401 m (1,315 ft) above sea level.

The train leaves Inverness round a left-handed curve and soon crosses the river Ness on a bridge replaced fairly recently after the original collapsed in severe flooding. A spirited run along the Beauly Firth provides fine views to the right before the train swings away from the water through the Muir of Ord to Dingwall. The line now heads north-west, following the coastal plain before swinging north-east to Tain on the picturesque Dornoch Firth, where it starts to climb alongside the Kyles of Sutherland to Culrain.

There follows a sharp climb at 1:70/72 as the line passes through a rocky gorge and past the small town of Lairg on its way to a summit 149 m (489 ft) above sea level, after which it swings east and drops down through pleasant scenery past the small Loch Fleet to reach the coast again at Golspie. A little further on is Dunrobin Castle, the seat of the Dukes of

Sutherland, which had its own private railway station and a shed to house the duke's own locomotive and carriage.

The railway follows the coast for another 24 km (15 miles) and, after Helmsdale, begins to climb again, in places as steeply as 1:60, toward the bleak but impressive uplands. At Forsinard, where a small group of houses and some trees cluster around the station building, the railway parts company with

the track, which goes straight on down Strath Halladale. The line swings sharply east, rising to 216 m (709 ft) at County Marsh summit, after which it descends until, 6.4 km (4 miles) further on, it is a surprise to come upon a station, Altanbreac. It then continues down to the wide coastal plain and the rail junction of Georgemas, where trains were divided, one section going to Wick and the other to Thurso.

● **ABOVE LEFT**
This small shop proclaims itself to be the first and last on mainland Britain. The house built by Jan de Groot (corrupted to John o' Groat) is nearby.

● **ABOVE RIGHT**
The striking blue of the erstwhile Caledonian Railway adorns No. 828, once belonging to that railway, as it waits at the Boat of Garten to take its train to Aviemore on the main line to Inverness.

● **LEFT**
A view from the castle of Edinburgh's world-famous Princes Street. The park between the castle and the street is on the site of a long dried-up loch.

SETTLE TO CARLISLE

The Settle to Carlisle line, which transports the traveller from the Yorkshire Dales through the desolate mountain scenery of the north-west, is one of the most scenic in England. For most of the journey, which takes in 14 tunnels and 19 viaducts, the line runs at an altitude of over 305 m (1,000 ft). One of the tunnels, the 137 m (450 ft) deep Blea Moor tunnel, is a massive 2,404 m (7,887 ft) long.

The Yorkshire village of Settle, where the journey starts, lies about 137 m (450 ft) above sea level. Although work began on the line in 1869, it was not until 1876 that the first passengers were able to enjoy the stupendous views that the line commands. The building of the line was not without incident, as can be seen from the plaque in the village church. Erected by the Midland Railway, it commemorates the men who lost their

● **LEFT**
No. 4498 Sir Nigel Gresley leaves Rise Hill tunnel on the approach to Dent station.

● **BELOW LEFT**
The West Yorkshire Dalesman, hauled by locomotive No. 5305, approaches the summit at Ais Gill Cottages *en route* to Carlisle.

lives while building the 27 km (17 miles) of track between Settle and Dent Head.

The first 21 km (13 miles) of the line travels through the Ribble valley to an elevation of 320 m (1,050 ft). After 18 km (11 miles) the train crosses the Ribblehead viaduct. Built out of limestone and red brick between 1870 and 1874, at 32 m (105 ft) high this handsome viaduct is one of the highlights of the journey. The remoteness of the

INFORMATION BOX	
Termini	Settle and Carlisle
Country	England
Distance	115 km (71 miles)
Date of opening	1876

● **LEFT**
The Ribblehead viaduct, built between 1870 and 1874 out of limestone and red brick. At 32 m (105 ft) high, this is one of the high points of the journey.

● **BELOW**
The Flying Scotsman heads the Cumbrian Mountain Express. It is seen here at Great Ormside heading south *en route* from Appleby to Hellifield.

line can be gauged from the fact that Blea Moor signal box stands some 1.2 km (3/4 mile) from the nearest road, and that Dent station is 6.4 km (4 miles) and 213 m (700 ft) above the village it serves. In winter the weather can be worse than anywhere else in England, with prolonged bouts of heavy snow. To prevent the snow from drifting on to the line, fences have been erected in the exposed mountain areas.

From Appleby to Carlisle the train passes through the Vale of Eden. Never encountering gradients of over 1:100, the line is laid some 15–30 m (50–100 ft) above river level. This makes it less liable to flooding, an important factor as the annual precipitation in this area can be over 2.5 m (100 in) per year.

The end of the journey is Carlisle station, which, in the early part of the century, with many railway companies jointly using it, was bustling with activity. Once an important artery between the city of Leeds and the north-west, the line is now one of the country's foremost lines for seeing, and travelling by, preserved steam locomotives.

The Settle and Carlisle is one of the finest preserved lines in Britain. A journey on these tracks is a trip back in time that every rail enthusiast should experience at least once in their lifetime.

LONDON EUSTON TO GLASGOW

This is one of the most historic lines in Britain, including, as it does, major lengths of Robert Stephenson's London & Birmingham and Joseph Locke's Grand Junction Railway. Although the title of Royal Scot was not bestowed until 1927, the train that bore the name was one of the oldest established in Britain, having first pulled out of Euston for Glasgow in June 1862. Up until 1914 the train left London Euston at 10.00, stopping at Willesden Junction, Rugby, Crewe (where it divided, with one section going on to Edinburgh) and Symington, reaching Glasgow eight and a quarter hours later.

In the summer of 1927, the LMSR made the Royal Scot a train for through passengers between London, Glasgow and Edinburgh only. The double-headed train, hauled by a Claughton 4-6-0 and a George the Fifth 4-4-0, stopped only twice – once at Carnforth, 380 km (236 miles) from Euston, where two 4-4-0

compounds took over for the run over Shap and Beattock summits to the second stop, Symington, 209 km (130 miles) further on, where the Edinburgh part of the train was detached. In 1928, hauled by Royal Scot 4-6-0 No. 6113 Cameronian, the Glasgow train made a non-stop run of

645.8 km (401.3 miles), a British record for any type of locomotive.

The most scenic part of the journey is the stretch north of Wigan, which starts with a sharp climb of about 3 km (2 miles) at 1:104, and then one at 1:119 to the summit of Coppull. Although the

● ABOVE
A southbound Glasgow to Euston train leaves Proofhouse Junction, south of Birmingham's New Street Station.

● LEFT
A scene at Wolverhampton's No. 1 Lock as a Euston to Glasgow InterCity train, hauled by a Class 86 electric locomotive, enters the station.

● **RIGHT**
A Euston-bound
train near
Ecclefechan,
Galloway, on the
first part of the
journey.

● **BELOW LEFT**
A southbound
Glasgow to Euston
train beside the M1 in
Northamptonshire.

● **BELOW RIGHT**
An RES (Rail Express
Systems) liveried
Class 86 heads
southwards through
Cumbria on the West
Coast main line.

next section of the track was conducive to high-speed running, speed restrictions were necessary owing to subsidence (erosion) caused by mine workings. At Boars Head the subsidence was so severe that the windows of the station waiting-room sunk to the level of the platform.

After the almost level track through the Lune Gorge comes one of the steepest main-line inclines in Britain – the 6.4 km (4 mile) long 1:75 climb to Shap summit, 279 m (915 ft) above sea level. From the summit there is a 51 km (32 mile) long run of unbroken downhill running to Carlisle.

Until the 1923 regrouping, Carlisle station was one of the most colourful in the British Isles, with many companies' locomotives in their bright liveries to be

seen. These included the crimson of the Midland, the blue of the Caledonian, the bright green of the North Eastern and the yellow of the North British.

After crossing the into Scotland at Gretna, much of the ten tonnes of coal with which the train started off had been used and the "coal-pusher", a piston

INFORMATION BOX	
Termini	London, Euston and Glasgow, Central
Countries	England and Scotland
Distance	645 km (401 miles)
Date of opening	5 July 1841

operated by steam that shoved the coal forward from the rear of the tender, was set to work. A sign that the coal-pusher was in action was a jet of steam trailing from the top of the tender.

Just beyond Wamphray began the most gruelling climb on any British main line. Although most trains had to take on rear-end assistance, the Royal Scot charged unaided up the formidable 16 km (10 mile) long 1:74 grade to Beattock Summit, 318 m (1,043 ft) above sea level.

From here the train descended into Glasgow Central station, which opened in 1879. Although remodelled some 12 years later, it was still found to be inadequate for the growing traffic, and in 1906 it underwent further changes, to more than double the station's capacity.

LONDON KING'S CROSS TO EDINBURGH WAVERLEY
THE FLYING SCOTSMAN

The name Flying Scotsman entered railway language on 1 January 1923. When the first expresses from London to Edinburgh began in 1862, the journey took 10½ hours; today it takes 4 hours and 35 minutes. Up to 1935, Ivatt's Atlantics were usually at the head of the train between London and Leeds; an A3 Pacific between Leeds and Newcastle; and a Heaton Pacific between Newcastle and Edinburgh.

London's King's Cross station was designed by Lewis Cubitt and built by John Jay in 1852. Today this station is one of the smallest London termini with only eight main-line and two suburban platforms. As the train leaves King's Cross, it passes St Pancras train shed. Designed by W.H. Barlow, the 210 m (689 ft) long, 30 m (98 ft) high building has a glass and iron roof, which spans 74 m (243 ft). When this magnificent feat of engineering was built, it was the widest in the world.

After passing through nine tunnels, the train travels over the stately Welwyn viaduct. Designed by Lewis Cubitt, the structure contains 40 solid brick arches, which reach 27 m (89 ft) at their maximum height over the Mimram valley.

● **LEFT**
The Border Bridge at Berwick-on-Tweed. Built by Robert Stephenson, it was opened by Queen Victoria in 1850.

● **BELOW LEFT**
The colourful border sign between England and Scotland.

All the original GNR stations between King's Cross and Doncaster, such as Stevenage, Hitchin, Huntingdon and Peterborough, were built using local materials by the Leicester-born Henry Goddard. Shortly after leaving Peterborough, the train reaches the

24 km (15 mile) long Stoke Bank, the summit of which, 105 m (345 ft) above sea level, is the highest point reached by the train this side of the border.

Travelling north the gradient steepens from 1:440 to 1:178 until, at the top, the train enters the 805 m (2,640 ft) long Stoke Tunnel, after which it descends to the town of Grantham. This is the stretch of line on which, in July 1938, Gresley's Mallard reached the world steam record of 203 kph (127 mph).

There are several flat crossings on this part of the line. One of these, just before Retford, was the scene of an accident in which the driver of a down express saw a goods train ambling straight across his

● **LEFT**
This mid-1940s scene shows the Flying Scotsman leaving Newcastle.

path. Having no time to brake, the quick-thinking driver accelerated and cut the goods train in two, thereby saving his train at the expense of only two or three goods wagons.

After leaving Doncaster, the train runs along a curving viaduct into Wakefield, before beginning its 3 km (2 mile) climb of 1:122 to Ardsley. Following a descent of 1:50 the train enters Leeds Central terminus, from which, after a short halt, the train retraces its steps for a short way before bearing right to strike up the 1:100 8 km (5 mile) long Headingley Bank. Just past the summit, the train plunges into Bramhope Tunnel. At 3.42 km (2 miles and 234 yd) long, Bramhope Tunnel is the seventh longest tunnel in the country. Beyond it, the gradient alters sharply to a downhill 1:94.

The train approaches Newcastle over the Tyne by the High Level Bridge. Designed by Robert Stephenson for both road and rail, this was the first major bridge-building work on which James Nasmyth's steam-driven pile-driver was used. Begun in April 1846, with a total weight of over 5,000 tons, this is the earliest example of a dual-purpose structure. The upper deck was for the railway, the lower for the road.

The next big bridge to be crossed is the 658 m (2,159 ft) long Royal Border Bridge, also built by Robert Stephenson, which was opened by Queen Victoria in 1850. Over 2,000 workers were engaged

● **ABOVE LEFT**
This picture clearly shows the two famous arches that are a feature of King's Cross station, London.

● **ABOVE RIGHT**
An InterCity train passes Durham Cathedral, the last resting-place of St Cuthbert.

● **BELOW**
350 miles to go until London.

INFORMATION BOX

THE FLYING SCOTSMAN

Termini	London King's Cross and Edinburgh, Waverley
Countries	England and Scotland
Distance	650 km (404 miles)
Date of opening	1 January 1923

---

in building the fine 28 redbrick semicircular arches, each with a span of 18.7 m (61 ft 4 in).

After crossing the border, the railway hugs the coastline as it ascends the 6.4 km (4 miles) of 1:190 up to Burnmouth. On passing Grantshouse the train enters the Penmanshiel tunnel, which was closed temporarily in 1979 after a fall had killed two men who were working in the tunnel.

The train enters Waverley station through the Carlton tunnel, opened in June 1846. Edinburgh's first station was confined to the narrow valley between the old and new towns of the city, and became congested. A new station, covering 23 acres, said to be the second biggest in Britain, was opened in 1900.

LONDON PADDINGTON TO SWANSEA – *THE RED DRAGON*

● **BELOW**
A Class 143 Regional Railways train outside Ragnor, near Cardiff.

The Red Dragon service, between London Paddington and Swansea (Abertawe), was first run in the winter of 1950–51. Departing Swansea at 08.45, the train made stops at Cardiff (Caerdydd) and Newport (Casnewydd-ar-Wysg), before completing the final 214 km (133 miles) of the journey to Paddington, non-stop in 165 minutes, arriving at 13.05. The return trip was 30 minutes longer. Leaving Paddington at 17.55, it made additional stops at Swindon and Badminton, so that Swansea was not reached until 22.45.

Reading station was the first of Brunel's one-sided stations, and one of the last survivors. All that remains of the original is the building on the southernmost platform. It was here that one of the first accidents on the Great Western occurred. While the station was being built, Henry West, a carpenter, was fatally blown from the roof by a "whirlwind".

About 14 km (9 miles) from Reading the train crosses Basildon Bridge, which was built in 1839 and extended in the 1890s. Its four redbrick 19 m (62 ft)

INFORMATION BOX

THE RED DRAGON

Termini	London, Paddington and Swansea
Countries	England and Wales
Distance	307 km (191 miles)
Date of first run	1950

arches cross the Thames uniting Berkshire and Oxfordshire. The line soon returns to Berkshire by means of Moulsford Bridge.

At the western end of Steventon, 18 km (11 miles) further on, the line crosses "The Causeway". One mile long, this is a raised flood path lined with trees and 17th- and 18th-century houses. A further 16 km (10 miles) brings us to Uffington, famous for its "White Horse", which can be seen from the train. This is 114 m (374 ft) from nose to tail and is believed to have been first cut into the hillside about 100 BC. Although called a horse it is more than likely that it was meant to be a dragon, for nearby is Dragon Hill on which, so folklore tells us, St George slew the fabled beast.

Swindon station, 124 km (77 miles) from Paddington, was originally built in 1841–42. A feature of the station was the hotel and dining-room connected to it by a covered overbridge. The original agreement was that all trains passing through should have a ten-minute refreshment stop here. Swindon was the site of Brunel's Great Western works, which were completed in 1843. The last

steam engine built at the works was Evening Star, which entered service in May 1960.

Badminton station, 160 km (100 miles) from Paddington, was specially built for the Duke of Beaufort, who demanded that any train had to stop at his request – until, that is, an Act of Parliament put a stop to his right. It was here that the eponymous game was first played. A few miles out of Badminton, the train goes under the Cotswold Hills through the 406 m (1,332 ft) long Chipping Sodbury tunnel.

First sketched out by Charles Richardson in 1865, the Severn tunnel, after twice being flooded out, was finally completed in 1886 at the cost of nearly £2 million (then $3.2 million). Connecting Wales to England, at 4,064 m (13,333 ft) long it is the largest main-line railway tunnel in Britain. The tunnel

● BELOW
A driver's-eye view from the cab of an InterCity 125 as it approaches the up train on the line between Paddington and Swansea.

● BELOW
The "Welcome to Wales" sign that greets passengers as the train leaves the Welsh side of the Severn tunnel.

shortened the route from London to South Wales by 40 km (25 miles) and led to the popular belief that the initials GWR stood for the "great way round".

Just before Newport the line crosses the River Usk. The first bridge, one of Brunel's wooden viaducts, was damaged by fire during construction. Remarkable as it sounds, out of the many wooden viaducts built by Brunel, this was the only one to suffer such a fate. It was later

rebuilt, but this time in wrought iron.

Cardiff Central station, 233 km (145 miles) from Paddington, was first built in 1850. To create a site for the station, the River Taff had to be diverted. The station was modernized in the 1920s. On leaving the Welsh capital, the line turns inland until it regains the coast near Margam, after which it skirts Swansea Bay, passing through Port Talbot and Neath before arriving at Swansea.

● OPPOSITE
The English portal of the Severn tunnel, connecting Wales and England.

● RIGHT
A scene near Sonning Cutting. Although passengers in the train do not get a good view of it, Sonning Cutting is an engineering achievement at 18 m (60 ft) deep and nearly 3 km (2 miles) long. It was built in the autumn and winter of 1839 and opened in March 1840.

LONDON EUSTON TO HOLYHEAD
THE IRISH MAIL

The London & North Western Railway's Irish Mail was the world's first named train. Known unofficially as the "Wild Irishman", it departed from Euston station for the first time in August 1848. After passing through the 1,080 m (3,543 ft) long Primrose Hill tunnel, the train entered Acton Lane station (named Willesden Junction in 1866), which was built in 1842. Owing to its two groups of completely separate high-level platforms, and the fact that nobody knew at which platform any particular train was to arrive at or depart from, the station was unofficially nicknamed "Bewildering Junction" by its passengers.

Some 27 km (17 miles) into the journey the train passes through the Watford tunnel. 1.65 km (1 mile and 57 yd) long, the tunnel was built so that the railway line did not cross over the land of the Earl of Essex.

After another 56 km (35 miles) the train passes over the Wolverton viaduct. Over 200 m (660 ft) long with six arches, each with an 18 m (60 ft) span, the viaduct is at the centre of an

● **LEFT**
A 20th-century InterCity train passes the 13th-century Conway Castle.

embankment 2.4 km (1½ miles) long and 15 m (49 ft) high. After a further 16 km (10 miles), Kilsby tunnel is reached. At 2,216 m (7,270 ft) in length, when it was built, at a cost of £290,000 (then $460,000), it was the longest railway tunnel in the world.

Passing Birmingham New Street, Manchester, Crewe and Chester, the train then runs along the North Wales coast. After going through Rhyl and Colwyn the line goes under the steep slope of the almost precipitous headland of Penmaen Mawr. As there was not enough room

between the mountain and the shore, in some places the rock had to be blasted and in others sea walls had to be built up to enable the line to be laid. A tunnel 211 m (693 ft) long was cut through the headland and, in some places, where the line ran close under the steep mountain face, covered ways were built as a precaution against falling stones.

During its construction, in October 1846, a north-westerly gale, combined with a spring tide of 5 m (16 ft), destroyed a large part of the work on the westward side of the headland. It was

● **LEFT**
An InterCity train approaching Crewe from the south.

then decided to cross the section by means of the big, curving, open viaduct that brings the train into Bangor. Work on the viaduct was eventually finished in 1849.

In the days of steam, in order to permit non-stop running between Chester and Holyhead, just before Bangor, near Aber, the speeding train would scoop up water from troughs laid between the tracks. Laid down in 1860, these were the world's first railway water troughs.

Next comes the Menai Strait tubular railway bridge leading to Anglesey. Built by Stephenson, the bridge spans 335 m (1,100 ft) of water near to Britannia Rock, from which it gets the name of Britannia Bridge. Stephenson's first plan

was to construct it out of cast iron. However, this was rejected by the Admiralty, who insisted that under no circumstances was the navigation of the Strait to be interrupted. After toying with various plans, in March 1845 Stephenson finally decided on the tubular wrought-iron beam with openings of 140 m (459 ft) and a roadway, formed of a hollow wrought-iron beam, about 6 m (20 ft) in diameter.

Built by a team of about 1,500 workers, the bridge has four spans, two of 140 m (460 ft) over the water and two of 70 m (230 ft) over the land. It was

opened for the public on 18 March 1850. Before the opening of the bridge, passengers had to disembark in Bangor and cross the Menai Strait by coach via Telford's suspension bridge.

The short run over Anglesey passes Llanfair PG, or, to give it its 58-letter name, coined by the local innkeeper in the 19th century, Llanfairpwllgwyngyll-gogerychwyrndrobwllllantysiliogogogoch. Renowned for having the world's longest railway sign, the station was re-opened in 1973. Then the train soon reaches Holyhead – and the ferry that conveys passengers to Ireland, the Emerald Isle.

INFORMATION BOX	
THE IRISH MAIL	
Termini	London, Euston and Holyhead
Countries	England and Wales
Distance	425 km (264 miles)
Date of first run	1 August 1848

LONDON PADDINGTON TO PENZANCE

One of the most exciting and interesting rail journeys in England is that from London Paddington to Penzance, at the south-westerly tip of Cornwall. When the line opened, in August 1859, not only did almost all the trains stop at all stations, but passengers also had to change at Exeter and Plymouth. On arrival in Truro, a horse-drawn bus took them on to Falmouth, where the travellers boarded the West Cornwall narrow-gauge railway for the 33-minute ride to Penzance. The fastest time for the whole journey was some 14 hours and 50 minutes.

1862 saw the introduction of the Flying Dutchman, a train which did the journey from Paddington to Churston,

INFORMATION BOX	
Termini	London and Penzance
Country	England
Distance	490 km (304 miles)
Date of opening	1859

on the Torquay branch of the South Devon Railway, at an average speed of 89.6 kph (56 mph), making it possible to reach Penzance in 10 hours and 19 minutes. The following year the line was extended from Truro to Falmouth,

● **BELOW**
Cornish Riviera Limited. The first train of this
name ran in 1904.

thereby making the equine transport
redundant. By 1867 the broad gauge was
extended to Penzance.

In 1890 the Great Western
introduced the Cornishman express,
which, by cutting out a number of
intermediate stations, was able to reach
Penzance in 8 hours and 42 minutes.
After the conversion from broad to
standard gauge in 1892, the Flying
Dutchman was able to cut a further 15
minutes off its time, so becoming the
fastest train in the world.

In 1896 the Cornishman posted a
time of 3 hours and 43 minutes for a

● **OPPOSITE ABOVE**
When the station was built Paddington was
still just a village. In the booking hall is a
diminutive statue of Isambard Kingdom
Brunel which was unveiled in May 1982.

● **OPPOSITE BELOW**
One of the few Brunel stations left, Dawlish
station, built in 1846, is lovingly preserved.
Here an InterCity train leaves the station *en
route* to Penzance.

● **ABOVE LEFT**
A section of the dramatic coastal track
between Dawlish and Teignmouth.

● **RIGHT**
An InterCity train crosses the Huntspil River at
the Somerset Levels. This is one of the wettest
areas in England with an average annual
rainfall of 101 cm (40 in). Much of the area is
below sea level and liable to periodic flooding.

Cutting, 18 m (59 ft) deep and 6.5 km (nearly two miles long), is another remarkable achievement, built in 1839 and opened in March 1840. The excavation was fraught with difficulties as torrential rain flooded the area and reduced the site to a quagmire.

One of the features of the line was Brunel's celebrated one-sided stations. With both platforms on the same side, but a short distance apart, the design obviated the necessity for passengers to cross the line. Examples of these, now totally rebuilt stations, which must have caused chronic operating difficulties, include Reading, Taunton and Exeter.

After the 998 m (3,274 ft) long Whiteball Tunnel, which marks the boundary of Somerset and Devon, there is a flat coastal run, taking in the five tunnels between Dawlish and Teignmouth – Kennaway, Phillot, Clerk's, Coryton and Parsons. In 1905 these tunnels were widened to accommodate double tracks.

Newton Abbot was where Brunel set up his atmospheric railway. The concept of this was that, instead of being hauled by steam engines, the carriages were

non-stop run to Exeter – then at 310 km (194 miles) the longest non-stop route in the world – cutting the time to Penzance to 7 hours and 52 minutes.

In July 1904, by running non-stop to Plymouth, the time was reduced even more when the Limited express reached Penzance in 7 hours dead. In May 1914, the time was cut to 6¹/₂ hours and, in 1927, with the introduction of the King Class, the most powerful engines in the British Isles, the Cornish Riviera reduced the time by a further five minutes to 6 hours and 25 minutes.

Soon after departing Paddington Station, which was designed by Brunel and opened in 1854, the train passes over the 274 m (899 ft) long Wharncliffe Viaduct. Built in 1838, the eight 21 m (69 ft) brick spans tower 20 m (65 ft) above the ground. The next point of interest on the route is Sounding Arch Bridge, which was built in 1838 and widened in 1891. Considered to be one of Brunel's finest bridges, it cost £37,000 (then $59,200) to build and consists of two of the largest, flattest arches ever built in brick, each with a span of 39 m (128 ft) with a rise of only 7.4 m (24 ft 3 in). It is this bridge that is depicted in Turner's painting, *Rain, Steam and Speed*.

Although passengers in the train do not get a good view of it, Sonning

● ABOVE
On getting off the train, visitors to Penzance are welcomed by this bilingual greeting in both English and Cornish.

● BELOW
The holiday is over. The train to Paddington leaves Penzance.

The 12.25 Great Western train from London to Bristol, showing the Great Western's new livery, at Swindon.

propelled by a vacuum caused by compressed air being pumped through a pipe between the rails.

Separating Devon and Cornwall is the 338 m (1,109 ft) long Royal Albert Bridge, which spans the River Tamar, the world's only chain-link suspension bridge to carry express trains. Widely regarded as Brunel's masterpiece, the two main tubular spans, each 137 m (450 ft) long and weighing over 1,077 tonnes (1,060 tons), are supported by three piers that allow a clearance of at least 30 m (100 ft)

above the water. The central underwater pier is anchored on hard rock 24 m (79 ft) below the high-water level and was built by masons working in a pressurized diving bell – the first such use in civil engineering. It took seven years to build and was opened by Prince Albert in May 1859, four months before Isambard Kingdom Brunel's death.

Over the 85 km (53 miles) between Plymouth and Truro, the train crossed 34 of Brunel's timber viaducts, now replaced by masonry ones. The viaducts,

which crossed the many deep and narrow valleys of the area, were constructed in two standard spans of 20 m (66 ft) for the Cornwall and Tavistock lines and 15 m (50 ft) for the West Cornwall structures.

The line reached Penzance in March 1852, when it opened to standard-gauge trains. Fifteen years later, in March 1867, the Great Western's broad gauge reached the town. The present station, which has a charming sign welcoming visitors in the now almost dead language of Cornish, was built about 1865.

The Mayflower entering Exeter St Davids station.

The train crossing the sea wall at Dawlish. The town of Dawlish is often the victim of fierce storms. One such, in 1974, washed away most of the down platform.

LONDON VICTORIA TO DOVER
THE GOLDEN ARROW

Although the Southern Railway (and its predecessor the South Eastern & Chatham Railway) had maintained a service from London Victoria to Paris, it was not until 15 May 1929 that the title Golden Arrow was bestowed upon the train. The first trains were hauled by 4-6-0 Lord Nelson Class and were exclusively for first-class Pullman passengers; however, two second-class cars were added in the 1940s . After World War II, the Lord Nelson Class was

● **LEFT**
The Golden Arrow travelling through Ashford, Kent.

● **BELOW LEFT**
The Golden Arrow coming into Headcorn station. This view is taken from Fritten Road Bridge.

replaced by Oliver Bulleid's Merchant Navy Class 4-6-2s. Bulleid, a New Zealander by birth, was the Chief Mechanical Engineer of the Southern Railway. Then, in 1951, Britannia 4-6-2 Standard Class 7s were introduced to the service. One of these, No. 70004, William Shakespeare, was exhibited at the 1951 Festival of Britain.

The Golden Arrow was one of the first trains in England to be fitted with a public address system, through which the international passengers were addressed in English and French.

Another feature of the train was the Trianon cocktail bar, reminiscent of a high-class club, where the rich were able to sup their way to the Continent. The exclusive first-class train lasted only two years, for by May 1931 the weight of the

INFORMATION BOX

THE GOLDEN ARROW

Termini	London Victoria and Dover
Country	England
Distance	113 km (70 miles)
Date of first run	15 May 1929

● **RIGHT**
The Golden Arrow
seen here between
Tonbridge and
Sevenoaks.

● **BELOW RIGHT**
King Arthur Class
4-6-0 No. 30794 Sir
Ector de Maris stands
at the night ferry's
traditional platform 2
at London Victoria.

● **BOTTOM
RIGHT**
The up Continental
boat express leaving
Dover Marine station
after collecting
passengers from the
cross-channel ferry.

Depression had persuaded the railway
company that their only course of action
was to admit second-class passengers.

Sporting a Union Flag and Tricolour,
the Golden Arrow departed London
Victoria at 11.00 a.m. The journey began
with a 1:62 climb on to the Grosvenor
Bridge. Subsequent gradients included
2.4 km (1½ miles) at 1:102 leading to
Penge tunnel, and 3 km (2 miles) at 1:95
to Bickley Junction, with slow running
round the curve to Orpington.

After passing Tonbridge the train was
faced with 6 km (4 miles) at 1:122 and 3
km (2 miles) at 1:144, the latter through
the Sevenoaks tunnel. From here to
Dover Marine, which was reached at
12.38, the line was fairly level and speeds
of 96 kph (60 mph) were possible.

The ferry, Canterbury, crossed the
English Channel in 75 minutes. After
transferring to the awaiting Flèche d'Or,
a four-cylinder Nord Pacific of the
French Northern Railway, the travellers
completed the last 296 km (184 miles)
from Calais to Paris in 190 minutes,
arriving in the French capital at 17.35.
You can still travel by rail and ferry from
Victoria to Paris, but not by steam.

BEDFORD TO BLETCHLEY

A rail journey from Bedford to Bletchley, two stations that connect the Midland main line with the West Coast main line, may not sound as romantic as a trip on the Orient Express, but the "friendly line", as many locals call it, is one of the finest journeys in the kingdom.

Since the first train ran on 17 November 1846, operated by the London & North Western Railway, the line has been vital to the people of the area. A journey along the route engineered by George and Robert Stephenson, now denominated the Marston Vale line and operated by National Express, is like a trip back to the 1930s. The 27 km (17 mile) journey,

which takes 50 minutes, is completely rural, with no mass urbanization to be seen. There are three manned level crossings and no fewer than six signal boxes that still operate semaphore

signals. The Fenny Stratford box houses a fine collection of old paintings and sepia photographs showing the area as it was.

At the beginning of the 20th century, the line was covered by a railmotor service. These were an early form of multiple unit and consisted of a self-propelled coach fitted with a steam boiler in one end. Because the passengers entered and left the coaches by means of steps, it was not necessary to build conventional platforms at the halts along the way. Today the trains are operated by Heritage DMUs. This is one of the last lines to use these units, which date back to the 1960s.

The journey begins at Bedford Midland station, which is on the Midland main line with services to Luton and Gatwick airports. The first part of the journey passes through Bedford St Johns, Kempston Hardwick, Stewartby (formerly Wootton Pillinge) and Millbrook. Here there is a crossing where the levers are housed in the open air by the side of the box. The crossing keeper has a collection of wheel hub caps that have fallen off cars as they ride over the bumpy crossing.

Part of the route goes over land belonging to the Duke of Bedford. The 10th Duke was a great supporter of the building of the line. He did, however,

● **ABOVE RIGHT**
Evening shadows lengthen as the two-car Class 117 DMU ambles through glorious countryside near Millbrook with a Bletchley to Bedford service.

● **RIGHT**
A Bletchley-bound train pauses at the delightful rural station of Fenny Compton, next to the A5 Watling Street, with a Bletchley to Bedford service. Note the semaphore signals and the high escarpment sweeping towards Ampthill in the background.

INFORMATION BOX

Termini	Bedford and Bletchley
Country	England
Distance	27 km (17 miles)
Date of opening	1846

insist that all the station buildings on his
estate (Fenny Stratford, Woburn Sands,
Ridgmont and Millbrook) should be of
half-timber design. Woburn Sands, the
coal depot for the line, was also
important for its brickyard, and the
railway was used to transport the bricks.

A feature of the journey used to be
the London Brick Works, whose many
tall chimneys were counted by
generations of children. There are now
only ten, which can still be seen from the
train. The old clay pits, now filled with
water, create a moonlike landscape. Some
of these sites were used as landfill for
London's waste, which was carried down
the line as far as Forders Sidings.

● **ABOVE**
The Derby Lightweight
two-car DMU Class 108
stands in the bay at
Bedford station with a
Class 319 Thameslink
EMU in the background.

● **ABOVE
RIGHT**
The traditional
country station
atmosphere of the
1930s is conjured up
in this typical scene
as a two-car Class
108 unit stands at
Aspley Guise station.

● **RIGHT**
"Ten Chimneys". A
two-car Class 117
DMU ambles past
the high escarpment
near Lidlington with
a Bedford to
Bletchley service.

LONDON TO COLOGNE

● **BELOW**
Electric BoBo locomotive No. 86.250 stands at
the head of its train in Liverpool Street station
in London.

There are three rail routes from London to
Cologne, one is via the Hook of Holland,
one is via Ostend, and the third is through
the Channel Tunnel.

● **VIA THE HOOK OF HOLLAND**
This used to be one of the pleasantest
ways to go to Cologne. A boat train,
usually with the best stock the railway
could muster and a gleaming locomotive
at the head, left London's Liverpool
Street station each evening. On arrival at
the special station at Harwich, where
facilities have been greatly improved
recently, passengers passed through
passport and customs controls and
walked straight to the ship. This route
can still be followed, but since June 1997
night ships for rail passengers have been
discontinued and replaced by catamarans
operating day services only.

The railway station at the Hook of
Holland is on the dockside. Connecting
international express trains ceased a few
years ago and the route via Venlo now
requires a couple of changes to get to
Cologne. Frequent local services run to
Rotterdam, which is a major port.

● **BELOW**
Electric BoBo locomotive No. 86.250 stands at
the head of its train in Liverpool Street station
in London.

● **LEFT**
The König Albert
was one of the
vessels that ferried
passengers from
Dover to Ostend in
the 1950s.

INFORMATION BOX	
Termini	London and Cologne
Countries	England, Belgium, Netherlands and Germany
Distance	via Ostend 595 km (370 miles); via The Hook of Holland 545 km (339 miles)
Date of opening	via Ostend 1861; via The Hook of Holland 1893; via the Channel Tunnel 1994

● **LEFT**
The Hook of Holland rail/ship station by
night. The large ships will soon be replaced
by large catamarans.

The terrain in the Netherlands is only difficult for rail construction to the extent that numerous rivers, many of them navigable, must be crossed. On the line to Venlo is the longest rail bridge in the Netherlands, at 1.07 km (3,510 ft), over the Hollandsch Diep at Moerdijk. Other places of rail interest are Tilburg, where the main workshops of the Netherlands railways are situated, and Venlo, on the border with Germany, an industrial centre that not only provides a wide variety of Netherlands motive power but also sees the hand-over of trains to German locomotives.

The route through Utrecht is the one now normally used to get to Cologne from Rotterdam. There is a good connecting train every hour to Utrecht, a major rail junction.

● VIA OSTEND

London's Victoria station was the starting-point to this once classic route to the continent, with boat trains depositing passengers virtually alongside ships. Today an electric multiple unit (EMU) runs to Ramsgate, and the bus provided by the shipping line carries passengers to the harbour. The night crossing used to bring them to Ostend early enough to catch the 06.34 train, giving passengers an arrival at Cologne by 10.42. The harbour at Ostend is host to myriad small

● BELOW
The smart way to get to Brussels and into Germany is to come from England by Eurostar from Waterloo station in London. A train arrives at Brussels Midi station, where connections can readily be made to most parts of Europe.

craft and fishing boats, and the town can offer a variety of places to sample continental fare. Just outside the station, a coastal tramway, part of the much diminished "Vicinal" system, runs southwards to De Panne and northwards to Knokke.

The elegant building and seven platforms of Ostend station are right alongside the quay. In addition to the usual local and inter-city services, international trains commence their journeys here, although the numbers have declined in recent years. At Ghent, the largest town in 13th-century Europe, there is a large railway station with an

● LEFT
A Sprinter on local services stands at Rotterdam Central station.

● **RIGHT**
Cologne's Hauptbahnhof is overshadowed by
the city's Gothic cathedral.

● **RIGHT**
Cologne's Hauptbahnhof is overshadowed by
the city's Gothic cathedral.

impressive old main building. In the early
morning and evening rush hours its many
tracks are very busy. A good range of
motive power and a variety of EMUs plus
the occasional freight train provide
constant interest.

And so to Brussels where the third
railway route to Cologne is met.

● **VIA THE CHANNEL TUNNEL**

The new London Eurostar terminal at
St Pancras is now the starting point for
trains serving Paris, Lille and Brussels.
The vast single-span roof has been
restored to accommodate the 400-metre-
long trains that will run on the first
high-speed line linking London to the
European high-speed rail network.
The interior of the trains bears a close
resemblance to the TGV on which it is
based. Once under way, the ride quality
is superb. It is so quiet and smooth that
the speed is hard to determine.

The train makes a slow start from
London, weaving its way through the
suburbs for many kilometres until it can
sprint along the fairly straight route
through Kent, passing hop fields and
oast-houses on the way to the entrance to
Dollands Moor sidings, where the live
current ceases to be collected from a
third rail and is taken from the overhead
line equipment. This operation is carried
out without stopping, and the train is
soon running at the maximum permitted
speed of 160 kph (100 mph) for about
20 minutes through the tunnel.

The train emerges in France with the
very extensive sidings for the car and
goods vehicle shuttle services away to the
left. The TGV line to Lille is joined and
having passed the specially built station
there is a locomotive depot to the right
and a large TGV and general repair depot
to the left. As the high-speed lines in
Belgium are completed it is possible to
see and appreciate the impressive
engineering feats which have been
undertaken in this ambitious project.

Brussels also has a fine Eurostar
terminal at the Midi station. From the
many platforms of the main station,
trains go to all parts of Europe. Below,
trams and a metro system serve the
environs of this bustling capital city.

The Belgium Government was far-
sighted when it supported the joining of
stations north and south of the city by a
tunnel – something yet to be achieved in
Paris or London. Brussel Centraal, as the
name implies, serves the city centre,
where there are many fine buildings. The
Gare du Nord is situated in the French-
speaking part of the city, in an area which
was once rather disreputable but is now
being sanitized by the construction of
many modern buildings.

● **RIGHT**
For passengers with some time to spare there is plenty to see and do in Brussels. Maybe a cup of coffee, or something stronger, in the Grande Place.

● **OPPOSITE BELOW**
The majority of short-distance inter-city and local passenger-trains are in the hands of EMUs in Belgium. Aum 75 Class 4-car unit heads a rush-hour train at Gent St Pieters.

● **BELOW**
The old Marloiban station in Utrecht has been turned into a fine railway museum. Railways in the Netherlands bought many locomotives from the UK. This outside-framed 2-4-0 No. 32 was built by Beyer-Peacock in 1864.

● **BOTTOM**
German Railways No. 140. 741 stands at the Dutch/German border at Venlo. It has taken over from its German counterpart and will soon set off for Cologne.

There are numerous trains from Midi station to Cologne, taking just under three hours, but this timing will be greatly reduced when the planned new lines have been completed. The approach by rail to Liège is down a very steep gradient, and even today a special electric locomotive is kept to bank heavy trains going in the Brussels direction. The station is very busy, with trains coming from all points of the compass, including the picturesque line to Luxembourg. The line climbs away from Liège following a sinuous course with some pleasant scenery on the way to Aachen. Beyond Aachen, the journey is largely through rural agricultural areas, passing the significant town of Düren. Increasing industry and urbanization heralds arrival at the outskirts of Cologne with large carriage sidings to the right and a massive locomotive depot at the left.

Cologne's main station is at a high level on the banks of the River Rhine. Its huge arched roof shelters passenger-trains of all descriptions, and traffic has increased to such an extent that the Hohenzollern bridge across the river now has a modern double track set of spans opposite the spans of the road and tramway part of the bridge that was destroyed in World War II.

Paris to Istanbul
The Orient Express

● OPPOSITE
A Kraus-Maffei Bavarian 18 Class 4-6-2,
No. 18470 L63, hauling the Orient Express
between Kehl and Stuttgart in about 1933.

What became the Orient Express sprang upon eight countries in 1883. Founded specially by Georges Nagelmackers, a Belgian mining engineer, La Compagnie Internationale des Wagons-Lits (The International Sleeping Car Company), the world's first multi-national, had been running through sleeping cars with wide buffers from Paris to Vienna since 1876. "Et des Grands Express Européens" was added to the name in 1883 when the train first linked Paris with Bucharest, as it still does today, via Munich, Vienna and Budapest. The journey took 77 hours one way and 81 the other – local time was unsynchronized.

Istanbul passengers were taken on to Giurgiu, ferried from Romania across the river Danube to Rustchuk in Bulgaria and then had another seven-hour train journey to the Black Sea port of Varna. From here an Austrian Lloyd liner took the travellers on the final part of their 82-hour journey.

From 8 August 1888, the train abandoned Giurgiu and diverted at Budapest to Belgrade and Nis in Serbia. It then travelled up the Dragoman Pass through the Northern Passara mountains by cornice and tunnel, on a gradient of 1:37, to Bulgaria; down to Sofia, up again

● ABOVE
The Military Orient Express in 1919. All the seats on this Allied military train were held by the French Army (note the tricolour on the tender), but civilians were admitted if seats were available. It is seen here crossing the River Limmat near Zurich.

● BELOW
The Orient Express as seen on the French Eastern Railway on 4 October 1883. The train of two passenger cars and a sleeper is being hauled by a 500 Class 2-4-0.

INFORMATION BOX	
THE ORIENT EXPRESS	
Termini	Paris and Istanbul
Countries	France to Turkey
Distance	3,212 km (1,996 miles)
Date of opening	1883

to Tatar Pazardjik, and through the mountains over the newly opened line to the city of Plovdiv, the furthermost point of the Oriental Railway from Istanbul. This journey took 67 hours and a few minutes.

Passengers from 1888 enjoyed the comfortable sleeping cars with velvet curtains, plush seating, lavatories at the car ends, and a tinkling hand-bell in the corridors, which summoned them to five-course French *haute cuisine* in the dining cars. Renamed the Orient Express in 1891, it made cursory frontier stops

to change engines. The clientele always included government couriers, chained to their diplomatic bags, but often royalty and diplomats also used the train. Indeed the story goes that a Romanian count caught the train just to enjoy the menu, remarking, "The express takes four hours to cross me" – meaning his vast estate!

Leaving Gare de l'Est, Paris, the train had an easy run up the Marne valley through Champagne vineyards, Epernay and Chalons, where, later, the Calais car was attached. The train then crossed the River Moselle at Nancy and continued on its way to the then German frontier at Deutsch-Avricourt.

The route across Alsace passes through the notable 1,678 m (5,505 ft)

● **ABOVE RIGHT**
One of the head attendants waits to welcome passengers aboard the Orient Express.

● **ABOVE**
The Pullman coat of arms.

● **RIGHT**
A British Pullman, taken at Kensington Olympia around 1987. The train manager stands in front of the dining car.

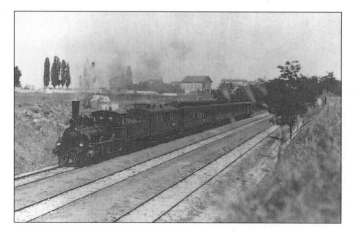

● LEFT
The Orient Express in Turkey about 1910. The train here is being hauled by an Oriental Railways Austrian-built 4-4-0. Note the "cow-catcher" on the locomotive.

The Orient Express was stopped abruptly in 1914 by the outbreak of World War I, when both sides used were forced to commission their passenger coaches for use as ambulance trains.

In 1916 the Germans started the rival Mitropa Company, using requisitioned Wagons-Lits cars, running the Berlin-Istanbul Balkan Express, to reach their Turkish allies. After the 1918 Armistice was signed in Wagons-Lits Dining Car No. 2419, destroyed by Hitler's SS troops in 1944, the Orient Express restarted with difficulty in 1921. In 1923, due to the Rheinland Occupation, the train was diverted via Zurich (Switzerland) and the 10.24 km (6 miles 650 yd) long Austrian Arlberg tunnel, which had been completed in 1884. This became a permanent route.

The Swiss-Arlberg-Vienna Express, renamed Arlberg-Orient Express in 1932, ran to Budapest via Hagyeshalom from Vienna, and to Bucharest via Sighisoara. A Paris-Athens sleeper ran

long Homarting-Arzviller twin tunnels – the twin carries the Marne-Rhein Canal. Eight km (5 miles) beyond Strasbourg (Strassburg) the Orient Express crossed the Rhine at Kehl, over a steel bridge destroyed in World War II, into Baden-Württemberg.

After travelling through Stuttgart, Augsburg and Ulm the express arrived in Bavaria's capital, Munich. Originally the express entered Austria at Simbach, but was soon diverted past Lake Prien to Salzburg and so on to Vienna, where, from 1894, it was joined by the Ostend-Vienna express.

The Orient Express then ran on through Bratislava to Budapest. The next section of the route, through to Bucharest, was via Szged and Timisoara, over the now disused 30 m (99 ft) high Biatorbagy viaduct, where, in 1931, the train was dramatically blown up by Hungarian fascists.

The Istanbul train ran south from Budapest, crossing the Danube at Peiterwarden bridge, and the Serbian frontier at Subotica. From here it was an easy run, through fields of sunflowers, to Nis-Plovdiv and the junction for Greece.

From Plovdiv, the Oriental Railway followed the Maritza valley near the Bulgarian frontier and so, after crossing the river several times, once over the

1,270 m (4,167 ft) long, 173-span bridge at Pithion, the train ran along the dramatic Aegean coastline to Thessalonika. It was on this stretch of the line that Ian Fleming's *From Russia with Love* was filmed. Then there are 1:66 gradients over the snow-clad hills to the Sea of Marmora and journey's end at Istanbul's Sirkeci station.

In 1900 Wagon-Lits tried a Berlin-Breslau (Wroclaw) to Istanbul express that avoided Vienna. This experiment, however, sadly only lasted two years.

● **LEFT**
An exterior view of
one of the Pullman
coaches, which form
the legendary train.

twice a week and a Paris-Istanbul service ran three times a week.

Disrupted again by World War II (there was a Zurich–Istanbul service for a time), the Orient Express was restarted in 1947 with ordinary coaches, one or two sleepers and the occasional dining car. In 1950, Captain Karpe, US Military Attaché at Bucharest, was murdered on the train as it was passing through a tunnel near Salzburg, in Russian-occupied Austria.

The Budapest-Belgrade sector ceased in 1963 when the Tauern-Orient sleeper was started from Ostend to Athens. This ended in 1976. The Tauern tunnel, which is 8.53 km (5 miles and 557 yd) long, was completed in 1909.

Today Wagons-Lits Austria still staff the Vienna-Paris sleeper, while a Hungarian Railways (MAV) dining car serves classic dinners between Budapest and Salzburg. Romanian Railways run the Budapest-Bucharest sleeper.

● **ABOVE**
Two stewards pose beside the open doors of the coaches of the Orient Express.

● **RIGHT**
Passengers dine in luxury aboard the Orient Express.

● **OPPOSITE**
The Arlberg-Orient Express at St Anton in the Austrian Arlberg in about 1932. Hauled by a ÖBB locomotive, the train has just emerged from the Arlberg tunnel.

CALAIS TO ISTANBUL
THE SIMPLON-ORIENT EXPRESS

● BELOW
The 1900 timetable cover showing the dining
car surrounded by compartments of (left) the
Orient Express and (right) the St Petersburg-
Cannes express.

In 1906, Wagons-Lits started the
Simplon Express (SE) from Paris to
Lausanne (Switzerland). The route took
in the recently opened 19.8 km (12 miles
557 yd) long Simplon Tunnel (Europe's
longest until 1991), Milan (Italy) and
later Venice (Italy) and Trieste (at that
time part of Austria). However, Vienna
would not let it proceed farther east,
which was precisely the SE objective.

At the end of World War I, the Allied
governments at the Treaty of Versailles
created the Simplon-Orient Express
(SOE). They asked Wagons-Lits to run
the route, which connected liberated
Romania, Yugoslavia and Athens with the
West, thereby avoiding Germany, Austria
and Hungary. They also compelled the
Germans to restart the Orient Express.

● LEFT
A replica of car No.
2439. The original,
in which the
Armistices of 1918
and 1940 were
signed, went by road
to Germany, where
it was destroyed on
the orders of Hitler.

● BELOW
The Simplon-Orient
Express at the
Turkish frontier
in 1950.

INFORMATION BOX

*THE SIMPLON-ORIENT
EXPRESS*

Termini	Calais and Istanbul
Countries	France to Turkey
Distance	about 3,460 km (2,150 miles)
Date of opening	1906

The Athens-Salonika main line, with its
numerous tunnels and viaducts through
and over the Greek mountains, opened in
1917. The second track tunnel was
opened in 1921.

The line from Calais Maritime to Paris
Gare de Lyon opened in 1870 and
crossed the 30 m (99 ft) high Chantilly
viaduct. From Paris the Simplon Express
followed the Seine valley to the Laroche-
Migennes engine-changing stop, after
which there was an easy rising gradient to

● OPPOSITE
The Venice Simplon-
Orient Express
travelling through
the Arlberg Pass near
the picturesque village
of Pettnau.

● LEFT
The Venice Simplon-Orient Express at Pettnau on the Arlberg in July 1984. The train is headed by ÖBB 1020 and 1010 Class locomotives.

After crossing the Orbe on the 30 m (100 ft) high Le Day bridge, at Daillens, the train joined the Swiss main line, electrified in 1906, from Neuchâtel to Lausanne, continuing along Lake Geneva through Montreux and following the Rhône valley to Brig at the mouth of the Simplon Tunnel. This last section was electrified in 1906.

The line emerged at Iselle, Italy, from where the Swiss-operated line drops 358 m (1,175 ft) in 28 km (17 miles) through the Trasquera tunnel, Iselle station, the 2,968 m (9,738 ft) long Varzo Spiral tunnel, five smaller tunnels and the 1,092 m (3,583 ft) long Preglia tunnel, to join the Italian railways at Domodossola. Passing Lake Maggiore, the train followed the flat line, built in

the Blaizy-Bas summit and a 4,100 m (13,451 ft) long tunnel before descending to Dijon. Here, turning east from Burgundy, it climbed from 288 m (945 ft) at Mouchard to 900 m (2,953 ft) at the mouth of the 6,100 m (20,013 ft) long Mont d'Or Tunnel, opened in

1915, which goes through the Jura mountains to Vallorbe (Switzerland). Before the tunnel was built, the trains ran via Pontarlier to Vallorbe on a line, which is now disused but whose claim to fame is that, in 1974, the film *Murder on the Orient Express* was made on it.

1848, from Milan to Venice, passing Lake Garda and Verona. After reversing at Venice the train crossed the causeway to Venice-Mestre, where the line rejoined the coast outside Trieste.

The Simplon-Orient Express, with its teak cars, took three nights and four days each way. Although all passengers had to change at Trieste, westbound passengers could sleep in the standing train and catch the connection to Paris the following morning.

From Trieste, where all passengers had to change, the line climbed from sea-level to 302 m (991 ft) at Poggioreale del Carso, the present frontier.

The SOE route through Ljubljana (Laibach) and Zagreb (Agram) ran daily to Vinkovci-Belgrade and Nis, where it divided – one part going to Istanbul (three times weekly) and the other to Athens (twice weekly). The Istanbul train also had connections to Bucharest, which it reached by using the notorious Vinkovci-Subotica branch line that crossed the Yugoslav-Romanian frontier over the Danube near the Iron Gates. Fuel shortages sometimes caused delays,

indeed it is said that on one occasion the passengers had to put money together to buy wood for the engine!

The famous blue-and-gold all-steel sleepers first appeared in 1926, four years after the Train Bleu (Calais-Nice-San Remo). By 1929 there was a daily service from Paris to Istanbul, which included a dining car, Calais-Istanbul sleepers and Calais-Trieste sleepers. In 1930 the SOE became the main prop of the Wagons-Lits London-Cairo service (known as the Taurus Express).

The train was re-organized in 1932, with the Ostend-, Amsterdam-, Berlin-, Prague-, Vienna-, and Paris-Orient or Arlberg-Orient sleepers joining the train at Belgrade on different days. This provided three daily Istanbul sleepers and two services daily (four from Thessaloniki) to Athens.

Romantic, dazzlingly mysterious, the train was used by all the Balkan grandees. King Boris used to drive the Simplon-Orient's engine in Bulgaria. British agents

● **ABOVE**
This rare picture shows the Venice Simplon-Orient Express on a diversion on the old Arlberg-Orient Express line via Zell am See. This was caused by a damaged bridge at Kufstein. The train is seen here in the 180 degree turn near Hopfgarten in Tyrol in July 1990.

● **RIGHT**
The Venice Simplon-Orient Express stands at Jenbach station in the Austrian Tyrol. A storm is brewing over the mountains.

● **RIGHT**
The Venice Simplon-
Orient Express at St
Jodock, between
Brenner and
Innsbruck.

● **BELOW LEFT**
This pre-war scene
shows the Simplon-
Orient Express on
the Gorgopotamos
bridge in Greece.

included Lord Baden-Powell, later
founder of the Boy Scouts movement. It
was on the train, just after World War II
broke out, that Royal Navy agents
murdered a German agent. Many novels
were written about the train, perhaps
most famously Agatha Christie's *Murder
on the Orient Express* and Graham Greene's
Stamboul Train. Mystery also reflected the
route's atmosphere, in which there were
always difficulties with the local customs,
who sealed one dining car's cupboard
supplies and broke the seals on another
at each border.

Wagons-Lits kept reserve supplies of
block ice, coal and vehicles along the
route, maintaining an almost out-of-this-
world glamorous elegance on board. In
summer the baggage van had a shower in
it. Wagons-Lits ran daily dining cars for
Lausanne-Trieste-Svilengrad, Nis-
Thessaloniki, Amfiklia-Athens and a
kitchen van for Uzunkopru-Istanbul.

World War II did not stop the
Simplon-Orient's glamorous journeys.
The warning that "Les Oreilles de
l'ennemi vous écoutent" (the equivalent
of the British World War II poster

"Walls have Ears") was pasted in the
cabins – the listening enemy ears still
travelling in the Berlin car, which lasted
until 1940. The train was finally stopped
in 1942, and individual sleepers with
neutral Turkish staff served most of the
overnight sectors until the SOE restarted in January 1946 (to Istanbul) and
1949 (Athens). After the war, dining cars
became a rarity.

The Simplon-Orient Express ended
in 1962, and, with much media coverage,
the last Paris-Istanbul sleeper ran on
22 May 1977.

● **RIGHT**
This 1907
photograph shows
the Venice Simplon-
Orient Express,
headed by a Swiss
steam-engine, at
Iselle di Trasquera
at the Italian portal
of the Simplon
tunnel.

GORNERGRAT TO ST MORITZ
THE GLACIER EXPRESS

Most people start this journey at Zermatt or St Moritz, but to miss seeing the Matterhorn while standing amid the snow 3,000 m (10,000 ft) up, with a panoramic view of other mountains, is to miss one of the finer sights in Europe.

It is not essential to take the Glacier Express itself to enjoy the wonderful scenery, but there are a number of advantages such as the provision of air-conditioned Panorama coaches and a restaurant car in which one can experience the novelty of having a wine glass with an angled base so that the stem and bowl remain upright on the steep gradients. It is recommended that, if at all possible, a seat is obtained on the right-hand side facing forward on this part of the journey.

There is pasture land in the valley from here to Randa. Look out for the houses built behind the huge boulders that fell from the mountains many years before. The Weisshorn, 4,506 m (14,783 ft) is off to the left. Between Randa and Herbriggen is a new section of rack line

● **LEFT**
A heavy express from Chur to St Moritz with coaches from the "Glacier Express" is about to plunge into the tunnel in the vertical rockface 213 feet above the Landwasser river.

● **BELOW LEFT**
A train from Chur to Arosa eases round the bend in the road by the Obertor gate in the city walls of Chur to join road traffic on the narrow Plessurquai along-side the river.

● **BELOW RIGHT**
The Gornergratbahn rack railway train is completing its descent to Zermatt. An electric taxi makes its almost silent way to a hotel.

constructed in the past ten years to circumvent the area where the whole mountainside collapsed, fortunately without causing any loss of life. This can be seen to the left where the route of the old line can still be seen in places.

The valley descends in steps at one place near Kalpetran, the line sharing a narrow gorge with the river. It then appears that the broadening valley with pastures and small vineyards heralds the end of spectacular views for the moment. Not so, for suddenly the train is perched on the edge of a deep cleft cut by the river, and following the contours, wheel flanges screaming.

Ahead and to the right appear two bridges leaping across the chasm. Both were built to carry the road from

Stalden-Saas, which the train is now approaching, to Saas-Fee.

The valley becomes wider and more populous, and at the large town of Visp the line shares a station area with the

Swiss Federal Railways main line down the Rhône valley. A short, brisk run on level ground brings the train to Brig. Watch out on the left for the trains of the Bern-Loetschberg-Simplon railway clinging to the valley side on their way to and from the Lötschberg tunnel.

Like most other towns strategically situated near the entrance to mountain passes, Brig has a long history and today watches over the northern entrance to the Simplon railway tunnel beneath the pass of the the same name, which links Switzerland with Italy. It has strong commercial and industrial interests and a growing tourist trade.

At Brig the train reverses in the station square outside the impressive Federal Railways building. A locomotive of the

● **ABOVE LEFT**
Andermatt looking toward Hospental and the distant Furka Pass.

● **LEFT**
The young Vorderrhein rushes alongside the line as both descend toward Hospental. In the far distance, road and rail zigzag up the mountainside from Andermatt heading for Disentis.

INFORMATION BOX	
THE GLACIER EXPRESS	
Termini	Gornergrat and St Moritz
Country	Switzerland
Distance	279 km (173 miles)
Date of opening	1926

● **LEFT**
The imposing Swiss Federal Railways station at Brig forms a fine backdrop to the station shared by the Furka-Oberalp and Brig-Visp-Zermatt railways. The "Glacier Express" reverses here.

using rack-and-pinion gear to climb. Be ready to look out to the right on emerging from the tunnel, for there is a wonderful view back down the valley toward Brig.

Lax sees the end of the rack for the present. Fiesch is a pretty tourist town in a sheltered location, from here the railway executes a 180 degree climbing turn on rack away from the town to reach Frgangen and yet another cable-car to Bellwald and the Fiesch glacier. One of the most picturesque parts of the journey follows as the train passes through or near many charming old villages, with their wooden houses packed closely together for shelter from the elements, watched over by an ancient church. Look out for the ancient wooden barns, which are raised above the ground on supports capped by large flat stones to prevent rats and mice from reaching the stored grain and fodder above.

At Oberwald, the present-day railway parts company from the old line. The latter passed Gletsch, with splendid views of the Rhône Glacier, the source of the

● **RIGHT**
Horse-drawn transport vies for business with battery-electric taxis outside the Zermatt station of the Brig-Visp-Zermatt railway. The station has been rebuilt since the picture was taken.

● **BELOW RIGHT**
The clear waters of the Matter Vispa tumble alongside a Zermatt to Brig train as it approaches Täsch station.

Furka-Oberalp (FO) Railway takes over, probably one of the 64 tonne (63 ton) rack-and-adhesion machines introduced in 1986.

Immediately after passing the BVZ locomotive depot at the station, the train swings right to cross the Rhône, known locally as the Rotten, on a girder bridge. Another sharp right turn, and the train is running alongside one of the main streets in Naters, just across from Brig. The valley narrows and is shared by road, rail and river.

Grengiols has the highest viaduct on the FO, it spans 31 m (102 ft) above the valley floor. When the train has crossed the viaduct, it enters a spiral tunnel still

● LEFT
The autumn tints are still on the trees as one of
the new and powerful locomotives of the
Rhaetischebahnen climbs with its train away
from Tiefencastel on its way to St Moritz.

and, of course, there are the regular
passenger-trains. About two-thirds of the
way through the tunnel, the train is
under the watershed of the Rhône and
Reuss rivers.

The line emerges near Realp and
follows the broad Urseren valley, passing
Hospental close by on the right.

Andermatt is a well-known holiday
centre and the junction for what used to
be the Schöllenen Bahn, now part of the
FO system. This runs down a steep rack
line in the narrow gorge to Göschenen

river, and entered the old tunnel to
emerge in a wild valley where the winter
conditions are so severe that through rail
services to Andermatt and beyond can be
suspended. Happily, a preservation
society is in the process of re-opening the
line between Gletsch and Realp for
summer use.

The present line uses a new tunnel,
much lower down the mountains. It was
opened on 26 June 1982 after a ten-year
construction period and with a length of
15.442 km (9.59 miles). Single-track
with two passing loops, it is the longest
metre-gauge tunnel in the world. Special
trains ferry cars and their passengers
through the tunnel in winter and summer

● ABOVE
Thusis is an important
rail and road
interchange point on
the line between Chur
and St Moritz. Its new
station reflects the
innovative style of the
Rhaetischebahnen.

● LEFT
Arosa is reached in
less than an hour by
a spectacular branch
of the Rhaetischebahn
from the station
square at Chur.

on the Federal Railways main line
through the Gotthard pass and tunnel.
Glacier expresses cross at Andermatt,
and much shunting is necessary to
change the restaurant car from one train
to the other.

The climb out of Andermatt is both
surprising and rewarding. A seemingly
impassable mountainside faces the train,
which heads straight for it, engages the
rack and swings right, climbing across the
face of the wall and giving views of the
valley to the right. Then it reverses

direction, opening up even wider views down the Urseren valley, now to the left. There are no fewer than four such reversals before reaching Nätschen, which is 407 m (1,335 ft) higher than Andermatt. Still climbing, the train passes through a long avalanche shelter to emerge with the Oberalp lake to the right and, just ahead, the station of Oberalppasshöhe at 2,033 m (6,670 ft) the highest point on the FO.

Between Tschamut and Dieni is the small and isolated chapel of St Brida, built in 1736. From here on there is no need for rack assistance as the valley broadens out with pleasant views. Sedrun is one of the access points for the construction of a new tunnel beneath the Gotthard pass which will revolutionize times on perhaps Europe's most important north-south axis.

Disentis's station has the attraction of being the meeting-point between the FO and Rhaetische Bahn (RhB) where, again, a locomotive change takes place with haulage probably being put into the hands of one of the fairly new 60 tonne (59 ton) Ge4/4 machines. The going is

now easy through pasture dotted with woodland. The next important feature is the Rhine gorge, which is entered around Castrisch, some 2 km (1¼ mile) beyond Ilanz. It was formed in prehistoric times by a landslide which filled the valley to a depth of 300 m (984 ft) through which the river gradually forced its way. The unusual rock formations are best seen from the left-hand side of the train.

The majority of passengers on the through trains are heading for St Moritz, and the coaches for that destination are detached from the train at Reichenau-Tamins and added to another train that has started at Chur.

Chur, the capital of the canton, is also the terminus of the standard-gauge Federal Railways and has a depot and workshops. The large station, recently rebuilt to incorporate the bus station, is shared by the RhB.

On the way back to Reichenau, the Ems Chemie works at Domat-Ems is seen to the left. For passengers coming direct from Zermatt, there is a further reversal at Reichenau, and after crossing

● RIGHT
The line between Disentis and Chur passes along a deep valley cut by the Vorderrhein through the prehistoric Flims landslip.

the Hinterrhein the train swings left to follow its course all the way to Thusis.

As the train climbs away from Thusis, on the right one can glimpse the fearsome Viamala gorge cut by the Hinterrhein, while on the left there is a good view back down the valley. The Schyn gorge cut by the Albula River is now followed right to Preda.

The line holds to the left side of the valley. Suddenly, round a curve, the remarkable Landwasser viaduct appears, carrying the tracks 65 m (213 ft) above the valley floor before plunging into a tunnel cut into the rock face.

Filisur is the junction for the shuttle trains to Davos and the starting-point for one of the most gruelling climbs in Europe for trains relying on adhesion only. It involves brilliant engineering, with the line now clinging to a vertical mountainside, then spiralling across the narrowing valley to gain height and then into spiral tunnels, one upon the other. Between Bergen and Preda at the Albula tunnel, the line rises from 1,376 m (4,514 ft) above sea level to 1,792 m

● LEFT
In February, the snow is beginning to melt on the rooftops of the ancient city of Chur, the capital of the Kanton of Graubünden.

● BELOW LEFT
The upper valley of the Vorderrhein near Tschamut-Selva in the grip of winter.

(5,879 ft) in about 12 km (7.5 miles) with a ruling gradient of 1:28.6. The Albula tunnel is the highest in Europe, with the summit in the tunnel at 1,820 m (5,971 ft). It was built between 1898 and 1902 under impossible conditions and has a length of 5,864.5 m (3 1/2 miles).

Samedan is a rail junction for Pontresina and the Bernina line and has a locomotive depot and workshops. It is only a short distance to St Moritz, passing through Celerina. The railway ends at St Moritz by the lake used for langlauf in winter. Above the lake are the hotels and restaurants of one of the most famous resorts in the world, a fine centre for exploring Switzerland's mountain scenery.

PILATUS
A ROUND TRIP FROM LUCERNE

● BELOW
The banner at Alpnachstad proclaims that the Pilatusbahn is the steepest rack railway in the world. Even the platform at the station is on a steep gradient.

Few visitors to Lucerne in central Switzerland can have failed to notice the imposing bulk of Pilatus, a massif of limestone virtually in the suburbs of the city. The massif comprises a number of peaks, the highest of which is Tomlishorn, 2,129 m (6,985 ft) high.

The mountain had an attraction for tourists long before the coming of the famous Pilatus railway, and several famous people have made the ascent, including Queen Victoria in 1868. Even then, she could obtain refreshment after the ascent, because two hotels had been built near the summit in 1860.

The success of the standard-gauge rack-and-pinion railway from Vitznau to the summit of the Rigi mountain prompted an application to the Federal Parliament in 1873 by the Vitznau-Rigi board to build a rack-and-pinion line up Pilatus. This implied using gradients no steeper than 1:4, the limit imposed by the Swiss authorities on the grounds that the vehicles might lift off the rack were the inclination to be greater. The line would have followed the route already

INFORMATION BOX

Terminus	Lucerne
Country	Switzerland
Length	4.27 km (2.65 miles)
Date of opening	1889

● **BELOW LEFT**
A small plume of cloud adorns the summit of Pilatus, seen from a ship on Lake Lucerne, which is heading for Alpnachstad at the foot of the mountain several kilometres away.

● **BELOW RIGHT**
Even the steep steps of the station platform at Alpnachstad fail to convey an adequate impression of the severity of the gradient on which the car stands.

An ascending car nears the upper station just below the summit of Pilatus.

● BELOW
A metre gauge train on the Brünig line of the Federal railways is arriving at Alpnachstad from Luzern.

● BELOW
The car to the left has just departed from Alpnachstad station. Those to the right are waiting to pick up passengers.

used by porters and horses. It was soon realized that this was so circuitous that the heavy construction costs would make it unlikely to return a profit. A shorter route would also be much steeper, and an obvious one was from Alpnachstad by the shores of Lake Lucerne, calling for a gradient of almost 1:2. The Locher rack-and-pinion system based on a concept by the famous mountain railway engineer, Riggenbach, utilizes a pair of vertically mounted pinions which engage in teeth on either side of the rack rail, thus providing a drive and preventing lateral movement. Beneath the teeth on the pinions, discs larger in diameter than the toothed wheels rotate beneath the broad base of the rack rail, thus preventing vertical movement. The conventional wheels on locomotives and carriages merely provide stability on the 800 mm gauge track. Turnouts are always complex on lines such as this, but the Pilatus is special. At six locations, heavy-duty

traverses slide curved track into the appropriate positions, while at two other points, one near the summit, the whole turnout is rotated horizontally.

The line, 4.27 km (2¹/₂ miles) long, opened on 4 June 1889 and runs from

Alpnachstad at 441 m (1,447 ft) above sea level to the upper station at 2,070 m (6,791 ft). Between 1886 and 1909, 11 combined steam locomotives and carriages operated the services until electrification at 1550V d.c. on 15 May 1937. One of the steam units is preserved at the transport museum in Lucerne.

Eight electric units were introduced at the start of electrical operation, followed in 1954 by a freight unit, which was provided with a "swap body" to convert it for passenger work, as required, in 1962. One more passenger unit arrived in 1968, and in 1981 another freight unit, diesel-powered, was delivered.

It is suggested that the journey is started at the ship terminus just in front of the main railway terminus at Lucerne and that a ship, possibly one of the old paddle steamers, is taken to Alpnachstad. In summer, there are six or seven sailings a day, and one can enjoy a meal and a drink while admiring the scenery and observing the considerable activity on Lake Lucerne. The alternative is to take the Swiss Federal Railways (SBB) Brünig line metre-gauge train to Alpnachstad.

Both train and ship deposit the passenger close to the Pilatusbahn station. The bright red trains await at a platform angled to correspond with that

of the train. It is advisable to choose the lowest compartment and, if possible, to obtain a seat on the far side facing downhill. Although sitting alongside the rock face on much of the lower part of the journey, you will be on the spectacular side on the upper section, where the line is perched on ledges as it nears the summit. Moreover, it is possible to look back down the line for the whole journey. Although facing rearward is advised, the journey is described as if facing forward. Shortly after the train departs, the depot and workshop are seen to the left. The depot is the only place where the tracks are on the level. Rail access is gained by one of the traverser type turnouts. Very soon the houses, the ship and the Brünig railway line look like small-scale models. Then the line enters beech woods, crosses a small mountain road and begins to dive in and out of a series of short tunnels.

After about eight minutes, the train crosses the Wolfort viaduct, which spans a deep gorge, providing a sudden view to the right and below across the arm of Lake Lucerne on which Alpnachstad is situated and toward the Glärner Alps. The train passes through more short tunnels, after which the nearby scene broadens into pasture dotted with contented cows and alpine flowers. Here at Aemsigen Alp is the passing loop and an opportunity to watch the traverser turnouts in action.

Craggy outcroppings of rock start to appear. The line follows the route of an ancient watercourse and levels out a little before reaching the Mattalp pasture, decked with flowers in summer and often with its own contingent of cows, bells

● **ABOVE LEFT**
The car seen at the cab window is descending and has been passed at the only loop there is on the line.

● **ABOVE RIGHT**
The car has just left the shelter of the summit station at Pilatus.

● **RIGHT**
One of the spectacular views from the top of Pilatus. The cables carry the car on the aerial ropeway, which descends toward Kriens near Lucerne.

The paddle steamer Unterwalden heading for Alpnachstad is glimpsed from a descending car.

jangling as they munch contentedly on the grass. There are few trees here, merely some stunted pines.

Through a tunnel and what a sensation! The train is crawling up a ledge on the sheer rock face of the Eselwand. Far below, little moving dots proclaim the presence of walkers on the mountain tracks, while above lies the col on which is situated the summit station. If there is a following train, it may be possible to watch the changing of the route by the rotating turnout before your train enters the covered station.

The saddle of the mountain has been levelled, and the hotels there provide restaurants and cafeterias as well as accommodation. There are numerous safe and well-made paths giving easy access to viewpoints, which, in fine weather, are difficult to beat. One can also watch arriving and departing trains edging along the Eselwand in the distance.

An interesting way to return to Lucerne is to take the large cable-car at the summit, which, immediately on departure, crosses an abyss on the east

face of the mountain before dropping down to Fräkmüntegg. The descent is quite steep, the car losing 650 m (2,133 ft) in a distance of 1,450 m (4,760 ft). There, transfer is made to a Gondelbahn, the little cars of which

swing just above the tree-tops to Kriens on the outskirts of Lucerne. Arrival is close to a trolley-bus route, which runs to the centre of Lucerne, passing on the way part of the route of the Kriens-Luzern-Bahn, an industrial railway.

● RIGHT
The hotel and restaurant near the summit of Pilatus.

● LEFT
The last few yards to the summit of Pilatus have to be tackled on foot.

LONDON ST PANCRAS TO BERNE
EUROSTAR AND TGV

This journey is one of the most technically exciting train routes of modern times. It begins at London's recently restored St Pancras International terminal for the Eurostar trains, which run regularly via the Channel Tunnel to terminals at Brussels and Paris.

The newly-restored terminal opened on 14 November 2007, at the same time as the opening of Britain's first high-speed line, meaning that the journey from London to Paris may now take as little as 2 hours 15 minutes. A new purpose-built terminal in Kent, Ebbsfleet International, opened that same month, offering easy access from London and the M25.

The international group responsible for design adopted the principles employed in the French TGV (Train Grande Vitesse), but numerous changes were necessary. The trains needed to operate in the much more restricted loading gauge found in Britain; electrical supply was to come from three different systems, including current collection from a third rail in Britain; there were to be four signalling systems; and stringent safety standards were demanded for operation through the tunnel.

The exterior design was British, one consequence of which is that future TGV and the "Thalys" have a central driving

● **ABOVE AND LEFT**
The original purpose-built Eurostar terminal at Waterloo station, London.

● **RIGHT**
The bustle of a Paris
terminal is captured
in this picture of the
Gare du Nord.

● **BELOW
RIGHT**
A Eurostar rests by
the buffer stops at
the Paris Nord
terminus after its
journey through the
Channel Tunnel
from London.

position and one window at the front of
the cab. The interior design was a joint
Franco-Belgian operation, and the result
appears to be that the Eurostar has more
space than the TGV, in spite of being
dimensionally smaller.

There were many mechanical and
electrical problems to be solved. For
example, safety requirements for the
tunnel demanded that passengers could
be moved from one end of the whole
train to the other. That ruled out
employing two units, so that the Eurostar
has just two power cars, situated at each
end of the 20-vehicle formation, with
additional motored bogies under the first
and last passenger coach to make up to
some extent for the loss of the power
that two equivalent TGV sets would
have had.

Bogies had to be reduced in overall
dimensions; the high overhead contact
line in the tunnel called for a higher-
reaching pantograph; carriage steps had
to be designed to match automatically the
differing heights of platforms in three
countries, and the complex signalling
requirements had to be met.

It is a credit to the international teams
that this was all achieved between
conception in 1987 and the start of
regular services in November 1994.

As yet, there is no dedicated high-
speed line in Britain, so the Eurostar
trains have to slot into the slower traffic
found in the south-east of the country. In
the urban area of London, lines built in
the earliest days of railways tend to be

sinuous, but at least it gives the traveller
the opportunity to glimpse the widely
changing patterns of life to be found in
any major city. Once into the Kentish
countryside, there is the opportunity to
increase the speed to 160 kph (100 mph),
especially on the fairly straight section
from Tonbridge to Ashford.

Certain Eurostar trains stop at the
rebuilt station in Ashford, which also

serves local and inter-city trains. This facilitates rail interchange and the gathering of passengers who have come by car and who would not have found it convenient to board in London.

It is a fairly short distance to the point at which the train swings left from the former British Rail lines to those of

Eurotunnel. The expanse of tracks, sidings, depots and loading docks for cars and heavy goods vehicles is called Dollands Moor. It is here that the shoes collecting current from the third rail are lifted and the pantograph is raised, although passengers will be unaware of it. The Channel Tunnel is 49.93 km

(31.03 miles) long and is the second longest rail tunnel in the world, as well as the tunnel with the longest underwater section. It lies 137.4 m (451 ft) below mean sea level.

French cab signalling passes instructions to trains in the tunnel and on the TGV lines beyond. Maximum speed in the tunnel is restricted to 160 kph (100 mph), and the riding is so smooth that, without any exterior point of reference, it is hard to detect movement.

Passage through the Channel Tunnel takes some 20 minutes and, on emerging from the tunnel into France, the immense yards of the Coquelles terminal can be seen to the left. The line to Paris passes through a newly built exchange station at Fréthun, and soon the Eurostar is running on the high-speed tracks through fairly level terrain with sweeping curves. On this stretch, an announcement is usually made that the train is running at its maximum authorized speed of 300 kph (186.4 mph).

Facilities for departing Eurostar passengers at the Gare du Nord generally leave much to be desired. Those passing through Paris on their way to Switzerland can either take a taxi (and make sure that it is an official one) to the large and impressive Gare de Lyon or take the relatively new underground link, which gets one there quicker and much more cheaply in some 15 minutes.

Finding the Swiss TGV – and it will probably be Swiss-owned, albeit in standard TGV livery – can be daunting among all the other TGVs, but once on board you can spot the differences between Eurostars and TGVs, which, for example, are wider and higher. The start from the Gare de Lyon is relatively cautious as the TGVs share the tracks

with numerous EMU, locomotive-powered push-and-pull services, both often formed of double-deck coaches, and the occasional locomotive-hauled express. As speed picks up, the train passes the immense marshalling yards at Villeneuve St Georges.

At Lieusaint the TGV joins the "Ligne à Grande Vitesse" (LGV), for the most part a new formation and alignment, purpose-built to permit the high-speed performance of these trains to be exploited. This is the Sud-Est LGV to Lyons, Valence and, ultimately, Marseilles.

The services to Berne and Lausanne follow the line only as far as Passilly, from

where there is a short link to the old main line at Aisy. Travel on the LGV is so smooth that the train's speed is hard to judge. There is little chance to study the local scene, however, because of the speed and the fact that the line is often in a cutting.

From Aisy to Dijon the alignment is good enough to maintain a good pace, and soon, a little to the right and below, Dijon comes into view. The TGV swings down the long grade, a stern test for man and machine northbound in the days of steam, and enters the busy main station, which is on a rather constricted site. The best trains take only 99 minutes to travel

● **LEFT**
A TGV in orange livery passes the exit of the huge marshalling yards at Villeneuve St Georges in the suburbs of Paris. Several TGV services now bypass this section of line using a new and much quicker route designed for TGVs, partly in tunnel, to reach southbound TGV lines.

● RIGHT
View of the Münster
in Berne from the
Kirchenfeld bridge
over the Aare.

● BELOW
RIGHT
Some light railways
in Berne terminate
in the streets. This
train has arrived
from Worb, a large
village outside
Berne, and is
waiting in Helvetia
Platz to return to
Worb. The service
has recently been
extended to a
terminal the other
side of the River
Aare at Casino Platz.

plain until it approaches the formidable mountain barrier of the Montagne du Lermont. The narrow defile through the mountains is guarded by the ancient town of Pontarlier, with its impressive castles perched high above rail and road as the Franco-Swiss border is approached.

The first village on Swiss soil is Les Verrières. A little further on and to the right, St Sulpice and Fleurier can be seen below in the Val de Travers, where the Scots engineer, MacAdam, saw the potential of the tar substance mined there as a surface for roads. The line winds through delightful scenery until, suddenly, panoramic views across Lake Neuchâtel are revealed to the right, the lake surface below dotted with yachts, small craft and passenger boats on regular services.

Neuchâtel, whose castle can be seen to the right on the approach, is an ancient city lying on the important main line between Basle and Lausanne/Geneva. Its large station mainly handles trains belonging to the Federal Railways

the 315 km (195.7 miles) from Paris to Dijon.

Soon after leaving Dijon, the TGV swings left away from the broad valley of the Saône and climbs toward the mountains, giving extensive views to the right. These give way to more restricted views as the track gets higher and woods and rocky cuttings close in.

Frasne, on a high plateau, is a junction. The main line runs straight ahead to Vallorbe, just over the Swiss border, from where it swings down with good views across villages and agricultural land until reaching Lake Geneva (Lac Léman) at Lausanne. The other line branches left and meanders across the

(SBB/CFF/FFS), but the livery of the
Berne-Loetschberg-Simplon Railway
(BLS) is also present. It is that company's
metals that are used to cross the generally
level and fertile broad plateau to Berne,
where the TGV service terminates in the
curving and rather gloomy station, well
situated near the centre of this small and
very pleasant capital city.

The journey from London to Paris has
until now taken 4 hours and 32 minutes.
With the new High Speed 1 (formerly
known as the Channel Tunnel Rail Link)
it is now possible for the journey to take
as little as 2 hours and 15 minutes.

● ABOVE
One of the electric
multiple units
arriving at Frasne
station.

● RIGHT
In the foreground is
one of the many
decorated fountains
to be found in the
heart of the old city
of Berne.

BUDAPEST TO LAKE BALATON

Budapest boasts three main-line termini, two of grand proportions and often featuring in period films, and Déli Pályaudvar (spelt Pú in timetables), a modern structure without much cover over the platforms. The station is close to Castle Hill and the large tram interchange at Moszkva tér and is thus convenient, although other services start at B. Kelenföld, a large suburban station. First-class travel is advisable and reasonably early arrival at the station is recommended, not only to get the right tickets but also to get a seat.

The train is likely to be hauled by one of the ubiquitous class V43 electric locomotives in a pleasing light-blue livery. The first batch of seven were built by Krupp in Germany, but the rest are from the well-known Hungarian firm of Ganz-Mavag. They are dual voltage but here operate on a supply of 25kV/50Hz providing an hourly rating of 2130 kW.

Loads are relatively light, and speeds, by Western European standards, are

● **ABOVE**
Buda seen from the Fisherman's Bastion on Castle Hill.

moderate, but this has the advantage for the interested traveller that the passing scene may be studied, whether it be architectural, agricultural or human.

The train sets off through the industrial and dormitory suburbs of Buda, keeping to the west of the Danube. It threads its way through the complex of lines serving people and industry before entering flattish countryside with small towns and villages, some of the latter surrounded by small fields worked

● **ABOVE LEFT**
A Russian-built CoCo diesel electric locomotive stands at Balaton central station, waiting for its next duty on a service to Keszthely.

● **LEFT**
The terminal station at Déli Pályaudvar is the starting-point for the journey to Lake Balaton. One of the ubiquitous Class 43 BB electric locomotives, mostly built in Hungary between 1963 and 1982, is the usual motive power for the main-line trains.

● RIGHT
The cool courtyard
of this café in old
Buda provides a
welcome relief from
the dry heat of mid-
summer.

"privately". In open areas one may see a collective farm enlivened by a few trees but surrounded by flat, tilled soil, but this style of farming is mostly found on the Great Plain to the east.

Streams meander near the line, with areas of marsh as well as tall grasses and some woodland. The 47 km (29 miles) from Budapest brings the traveller to Lake Velence, some 10 km (6 miles) long and shallow. It is seen to the right of the train, and its proximity to the city has attracted the usual lakeside cafés and stalls as well as holiday homes. The north end is a wildlife sanctuary, access to which requires a special permit.

Soon after, one reaches the large town and junction of Székesfehérvár, where connections from the north of the country are made. Only 10 km (6 miles) further on, and 77 km (48 miles) from Budapest, is Szabadbattyán, the junction where the lines to the north and south of Lake Balaton divide. This train is going south of the lake, and it is around here that the distant hills of Bakony Vértes can first be seen at the right.

It is not until after Balatonalig, 102 km (63 miles) from Budapest, that the blue waters of the lake, dotted with sailing craft, come into view on the right. It is the largest freshwater lake in west and central Europe, 77 km (48 miles) long and very shallow. It is no more than 1.5 m (5 ft) deep on the south side as far out as 1 km (.625 mile) from the shore, and it is said to be only about 3 m (10 ft) deep in the middle.

The north shore of Lake Balaton is significantly different from the south. After leaving the hills and lake shore round Keszthely, the railway curves inland across a small plain to Tapolca, an industrial town and rail junction whose prosperity began with the mining of basalt. The line then swings back to the more pleasant narrow coastal plain.

The line is now approaching the north-eastern end of the lake, which it follows closely before turning sharply inland to the junctions at Casjäg and Szabadbattyán, where the outward route is rejoined.

● ABOVE LEFT
A close view at
Keszthely of 2-6-2
No. 324-540, of a
class dating from
1909, which has just
finished a special
journey with a train
of vintage stock.

● RIGHT
The hub of the tram
system in Buda is at
Moszkva tér, seen
here in an "off-
peak" period!

FIER TO VLORE, SHKODER TO DURRES

This account of a journey describes a visit made to Albania in the early 1990s during the Communist regime of Enver Hoxha, the fanatical dictator of that small nation. Entry to the country was then exceedingly difficult; the only possible way was to attempt participation in a group tour run by a limited number of, usually, politically minded agencies. Upon arrival, moreover, the riot act was read to all Western visitors; virtually everything worth doing was not only forbidden but "punishable by execution". There was one exception: for travelling the state railway without government permission the penalty was a mere 25 years' hard labour. So one covered the country by rail.

Until the national railway network was inaugurated in 1946, there were only two lines: a 31 km (19 mile) Decauville track taking bitumen from the mine at Selence to Skele, the port 3 km (2 miles) south of Viore; and a much shorter line between

Shkozet and Lakaj, south of Durres. Today passenger-trains run twice daily between Shkoder in the north and Durres, the chief port, via Lezhe and Lac; six times daily between Durres and Eibasan (with one extending to

● **ABOVE**
Vlore Junction. It is from here that asphalt and cement are transported to Durres.

● **BELOW LEFT**
A freight-train waits in the rail yard at Durres.

● **BELOW RIGHT**
A train waits to depart from Tirana station.

INFORMATION BOX	
Termini	Fier and Vlore; Shkoder and Durres
Country	Albania
Distance	*c.* 700 km (435 miles)
Date of commencement of construction	1946

● **RIGHT**
The rather elegant,
slender structure of
the railway bridge
near Qukes.

● **BELOW**
The train from
Durres arriving at
Elbasan. This 30 km
(19 miles) of track
was opened in 1950.

Pogradec); and twice daily between Durres and Fier; in all some 700 km (435 miles) of track.

A line has long been under construction to link Fier with Vlore, and now, with the help of "volunteer" labour, it is at last complete. However, the much-vaunted connection of the Albanian rail network to the European system south of Titograd in Montenegro has still not materialized. Nor has the link with Bar in Yugoslavia yet been made. Thus the Albanian Railways network remains isolated and detached.

The track is in poor condition, but in 1991 the rolling stock was renewed from Italian sources. Previously most of it originated from Romania, Hungary and the then Czechoslovakia, and the condition was deplorable, with broken seats and overflowing toilets. In fact, even while in operation, the seats and fittings were being used for fuel by chilly passengers and, without the metal replacements, by now there would doubtless have been nothing but the steel bogies left!

Only one class of travel is available, trains are diesel-powered, and because of the mountainous terrain the builders of the line had considerable obstacles to overcome.

The taking of photographs of anything to do with the railway or its routes carried severe penalties, which made the photographs shown on these pages extremely difficult to obtain. As it was, on a second visit, the author was finally arrested for boarding a forbidden train in possession of a camera and was taken before the Ministry of the Interior in Tirana for a severe reprimand and threat of expulsion before being released.

TUNES TO LISBON

The journey commences in Tunes and is a wonderful way to experience the fertile landscape of Portugal. Tunes is a town that has avoided so far the refurbishment or modernization that has afflicted other parts of the network. Much of the investment has come from EU sources, and the accompanying requirements and dictates do not always sit easily with the relaxed local way of life. Welcome track improvements have been made, together with track rationalization and the withdrawal of freight-yards. Expensive and impressive refurbishment of stations has been coupled with de-staffing and the appearance of graffiti and vandalism.

As a junction serving single-track routes to Barreiro, along the Algarve through Faro to the Spanish border and the Algarve branch to Lagos, Tunes sees considerable activity. At times six or more locomotives and four trains may be in the station at once, with complicated shunting of stock between various services. The three-coach train to Lisbon, headed by a French-designed 3,000 hp locomotive, is soon under way, rattling

INFORMATION BOX

Termini	Tunes and Lisbon
Country	Portugal
Distance	259 km (161 miles)
Date of opening	July 1989

● **BELOW**
No. 1933 on train IC582, passing the vineyards in the hills south of Sao Bartolomeu de Messines, having travelled some 11 km (7 miles) from Tunes.

across the turnouts and over the broad level crossing at the Barreiro end of the station. This distinctive crossing, which has a road junction in one arm between the Lagos and main lines, is still operated from a hut by a woman crossing-keeper who shows flags or lights to the train crew as they pass.

The journey provides a great variety of generally sparsely populated landscape ranging from fertile pastures to quite bleak hillsides, that in summer would offer little protection from the sun. Having crossed the flat pastures and small orchards near Tunes, the train soon starts its sinuous course through the first range of hills. Fresh vegetation contrasts with the white walls of isolated farms and the reddish-orange of the soil. In places, grey rock cuttings and cactus bushes add variety.

As the train climbs higher, pockets of mist hang in the hollows, and clear streams and rivers curl around the contours of the hills. Near Sao Marcos da Serra, 27 km (17 miles) from Tunes, the train crosses the Ribeira de Odelouca, from whose banks a deafening chorus of frogs can be heard. Formerly, the hills around here were the harmonious domain of sheep and cork oaks, but increasingly the harsher culture of eucalyptus is becoming dominant. Near

● **OPPOSITE TOP**
The attractive tile-decorated station at
Grandola shows signs of life as the train IC580
rolls in to a stop.

● **RIGHT**
IC583 raises dust from the ballast as it
accelerates through the isolated station of
Santa Clara-Saboia. A line of wagons awaits
the next load of timber in the adjacent siding.

● **RIGHT**
Train IC583, behind
a 1931 Class
locomotive, disturbs
the rural tranquillity
and interrupts the
chorus of frogs,
having crossed the
Ribeira de Odelauca
some 25 km (16
miles) from Tunes.

Pereiras, the train crosses an impressive
stone-arched viaduct, the 123.5 m (405
ft) long Ponte de Mouratos, one of the
tallest structures on the line.

After the train has growled its way
round more curves and through the
station, the landscape, although
undulating, becomes more open. Next
we come to Santa Clara-Saboia, its
attractive station some distance from
either of the communities it purports to
serve, after which the train heads

● **BELOW**
In the tranquil setting of the valley of the
Mouratos, a 1931 Class diesel heads a well-
laden IC582 across the imposing Ponte de
Mouratos viaduct.

● **LEFT**
The fortified town of Alcacer do Sol is seen across the floodplain of the Rio Sado as a train approaches the 274 m (900 ft) long bridge over the river. One of the more distinctive crops in the area is rice.

towards the short Tunel da Horta. The line remains fairly sinuous, providing a vista of an impressive villa near Torre Va.

More open terrain allows the train to gather speed. Lighter soils lead to further variety of vegetation, with pine-woods and heathland interspersed here and there. At Alvalade, 111 km (69 miles) from Tunes, the train encounters orange orchards and in places lupins abound, while white egrets, storks and buzzards can sometimes be seen.

Having left the plain, the train encounters a lush rolling landscape of fields and meandering rivers. Broom, flat-topped pines and firs being tapped for resin attract the eye before an even more impressive sight is met. At Alcacer do Sal, the line takes a broad sweep

● **LEFT**
Two of the ubiquitous 1201 Class rest between duties at the Lisbon end of Tunes station.

● **BELOW LEFT**
SOREFAME-built No. 1939 thunders across the points to the south of Santa Clara-Saboia, with IC582 *en route* to Barreiro.

around the hilltop town and castle before crossing the Rio Sado on a girder bridge. Until a few years ago this view was absolute perfection, but today it is marred by a major highway that shares the locality.

The lazy Rio Sado meanders towards its estuary, which incorporates one of the prime wetland nature reserves in the country. Mudflats, marshland, water meadows and low wooded hills provide a rich prospect for both humans and birds. The line swings away from the water eventually, and we are back to a sandy landscape of large fields fringed by cork oaks and pine.

At Pinheiro, 191 km (119 miles) from Tunes, the station buildings are well maintained but somewhat remote from the tracks – and positively distant from the community they purport to serve. Not surprisingly, services are sparse; only two northbound trains per day are booked to stop and search for passengers.

From here, the train takes the more northerly route via Valdera, whereas on the return journey in the evening it serves the historic town of Setubal. Having joined the line serving Vendas

● **RIGHT**
The Fridays-only
Algarve to Porto
sleeping-car express
approaches the
Tunel da Horta,
some 50 km (31
miles) from Tunes,
behind a British-
built 1801 Class.

● **BELOW
RIGHT**
The train IC580
basks in the
morning sun, as it
waits to pass inter-
regional service
IR871 at Grandola.
Not surprisingly
with such a
relatively light load,
the locomotive 1937
has made good time.

displays, not always providing relevant
information, have changed the old
ambience somewhat. There has been talk
of moving the tracks nearer to the new
piers, but not, one hopes, at the expense
of the old station structure.

The ferries provide a frequent and
pleasant voyage across the Tejo (Tagus),
especially if you are able to secure some
of the limited open deck space. The
upper deck was formerly reserved for
first-class passengers, but these days the
accommodation is open to all. Sitting in
the sun at the stern for the half-hour
crossing serves as a welcome appetizer
for lunch. One can watch the activities of
other ferries and catamarans criss-
crossing the harbour and survey the naval
dockyard and commercial yards at
leisure. Dominating all, on a clear day, is
the impressive suspension bridge high
above the waterway.

All too soon the journey is over.
However, just as the Algarve exerts its
annual charms, so too does Lisbon, and
there is no finer way to link the two than
by inter-city express from Tunes and
ferry from Barreiro.

Novas and Casa Branca near Poceirao,
the train races towards the fascinating
junction at Pinhal Novo, which is 233 km
(145 miles) from Tunes. This station still
enjoys an array of semaphore signals and
a commuter service provided, in part, by
elderly ALCO diesels dating from 1948.

On the final stage of the rail journey
to Barreiro, the driver maintains both a
high speed and frequent blasts on the
horn as this area has many official and
unofficial level crossings, as well as
people who use the trackside as an
extended footpath. Barreiro itself boasts
a major locomotive works and extensive
sidings for both locomotives and rolling
stock. The station has an attractive overall
roof and associated metalwork, but
surprisingly few platforms considering
the area it serves.

Until recent years, the ferries to
Lisbon used to depart from jetties

immediately adjacent to the station.
However, as part of a major new
investment, they now leave from opposite
the bus station, a short walk away. New
turnstiles, ticket machines and dot matrix

CALAIS TO MILAN
ACROSS EUROPE BY MEDLOC

Any reference to rail journeys from the Channel coast to Italy conjures up delightful visions of the Orient Express speeding across frontiers while passengers dine on *cordon bleu* meals in Pullman comfort. My own experience, however, as a serviceman in the aftermath of World War II, could hardly have been in greater contrast.

In late March 1946, after a spell of home leave, I reported back to a transit camp outside Southampton, anticipating a return voyage by troopship to Port Said. But the ways of the Military are ever unpredictable, and after whiling away a fortnight, a party of us were bundled aboard a Waterloo-bound train at Southampton Central, hauled by nothing more prestigious than an N Class 2-6-0. On arrival we were promptly transferred to Victoria station, where I had my first glimpse of a West Country Pacific before departing on a semi-fast to Dover Priory. The next day, after a mercifully smooth Channel crossing, we docked at Calais alongside the war-torn remains of the Gare Maritime.

● **LEFT**
The Sacré Coeur in Paris

● **BELOW LEFT**
A view of Savona station in 1975, showing a four-car EMU.

● **OPPOSITE BELOW**
Not a museum or a palace, but the exterior of Milano Centrale station, the end of one stage and the beginning of another on the 1946 Medloc marathon.

Here I should explain that, to expedite the transit of service personnel between the UK and various Continental destinations, the railway Operating Division of the Royal Engineers had organized the "Medloc" (Mediterranean line of communication) service of troop trains. I was about to experience Route B, which went from Calais to Milan, with feeders onwards to Southern Italy. Route A, meanwhile, linked Dieppe with Toulon, and Route C went from Calais to Villach in Austria. As Route B was discontinued shortly afterwards, I count myself fortunate since, despite the discomforts, it was an unforgettable and unrepeatable journey.

● **RIGHT**
What better locomotive to tackle the gradients between Dijon and Vallorbe than one of the fleet of ex-PLM Mountains? No. 141-F-177 of this large locomotive family is portrayed at Périgueux in 1962.

● **BELOW LEFT**
Haulage of a British troop train was an unusual assignment for a Swiss Federal Railways locomotive, but an Ae4/7, as shown here at Lucerne, was so employed on the Medloc special in April 1946.

● **BELOW RIGHT**
An SNCF Class BB8100 passing through Villeneuve-St-Georges.

The train in which we were to spend the next 37 hours consisted of 11 FS (Italian) corridor coaches – somewhat lacking in such luxuries as upholstery – plus two vans and a silver-painted FS NAAFI car, decorated with army insignia and named Lancastrian for the essential supply of "char and wads" (tea and cake). I was eager for my first sight of a French locomotive, and I was delighted when the former Nord Collin Pacific No. 231-C-43, of a type renowned for pre-war haulage of the Flèche d'Or, backed on to the train. Also in view in the dock

area were numerous War Department 2-8-0s awaiting repatriation.

We left Calais around 13.00 and made slow progress, hindered by the vast amount of reconstruction work arising from the ravages of war, along the main line towards Paris. Engines were changed

at Amiens. At Boves we had a meal halt, where we were fed and watered beside the line. Another lengthy stop was made at Creil, where a line of 141R Mikado 2-8-2s, newly delivered from America, stood outside the locomotive depot. After the war, a fleet of over 1,300 of

INFORMATION BOX	
Termini	Calais and Milan
Countries	France, Switzerland and Italy
Distance	Calais-Milan: 2,392 km (1,486 miles)
Date of opening	1866

● LEFT
The Piazzo della Scala in Milan.

SNCF Region 5 (PLM) steam traction. There were Mountains (4-8-2s), including one resplendent in olive green, and a selection of mixed traffic 2-8-2s dating from 1919 onwards, although, curiously, only one example of the fleet of over 300 Pacifics was seen at close quarters. Other attractions included the distinctive French signals, notably "chequerboards" controlled from high cabins designated "Poste 1", "2" etcetera, and goods rolling stock including elderly vans with brakemen's cabins perched high on the ends.

A 2-8-2, No. 141-E-173, took over for the more demanding section to

these rugged machines was to prove of immense help to the SNCF during the years of transition to widespread electrification.

From Creil we diverged from the main line as darkness fell, and my scanty notes tell me that our route thereafter took us through Epluches, Ermont, Eaubonne and round the outskirts of Paris via the North-South Ceinture link line. There were tantalizing glimpses of vast marshalling yards and strange locomotives under the arc lights, including one of the Mallet 031-130TB tanks used for local heavy-freight trains and shunting.

A period of fitful sleep followed – the unyielding seats and persistent draughts were not conducive to slumber, though one enterprising fellow-traveller took to the luggage rack – and daybreak found us making steady progress south-eastwards along the former PLM main line towards Dijon. Superbly engineered, the line closely followed the course of the Yonne and Armençon rivers. This route would in years to come provide a race track for fast expresses such as the Mistral; our speed, however, was restricted to a maximum of around 80 kph (50 mph). Even in a bleary-eyed state, one's interest was soon aroused when passing places such as Laroche-Migennes and Les Laumes-Alésia, both with well-stocked

locomotive depots and busy yards.

During a long halt at Dijon, an important junction where the lines to the Mediterranean and to Switzerland part company, I feasted my eyes on a variety of

● LEFT
The US Army S160 2-8-0s were invaluable in the haulage of troop trains in Italy during and after the war. This example, as FS No. 736.205, sadly ended its days at Milano Smistamento.

● **RIGHT**
The statue of Victor Emmanuel II in the Piazza
Domo, Milan.

Vallorbe, leaving Dijon at 08.30 and
reaching the Swiss frontier at 15.00.
There was a break in the journey when
we backed up a branch line at Villers-les-
Pots for a meal of stew eaten from our
mess tins at another line-side fast food
outlet. On this section, locomotives
recorded included a 4-8-0 with V-shaped
fronts to the cabs. Most impressive to
British eyes were local passenger 4-8-4
tanks, as big as a pair of LNER N2s
coupled together.

At Vallorbe, a Swiss Federal Railways
Ae4/7 4-8-2 electric locomotive took
over. The next 241 km (150 mile) stretch
was the highlight of the journey. We went
down to Lausanne, then along Lake

Geneva and eastwards through the Rhône
valley to Brigue. The superb scenery
along this section of the route was bathed
in bright sunshine and made a lasting
impression, and a nice touch was that
some of the good citizens of Lausanne

were kind enough to hand us chocolates
while our train waited under the station's
overall glass roof. Even with the addition
of a steam-heating van to an already
heavy train, the 3,120 hp steed gave a
lively performance, non-stop to Brigue,
with the level-crossing bells sounding
merrily as we sped past.

At this time, steam traction had not
been banished from Swiss rails, and a trio
of 4-6-0s and a neat little 2-6-0 had been
observed outside the depot at the end of
Lausanne's platforms. Elsewhere,
however, the scene was all electric with
glimpses of metre-gauge lines at the
stations of Montreux, Aigle and
St-Maurice. As twilight fell we threaded
the Simplon tunnel, emerging at the
other end into Italy.

During a prolonged stop, another
meal was consumed at Domodossola
before departure for Milan at 21.00
behind FS Pacific No. 601.010. This
locomotive, rather more impressive in
looks than in performance, was one of
only 33 built just prior to World War I.
With modifications in the 1930s, most
FS main-line passenger work was
entrusted to the more numerous and
dependable Compound 2-6-2s.

Little was seen during the run to
Milan, where we arrived in darkness at
the great 22-platform terminus at the
unsociable hour of 02.00.

● **RIGHT**
The Gallerie
Emanuelle in Milan.

● **OPPOSITE
BOTTOM**
The FS Italia electric
locomotive, which
took over at
Domodossola, was a
1-Do-1, identical
with No. E428-028,
recorded at the
same station 15
years later.

MYRDAL TO FLÅM
THE FLÅM RAILWAY

The Flåm Railway, part of the Norwegian
State Railway system, or Norges
Statsbaner (NSB), runs between the
towns of Myrdal and Flåm, a distance of
20 km (12 miles). The railway's claim to
fame lies in the fact that Myrdal is 865 m
(2,838 ft) higher than Flåm, making this
line one of the world's steepest non-
rack-operated railways. Since the late
1950s, NSB has been selling an excursion
ticket called "Norway in a Nutshell" for a
round trip from Bergen by train, boat
and bus via the Flåm railway. This is the
journey described.

However, before boarding a train, a
little history of the Flåm railway.
Flåmdalen – the Flåm valley – starts from
Myrdal with a 350 m (1,148 ft) drop,
and it is this that causes the major
engineering work as the railway must
negotiate it by tunnels, ledges and hairpin
curves. The first survey for the line was
in 1893, which produced a proposal for
an 18 km (11 mile), 3 ft 6 in gauge rack
railway with gradients of 10 per cent on
the rack section. However, after

Preserved electric locomotive No. 9.2063 of
1944, on display at Flåm. Adjacent is the old
station building, which houses a small
museum about the Flåm railway.

● **BELOW**
NSB electric locomotive No. 11.2110 at Flåm
on the stock of the overnight sleeper service to
Oslo. This is the Flåm branch's only through
train to the rest of the network, the coaches
being attached to the overnight Bergen to
Oslo train. The Flåm branch is one of the last
outposts of the Class 11 locomotives.

government approval, the plan was
modified to the current, standard-gauge,
electrified adhesion route in 1923. The
purpose of the line was to link the
Bergen to Oslo line, itself completed in
1909, with the Sognefjord. This route
was already popular with tourists,
although the limit was one person per
chaise on the uphill journey, limiting the
number of people that could be handled.

The Flåm railway has a ruling gradient
of 5.5 per cent for 80 per cent of the
line's length. There are 20 tunnels
totalling 5,692 m (over 3½ miles), which
is over a quarter of the line. The
minimum curve radius is 130 m (427 ft).
All trains operating over this line are
fitted with five different braking systems,
each of which alone can stop the train.
Unsurprisingly, maximum speed is
limited, to 40 kph (25 mph), giving a
journey time of 53 minutes. However,
the scenery is so spectacular, that this
seems too short a time, not too long!

It had been intended to open the
railway in 1942, but wartime measures
meant it was opened in August 1940,

● **RIGHT**
A view from Stalheim Hotel, towards Gudvangen and the Nærøyfjord. The pass road leaves the new road where it crosses the stream in the middle of the photograph, and then crosses the stream a little to the right.

although steam-operated. The electric locomotives ordered, on the other hand, were delayed by the war, not arriving until 1947. These locomotives, designated Class E19, survived until 1984. One has been put on display at Flåm station.

Despite threats of closure in the 1960s, traffic on the line has grown, reaching 315,000 in 1992. The passenger service is seasonal, with only four trains operating each way in winter, but 12 services each way in summer.

The day's journey starts from the terminus station in Bergen, Norway's second city. This is an imposing stone-fronted and very solid-looking building with a curved roof over the four main tracks. The journey to Myrdal is by

INFORMATION BOX	
THE FLÅM RAILWAY	
Termini	Myrdal and Flåm
Country	Norway
Distance	20 km (12 miles)
Date of opening	1940

● **RIGHT**
Fylkesbaatane's boat *Skagastøl* arriving at Flåm. Its previous use as a car ferry can be discerned, the raisable bow continuing to be used for embarking.

stopping train, which is formed of a suburban electric multiple unit (EMU). These are not as comfortable as the long-distance trains, but the low seat-backs and large windows allow good views of the passing scenery.

While the journey to Myrdal is not as spectacular as the Flåm railway, nor the countryside as barren as that on the central part of the Oslo to Bergen railway, there are some very attractive views on the first 86 km (53 miles) to Voss. Best of all is the stretch between Takvam and

● LEFT
NSB three-car EMU No. 69625 at Myrdal,
having worked from Bergen.

Stanghelle, where the railway follows one of the minor fjords.

From Voss, the railway starts to climb. The line to Oslo will reach 1,300 m (4,265 ft) above sea level at its highest point, but this journey only goes as far as Myrdal, 867 m (2,845 ft), two hours and 135 km (84 miles) from Bergen.

Myrdal is situated between two tunnels and seems to exist purely for the purposes of a railway junction. The only visible habitations are a few houses, quite probably built by the railway. The steepness of the Flåm railway is obvious from the start, when one sees the way the railway track disappears downhill from the end of the platform. During the journey, anyone walking up and down the carriage – literally – will realize just how steep the track is, one end of the 24 m (79 ft) coach being 1.4 m (4½ ft) below the other.

The first view comes after one kilometre (²/₃ mile) at Vatnahalsen, where the Kjosfossen power-station lake and waterfall can be seen below. Three kilometres (2 miles) later, the train stops at Kjosfossen to allow passengers to leave the train and photograph the waterfall, now pouring down from several hundred feet above.

A couple of kilometres (1.24 miles) later, the highest settlement in the Flåmdalen comes into view. At several points, between tunnels and snow shelters, spectacular views are available, both down and upwards, where you can see parts of the route taken by the railway. In particular, the "window" out from one of the tunnels inside the rock face can be seen above the snow shelter on the lower level of the line. At Berekvam, slightly under half-way, there is a passing loop, the only place on the line where trains can pass each other. Below Dalsbotn, Flåm church can be seen along with some farms in the flatter valley floor. Soon after Hareina, the gradient slackens as the valley floor is reached, and the last couple of kilometres are relatively flat, passing through farmlands, but still overhung by the towering sides of the fjord. The "port" of Flåm is finally reached after negotiating a narrowing and curving of the valley, such that the fjord cannot be seen from the train on the journey down from Myrdal.

The area around Flåm station is clearly aimed at tourists, with a number of gift shops and restaurants. However, a short walk brought relief from the throng! The two-hour connection is more than adequate to see the area around the railway station and, with a little effort, there may be enough time to walk some way up the valley towards the Flåm church. Some of this time should be spent on a visit to the interesting Flåm railway museum, situated in the old station building, which explains the history of this extraordinary railway.

● RIGHT
A view of Flåmdalen from below Dalsbotn,
seen from a train on the Flåm railway. Flåm
church is in the small settlement in the middle
of the view. The Aurlandfjord is off to the right
after the valley narrows.

Preserved electric locomotive No. 9.2063, of the type built for the Flåm line, is displayed on the station platform. The adjacent small railway depot is home to an unusual battery shunting locomotive.

Gudvangen is on the Nærøyfjord, a branch off the Aurlandfjord. The village appears to be little more than a couple of farms, a jetty for the ferries and a tourist shop and restaurant, albeit in an attractive setting.

From here our trip continues by coach to Voss. The coach trip is dramatic in itself. The first section is along the valley at the end of the fjord, but the coach turns off the main road to take the pass road up to Stalheim. This road is very narrow and steep and has frequent hairpin bends. These are a struggle for the coach, even without the distraction of downhill traffic. This is fortunately light, as a new road tunnel has been constructed to avoid this section. The views from the coach are spectacular, but are as nothing compared to those from Stalheim. This is a hotel perched on a saddle between two valleys. On one side is the steep drop down to Gudvangen; on the other, the much shallower drop towards Vinje.

The run on to Voss is much less dramatic. The scenery is no less attractive, although the height of the land allows only a minimal amount of vegetation to grow, which shows one a different side to the country. Voss is a lakeside town and skiing centre, with an imposing church. It used to be the junction for a branch line to the Hardangerfjorden, since closed. Finally, a train is joined for the return to Bergen.

Great Journeys of the East

This section takes the reader on some of the most exciting rail journeys in the world, from the romance of the Trans-Siberian Express to the fabulous luxury of the South African Blue Train. The reader will experience the deserts of Iran and the plush jungles of Ghana where, if not attended to, within months the flora and fauna overgrow the railway line itself. This section also brings to life historical figures such as Lawrence of Arabia whose destruction of the railways in Saudi Arabia still has not been repaired, and we go to China, the last bastion of the steam locomotive.

India is not forgotten as we travel the length and breath of the sub-continent, riding on trains ranging from the luxurious Palace on Wheels to the "toy train" that takes us up the foothills of the Himalayas to the town of Darjeeling. We visit Australia where we remember the pioneers of the 19th century through whose efforts the railways of that vast continent were laid, and lastly New Zealand for, among others, its spectacular Transalpine journey.

● **OPPOSITE**
The Eastern and Oriental Express near
Kanchanaburi, Thailand.

● **ABOVE**
The afternoon train leaves Pachegaon station, in
India, which amounts to little more than a sign
board set amid the scrub.

CASABLANCA TO GABES

The trains on this line will take the rail traveller all along the Mediterranean coast of North Africa from Morocco's Casablanca, via Tangier, to Gabes in south-eastern Tunisia, some 1,778 km (1,105 miles) in all. French from 1840 to 1960, Algeria was treated as a *département* of France, and its railway – the Société Nationale des Transports Ferroviaires (SNTF) – was constructed and run accordingly. Built to standard gauge, the trains ran with a pre-war speed and efficiency admired by many countries. The system is basically coastal, to provide a link between Casablanca in Morocco and Tunis, at one time all French.

Neither Moroccan nor Algerian Railways are the slightest mite house-proud. Some of the trains are a disgrace. From Fez to the Algerian border, compartments are a mass of sprawling bodies trying to get some sleep on wooden seats.

Pink *wadis* show in the dawn. Taza Haut brooded on a hill and, nearby, an amazing conglomeration of buildings

● **ABOVE**
Ouja railway station on the border between Algeria and Morocco.

INFORMATION BOX

Termini	Casablanca and Gabes
Countries	Morocco to Tunisia
Distance	1,778 km (1,105 miles)
Construction began	1915

called the Kasbah of Taourirt scowl at the train. Ouja is the border town, a dull but not unpleasant place of wide streets and solid European-style houses.

Rusty train wrecks lay beside the line to Oran. Tiemcen, however, shows a face of Andalusian elegance and Moorish arcades. Sidi-bel-Abbas smells of Foreign Legionnaires. The most Moorish-looking building in Oran is the chaotic railway station, where a corner seat on the train may be won by starting a rumour that it is to arrive at an adjacent platform.

● **ABOVE**
The Casablanca to Tangier express waits at Sidi Slimane.

● **LEFT**
The through diesel express of Moroccan Railways on its way from Marrakesh to Tangier via Casablanca and Rabat.

In Tunisia, however, things change dramatically and abruptly. The trains are reasonably clean and in better order, even though the general feeling is that foreign tourists are not expected to use such lowly vehicles. On the train to Tunis, the customs officers have the habit of searching bags by the simple expedient of turning them upside down.

The 190 km (118 miles) of line between the border and the capital is narrow – metre-gauge – which explains the change of train. Though a fraction of the size of its massive neighbour, Tunisia can boast a track mileage of 2,200 against Algeria's 2,570.

In the south of the country, at Sfax, one has to change trains again. However, the onward connection to Gabes is poor, and the trains that eventually arrive seem as reluctant as the traveller is eager to reach the end of the line.

As in many industrial countries, the railway route into the capital is not the most attractive. The line sneaks in by the back door through the dingiest of industrial complexes. Onwards to Constantine and its amazing rock formations and a deep ravine traversed by slender bridges. The next main station is Annaba – once known as Bône. The trains that creep out of Annaba are equipped with third-class coaches, which are fit only for the knacker's (junk) yard, several compartments being both windowless and seatless. Souk-Ahras is the border town, some 16 km (10 miles) from the Tunisian frontier. Here, on the fringe of war, the border police sport brigand-style uniforms and swaggers.

● **ABOVE**
A modern passenger train passes Bab Tisera (Sidi Kacem) *en route* from Casablanca to Fez.

● **RIGHT**
A passenger train arrives at Rabat.

CAIRO TO ASWAN
THE STAR OF EGYPT

Although the all-sleeper express has lost its name today, tourism up the River Nile is 120 years old. Thomas Cook & Son (more particularly his son John) organized tourist river steamers on the Nile from about the mid-1870s. They were based in Cairo, which was connected with Egypt's main port Alexandria by the first railway in the Middle East, built in 1855. It included a bridge over the Nile outside Cairo, also used by the Star of Egypt on leaving Cairo Main. Wagons-Lits, creators of the Orient Express, celebrated their Silver Jubilee in 1898 by expanding simultaneously into Russia and Egypt.

Here the cars were painted white to reflect heat and had double roofs, while dining cars, built by Ringhoffer in Prague, had primitive air-conditioning, with blocks of ice cooling the air circulating between the skins of the roof. The great rival of Cook, whom they bought up in 1928, but lost during World War II, Wagons-Lits started sleepers with a diner in 1898 from Cairo to Luxor. At least until 1908, the lines which ran on up the Nile to Aswan remained narrow-gauge. The 1908 night train left Cairo on

● **RIGHT**
A typical village market, or souk, of which many are seen on the journey.

● **BELOW**
Part of the frieze on the Thomas Cook office building in Leicester, depicting Cook's first full Egyptian tour begun in 1884.

● **BELOW**
An Egyptian Railways 1,500hp Bo-Bo waits to take its carriages to pick up Cairo-bound passengers at Aswan.

Mondays, Wednesdays and Saturdays, returning from Luxor on Tuesdays, Thursdays and Sundays.

The line leaves Cairo, crosses the Nile on the Alexandria line bridge and then turns upstream along the Nile's left bank through Assyut. It crosses the Nile at Nag Hamadi, and thereafter follows the right bank to Luxor and on to Aswan.

In 1906 Lord Dalziel bought from the executors of George Mortimer Pullman their British operations together with the exclusive rights to the name Pullman on railway cars throughout Europe and

● LEFT
A French-built turbo train on the Cairo to Alexandria run in Egypt.

The Sunshine Pullman ended its life in 1939, but the sleeping cars were revived after the war, and the Star of Egypt continued until around 1958-9 when Wagons-Lits was sequestered. The Egyptians found they could not really manage without them, and the Egyptian Republic Railways allowed them back, setting up a joint company to run the train. The Hungarian sleeping cars that ERR had bought were relegated to slow trains, and the modern-day all-sleeper train, with lounge car, now has German vehicles built in the 1980s by Messerschmidt MBB. A supply car replaces the diner, and meals are served in the cabins.

At present one train suffices on the route – most people either cruise on the Nile or fly. Thomas Cook still run the Nile cruise ships, but mostly these belong to other companies. Now the journey by all-sleeper train, which terminates at Aswan, takes some 16 hours – the 1938 journey was half an hour faster.

Egypt. Lord Dalziel gave these rights to Wagon-Lits, of which he was a director, in 1907. Wagons-Lits started using Pullmans in about 1925 and those for Egypt were shipped, newly built, direct from England. Lord Dalziel died in 1928, a few weeks after Wagons-Lits had swallowed up Cook, in the pretence that it was a merger.

Further Pullman cars were sent out in 1929, when the Sunshine Express, an all-Pullman day train from Cairo to Luxor, was started. New sleeping cars now ran in the night train, named Star of Egypt. At Aswan it continued to El Shallal, above the cataracts and the Aswan Dam, connecting with steamers to Wadi Halfa, in the Sudan, where the Sudanese Railways line to Khartoum avoids a big bend in the river. When the new Aswan Dam was built, the Aswan terminus was forced to move to El Sadd el Ali.

● ABOVE
A mechanized maintenance train in Egypt.

● BELOW
For much of the journey, the train travels by the Nile, seen here near Cairo.

INFORMATION BOX

THE STAR OF EGYPT

Termini	Cairo and Aswan
Country	Egypt
Distance	960 km (597 miles)
Date of opening	1908

NAIROBI TO KAMPALA

When construction of the then East
African Railway began in 1898, it
appeared to be going "from nowhere
through nowhere to nowhere", and so
they called it the "Lunatic Line". But
there was a purpose. The aim, besides
building a railway line through unknown
East Africa to the once remote inland
country of Uganda, was to help put down
the detested Arab slave trade.

Victorian crusading enterprise in East
Africa was chiefly directed at Uganda.
Kenya was an afterthought. The crusade
needed a railway so, with the matter-of-
fact approach characteristic of the times,
a railway was driven all the way from
Mombasa on the Indian Ocean. If the
track had to rise many metres up and
down again, what did it matter? So it was
successfully driven across hundreds of
kilometres of bush alive with marauding
wild animals, disease-carrying swamps
and the lunar trough of the Great Rift
itself, to Lake Victoria.

The line reached Kisumu after
unbelievable feats of human endurance
and engineering, and was later pushed
forward to Kampala and beyond. From

● ABOVE
Locomotive No. 5932 "Ol' Donya Sabuk" seen
here hauling a Mombasa to Nairobi freight at
Athi River.

INFORMATION BOX

Termini	Nairobi and Kampala
Countries	Kenya and Uganda
Length	1,338 km (831 miles)
Date construction commenced	1898

the coast, the line snaked through the
uplands, infested by lions that killed
some 200 construction workers, to reach
a well in the deserted Kikuyu country. It
came to the great Rift Valley escarpment,
down which trains had to be lowered on
an inclined plane assisted by rope
haulage, and then continued over the
Mau Summit to Kisumu on the shores of
Lake Victoria. Here a prefabricated ship
was launched, and Kampala, capital of
Uganda, became accessible to the outside
world via a journey of under five days.
Nowhere else in the world, and at no
time in history, has a journey been so
dramatically shortened from six months'

● ABOVE
Derailed on the soggy Kasese Extentions,
this locomotive was back in service within
three months.

● LEFT
A train approaches Jinja bridge near the Ripon
Falls, the source of the Nile.

● **RIGHT**
● **RIGHT**
An East African
Railways Class 59
4-8-2+4-8-2
Mountain Class
Garratt pulls heavily
away from Voi at the
edge of the Tsavo
game reserve in
Kenya with a heavy
freight from
Mombasa, bound
for the Kenyan
capital, Nairobi.

● **BELOW LEFT**
An East African Railways Class 59 4-8-2+2-8-4
Garratt locomotive, built by Beyer Peacock of
Manchester in 1955, rounds the spiral that
forms part of the steep climb up the coastal
escarpment from Mombasa on the Indian Ocean.

Notwithstanding the many stops at the
wayside stations, the train did its best to
make up for lost time. Each station was a
colourful pageant of people, though few
seemingly had any business with the
railway; it was just that the station was
the community centre – the place where
the action was. At Jinja we crossed the
River Nile.

It was raining when we reached
Kampala and, climbing the stairs towards
the exit, I was intercepted by what I later
learned was a plain-clothes agent of the
security service. The ensuing
developments form no part of this rail
narrative but, briefly, entailed my being
arrested as a likely spy (for showing an
interest in the railway), my interrogation
in Kampala's grizzly central police station
and prison, which took place over several
days and nights, and my final release.

I was put aboard (i.e. left clinging to
the step of a packed coach of) the
seemingly very last train allowed through
to Nairobi, where I arrived none the
worse for my ill-fated Kampala visit
except for a deficiency of sleep and a
good meal.

dangerous walking to a four-day ride in
what was then comparative comfort. At
the same time, the line opened up both
Uganda and Kenya and was instrumental
in the development of East Africa's major
metropolis, Nairobi.

By early 1997 all rail services except a
once-weekly international one terminated at the Kenya-Uganda border, but
on this particular journey, 20 years or so
earlier, the train was the last non-
intercontinental through service to
operate for some time. A military crisis
had arisen, and President Idi Amin's
army was poised to invade Kenya.

Deciding to press on regardless, the
journey had to be confined. The train out
of Nairobi was a lesser animal than that
of the Mombassa-Nairobi Express, but
adequate enough. And when one has the
stupendous sight of the Rift valley *en
route*, a reasonably clean and openable
window is all that you really require.

On the floor of the Rift valley lies the
town of Nakuru and, to the south of it,
Lake Nakaru, an expanse of shallow,
saline water, the shores of which are the
sacred nesting ground of over 10,000
flamingos.

Unfortunately, the train was kept
standing at the Kenyan border station of
Malaba for five hours, following which it
drew into Tororo. Between these two
points the train was virtually empty – a
somewhat lonely experience in a
potential war zone. But the coaches filled
up at Tororo.

● **BELOW**
East African Railways Class 59 4-8-2+2-8-4
Garratt No. 5922 "Mount Blackett" climbs the
steep coastal escarpment away from Mombasa
with a Nairobi-bound freight.

A NETWORK IN DECLINE

Rail travel in Ghana is now, alas, almost a thing of the past. In its heyday, however, passenger travel was luxurious with restaurant and sleeping facilities on many trains. By 1985, owing to the general decay of the system as well as the permanent way, steam was extinct. This was much to the chagrin of the railway workers, who liked the simplicity of steam; diesel locomotives are much more difficult to maintain. This has resulted in much of Ghana's railway being almost at a complete standstill, with hardly any passenger trains running at all.

Although the total route length of railway in Ghana was only 953 km (592 miles), a journey on its tracks was an unforgettable experience. The system was in the form of a letter A, with Kumasi at the apex, the two feet at Takoradi and Accra, and the chord of the A connecting Huni valley and Kotoku. One of the notable features of the network is the excessive curvatures. A prime example of this is the section between Kumasi and Takoradi, where there are about 504 curves in a section of 270 km (168 miles).

It was the discovery of gold that caused the British to begin building the first railway in the country, which was then called the Gold Coast. Starting from the coastal village of Sekondi in 1899, the line progressively embraced the communities at Tarkwa, Dunkwa and Obuasi, and in September 1903 it finally reached the Ashanti kingdom of Kumasi, an incredible 265 km (165 miles) inland. The original Sekondi station is still there, with its Gents clock from Leicester still on the wall – long since stopped.

INFORMATION BOX	
Termini	Accra, Kumasi and Takoradi
Country	Ghana
Distance	953 km (592 miles)
Date of commencement	1899

● **TOP**
British steam locomotives lie derelict in the overgrown yard at the Location works.

● **ABOVE LEFT**
A decrepit diesel-electric locomotive undergoing overhaul at the Location works.

● **LEFT**
The historic railway station at Sekondi, which would have made the perfect site for a national railway museum, complete with defunct clock from Gents of Leicester.

Ghana's coast is hemmed in by a belt of jungle 240 km (149 miles) deep, and building the railway through the gloomy forests and the vast tracts of fever-laden jungles of the interior was a superhuman achievement, costing many lives as workers fell victim to diseases. In many places there was less than 30 m (100 ft) of clear view ahead. There were many depressions filled with swamp water, concealed from sight by the overgrowing scrub. Another, not so obvious, problem, was caused by the pegs that the engineers placed 30 m (100 ft) apart to indicate the centre of the proposed track. As these stakes were cut from green wood, they soon started to sprout, causing the survey line to be obliterated in a short space of time.

Extensions to the network made the Gold Coast Railways the pride of Africa. Apart from opening up the gold fields, the railway helped to exploit Ghana's vast potential for cocoa, which developed the Cadbury empire, while manganese from Nsuta, bauxite from Awaso, and timber from Kumasi all flowed down the west line to the coast for export. The circuitous line from Accra to Kumasi was begun in 1909 but did not reach Kumasi, 583 km (362 miles) away, until 1923.

One of the more impressive bridges on the network was that at Ancobra, on the 31 km (19 mile) long branch line from Tarkwa to Prestea. The bridge, supported on 12 m (39 ft) high concrete piers, has four spans, the central one

being 55 m (180 ft) long. In 1985, when the railway photographer and historian Colin Garratt visited Ghana, he found Accra's railway station mouldering in an aura of decay. The huge marshalling yards had been turned into a fruit and vegetable market, the sidings were rusty and unused, and the only passengers were market women who had come to the city from the country to sell their produce in the capital.

Garratt appealed for the heritage to be conserved – Sekondi station would have been ideal. However, all was destroyed in exchange for instant revenue from the sale of scrap to the steelworks at Tema. Thus Ghana lost the chance of a fine cultural/tourist opportunity.

● **ABOVE LEFT**
The infrastructure of Ghana's railways degenerated into such a poor condition as to threaten survival of the whole network. During the 1980s, huge numbers of volunteers were mustered to form work gangs in a desperate bid to save the network.

● **ABOVE RIGHT**
Industrial history, all imported from Britain, in the forge at the Location locomotive works – a piece of industrial Lancashire grafted on to the primeval jungle.

● **BELOW**
The abandoned locomotive depot yard in Accra has long since been illegally taken over by marketeers. Forming a backdrop to the merchandising is (left) a Hunslit 0-8-0 tank engine along with a Vulcan Foundry 4-8-2.

CAPE TOWN TO PRETORIA
THE BLUE TRAIN

The first luxury train to run the 3 ft 6 in gauge route from Cape Town to Pretoria was started in 1903. This was operated by the Cape Government Railway and the Central South African Railway. In 1910, on the formation of the Union of South Africa, all the country's independent lines amalgamated to form South African Railways, and the train was named the Union Limited. Although the train was a luxury one-class express, which required supplementary fares, it was extremely popular, so much so that in the 1930s more coaches had to be added and the smart Pacifics, which were used to haul the train, were replaced with 4-8-2s.

The twice-weekly train was renamed the Blue Train (Bloutrein) in April 1939. It was, of course, not the first time a train had been so named, for the Train Bleu had been running from Paris to the Côte d'Azur since the 1920s. This change of name coincided with the introduction of new blue-and-cream carriages with clerestory roofs; the locomotives, however, continued to be in the black of South African Railways. The compartments were super deluxe,

- **LEFT**
The Blue Train at Johannesburg station.

- **BELOW LEFT**
A head-on view of the Blue Train.

INFORMATION BOX	
THE BLUE TRAIN	
Termini	Cape Town and Pretoria
Country	South Africa
Distance	1,607 km (999 miles)
Date of first run	1910

- **BELOW LEFT**
The Blue Train traversing the Hex River valley.

- **BELOW RIGHT**
The Blue Train is not without luxuries, such as facilities for a wash and brush up.

dust-proofed and air-conditioned with blue leather upholstered seats, loose cushions and writing tables with headed notepaper. At the rear of the train was an observation car. In spite of the 3 ft 6 in gauge the body width of these coaches was 3 m (10 ft).

Such was the popularity of the train that, in spite of the high prices, reservations had to be made far in advance. To provide room for the various on-board services, including fully equipped bathrooms, only 100

passengers could be catered for on each journey. The train was electrically hauled by blue locomotives between Pretoria and Kimberley, and again between Beaufort West and Cape Town, and scheduled to do three round trips weekly from October to March and one from April to September.

President Nelson Mandela inaugurated the "new" Blue Train in June 1997. Built from the undercarriage of the original Blue Train sets, these two new trains feature only two grades of on-

board accommodation – luxury and deluxe – as opposed to the previous four.

The luxury suites differ from the deluxe in that they are more spacious and offer larger bathrooms – deluxe ones have private shower or bath, luxury ones all have baths. There is 24-hour butler service, laundry service and two lounge cars, and while all the suites are equipped with televisions and telephones, the luxury suites in addition have CD players and video recorders. There is also live footage on TV from a camera positioned in the front of the train, giving passengers a "driver's-eye" view of their journey.

With this impressive level of upgrading of the Blue Train, capacity on board has inevitably been reduced from 107 to 84. The Blue Train no longer serves Johannesburg, routing via Germiston instead as it travels between Pretoria and Cape Town. There are several departures throughout the year between Pretoria and Victoria Falls.

● **ABOVE**
The Blue Train running through the beautiful Hex River valley.

● **LEFT**
The Blue Train with the unmistakable Table Mountain in the background.

CAPE TOWN TO VICTORIA FALLS

Railways in the Cape Colony date back to 1857, when a pioneering line was opened from Cape Town to Wellington – a 72 km (45 mile) journey. In 1873 the first trains completed the 1,036 km (644 miles) from Cape Town to Kimberley across the Karoo, and as Cecil Rhodes progressed through Africa, the iron road was laid northwards, the 235 km (146 mile) section from Kimberley to De Aar being laid in an impressive 20 months between March 1884 and November 1885. The route of the Pride of Africa is from Cape Town, via Beaufort West, De Aar, Kimberley, Klerksdorp, Johannesburg, Pretoria, Mafeking (border), Gaborone, Plumtree (border), Bulawayo, and Hwange to Victoria Falls.

The modern flat-roofed station at Cape Town seems an improbable place to

● **LEFT**
The observation car of the Pride of Africa allows unimpeded views across the African bush. Comfortable armchairs make this an ideal venue to watch the passing scenery, while the open platform gives photographers superb views of the passing landscapes.

INFORMATION BOX

Termini	Cape Town and Victoria Falls
Countries	South Africa to Zimbabwe
Distance	3,200 km (2,000 miles)
Date of completion of first section	1873

embark on one of the world's most entrancing railway journeys, but on Platform 24 stands no ordinary train. Drawn up like guards on parade, the Pride of Africa, resplendent in bottle-green livery, evokes the sublimity of a truly grand occasion. At the head of the train, a pair of Class 6E1 3,000V DC Bo-Bo electrics, in the rather old-fashioned rusty-brown colours of South African Railways, look purposeful and

● **LEFT**
A double-headed train crosses over the Kaaiman River bridge.

● **BELOW**
Locomotive No. 519 returning from the cement
works at Gwanda, Zimbabwe.

● **BOTTOM RIGHT**
An impressive line-up of Garratts at Bulawayo shed.

● **BELOW**
Rovos Rail owns four steam locomotives. No. 439, Tiffany, is the oldest,
built in 1893 and restored by Dunns Locomotive more than 90 years
later. Numbers 2701, 2702 and 3360 are all Class 19D locomotives.

ready to haul their charge over the 708
km (440 miles) to Beaufort West, from
just over sea level at Cape Town to over
1,219 m (4,000 ft) across the Karoo.

The dignified welcome for the
passengers is in stark contrast to the local
Metro trains busily heading off into the
suburbs, their human cargoes packed
tighter than sardines. Rohan Vos, owner
and visionary behind the Pride of Africa,
is often on hand to give a few handy hints
on how to get the most out of the pan-
African odyssey, before he bids the train
farewell, toasting the travellers with fine
South African sparkling wine.

Nestling beneath the distinctively flat-
topped massif of Table Mountain, Cape
Town enjoys one of the most spectacular
settings on earth. As the Pride of Africa
begins its journey northwards, it soon
leaves the compact patchwork of red-
and white-roofed houses and modern
office blocks behind as the tracks follow
the mighty circle of Table Bay with its
encircling ocean before heading inland.

In the wine country of Paarl and the
Hex River valley, tangled vines grow in
the foothills of starkly chiselled
mountains. These are modest farmsteads,
their white porticoes guarded by
cypresses at the end of rutted dirt roads.
Here and there, roosting in the scrub,

ostriches preen their feathers among
indifferent sheep and horses.

Africa has been a magnet for
adventurers ever since Xenophon's men
took time out to hunt the wild ostrich,
and in our own times Rohan Vos has
single-handedly created one of southern
Africa's most romantic travelling idylls.
Rovos Rail is his dreamchild, and in 1986
he started lovingly restoring ancient,
abandoned railway coaches and proud
steam locomotives.

Dating from 1919, each sleeping car,
observation car, bar and lounge car, as
well as the atmospheric Victorian and

Edwardian dining cars, combines the
opulence of pre-war style with subtle
modern innovations. Sleeping
accommodation is in suites with double
or twin beds, together with private
showers and toilets.

As the sun all but disappears, leaving a
last explosion of light along the earth's
rim, the train arrives at Matjiesfontein.
Here an hour-long visit can be made to
the historical hamlet where, over one
hundred years ago, Laird Logan set up a
small refreshment hotel to revictual the
hungry and thirsty travellers of the Cape
Government Railways. The graceful

hotel, named after Lord Milner, provides an opportunity to take the evening air and enjoy a small draught of the famous Castle beer.

As the train continues its journey, the Karoo's horizon becomes scarlet, the sky salmon, the earth blood – it is the drunken dusk of the desert. Passengers become ensconced in the observation car, aperitif in hand, watching the African night creep up on the train.

Coach No. 148, Pafuri, was originally built in 1911 as an A-17 type dining car comprising a small bar, a 24-seat dining section, and a kitchen. In 1924, she was converted into a full 46-seater, responding to an increasing percentage of

passengers taking meals on the great trains of Africa, such as the Diamond Express, the Imperial Mail and the African Express.

Today's passengers enjoy evoking the nostalgia of the great days of travel in this most romantic of settings, surrounded by seven pairs of carved roof-supporting pillars and arches. Later, the travellers fall asleep to the rhythmical, hypnotic motion of the train's wheels. Despite the narrow 3 ft 6 in gauge of South Africa's railways, the ride is surprisingly smooth.

Unnoticed at Beaufort West the current changes to a.c., and now two Class 7E Co-Co locomotives are attached

to haul the train to De Aar. During the night, the 235 km (146 mile) stretch of non-electrified line from De Aar to Kimberley is reached, and a pair of Class 34 Co-Co diesel electrics put in charge.

The following day sees the train arrive at the fine old Victorian station of Kimberley. This city of diamonds is set in the flat, austere landscape of the Karoo. History is rekindled as lunch is enjoyed in the famous Kimberley Club, wistfully recapturing the spirit of the reign of Rhodes and Jameson, who clinched so many deals on these premises. Now with two powerful, high-speed 3,000V d.c. Bo-Bo Class 12Es in command, the Pride of Africa speeds towards Pretoria.

The following day, after a sightseeing tour of Pretoria, the 17-carriage train heads north through groves of orange, papaya and avocado, past depressing townships where flocks of children run down to the tracks smiling and waving. In the observation and lounge cars the rail-borne safari begins in earnest as sightings of impala, kudu and zebra give us a foretaste of this unforgettable close encounter with Africa.

Crossing into Botswana at Mafeking the Pride of Africa undergoes one of a series of no fewer than seven locomotive changes between Pretoria and Victoria

Falls. The mood on board is one of
anticipation as passengers savour Cape
crayfish and Karoo lamb washed down
with Chardonnays and Cabernets.

The steepest gradient encountered is
1:50, as the train makes its assault on the
steep-sided mountains that separate the
lush, fertile Hex River valley and the
elevated, arid Karoo. The climb of 533 m
(1,750 ft) over 82 km (51 miles) is the
most spectacular section of the journey;
its highest point lies just south of
Johannesburg at 1,834 m (6,017 ft). The
series of four tunnels in the 16.4 km
(10.2 mile) long Hex River tunnel system
are ranked as the fourth largest in the
world and are by far the single most
outstanding feature of the journey
between Cape Town and Victoria Falls.
The tunnels are dead straight, and the
longest of them, the northernmost, is
spectacular when viewed from the
observation car – you can still see the
entrance as you leave the exit.

The last complete day on the train is
filled with spectacular views of the
African bush. After crossing into

Zimbabwe at Plumtree, an afternoon visit
is made to Bulawayo. Home to
Lobengula, King of the Matabele nation
in 1870, the city went on to become
synonymous with mining. Here a Class
15 Garratt articulated steam locomotive
takes charge. This huge 28-wheeler hauls
the Pride of Africa through the night
along one of the longest stretches of
straight railway line in the world – the
116 km (72 miles) between Gwaai and

Dete on the eastern edge of the Hwange
National Park. Musi-oa-tunya ("smoke
that thunders") – the African name for
the Victoria Falls – heralds journey's end.
The screaming of the wheels as the train
rounds the final curve adds to the
dramatic sense of theatre that this
3,218 km (2,000 mile) pan-African
adventure has created. Truly, the Pride of
Africa is an iconoclast, following in the
footsteps of empire.

CAPE TOWN TO PRETORIA
THE TRANS KAROO

● **BELOW**
Cape wine area farms near Paarl,
seen from the Trans Karoo.

The Trans Karoo is named after its crossing of the Karoo Desert, which covers around one third of South Africa, and is larger than Great Britain and Ireland. Although the Karoo is not of the sand dune type, it proved to be a difficult barrier to cross. Another kind of barrier is the altitude of the Highveld on which Johannesburg is situated; the city is over 1,524 m (5,000 ft) above sea level. The combination of these two factors continues to make operation of trains between these principal towns of the Republic of South Africa (RSA) a continuing challenge, even after electrification of the line.

The lack of water in the desert led to the introduction of a feature unique to South Africa, the condensing tender. These elongated vehicles contained steam-condensing equipment and were used with many Class 25 steam locomotives to reduce water consumption by recycling as much steam as possible. The result was that the British-built locomotives could travel over 1,100 km (700 miles) on one tender of water.

Modernization has shortened the Cape Town to Pretoria journey from the 30 hours taken in 1978, and the Trans Karoo now runs daily rather than five days a week as it did then. However, a second train over the route, running to a schedule 12 hours later on four days a week, has been deleted. The reduction in passenger rail travel has been repeated across the country and is well illustrated by the long lines of stored passenger-coaches outside Cape Town.

The Trans Karoo runs daily between Cape Town and Pretoria via De Aar, Kimberley and Johannesburg, taking 26 hours for the 1,600 km (1,000 mile) journey. The famous Blue Train continues to operate over the same route three days per week, but is now aimed at the luxury travel and tourist market, whereas the Trans Karoo operates the "genuine" passenger service.

The Trans Karoo departs the large Cape Town terminus station from platform 24, which is reserved for this and the few other long-distance services.

SAR Class 6E electric locomotive No. E1184
outside Beaufort West depot sporting the
latest Spoornet livery. These 3,340 hp
locomotives were built in 1970–1 by Union
Carriage and Wagon Co. (UCW), at Nigel,
Transvaal, with equipment from AEI in
Manchester, England. Double-headed
members of this class haul the Trans Karoo
from Cape Town to Beaufort West and from
De Aar to Pretoria.

● BELOW
The SAR steam
locomotive dump at
Millsite. The large
locomotive in the
centre of the picture
is one of the large
Bayer-Garratt
articulated
locomotives.

INFORMATION BOX

THE TRANS KAROO

Termini	Cape Town and Pretoria
Country	South Africa
Distance	1,600 km (1,000 miles)
Commencement of building	1892

● OPPOSITE BELOW
A steam-hauled Trans Karoo passing Millsite.
The locomotives are 4-8-4s of class 25NC,
Nos. 3476 and 3404. These locomotives
were constructed in 1953–4 by North British
in Glasgow, Scotland, and Henschel of
Kassel, Germany.

● BELOW
The Karoo near Beaufort West. The
background hills are of a shape common
in the desert.

The train the author travelled in was
made up of 15 coaches, a car-carrying
van, a steam-heating van and two electric
locomotives of Class 6E. The weather was
cool enough for wisps of steam to be seen
emanating from the steam-heating van.
The locomotives would be changed a
couple of times en route, at Beaufort West
and De Aar. A Class 7E was used between
these points as this route is electrified at a
different voltage, 25kV a.c. as opposed to
3,000V d.c. from Cape Town and into
Pretoria. The Friday departure from
Pretoria as far as Klerksdorp, and the
Saturday return, were steam hauled using
double-headed 4-8-4s of Class 25NC.

First impressions of the train are not
helped by the tatty appearance of the
paintwork, which belies the state of the
interior. Inside, the coaches are clean and
simply but effectively furnished. The
train was formed with three classes of
accommodation. The first and second
class were sleeper coaches marshalled
each side of the restaurant cars. The third
class, mainly day coaches, was separated
from the rest of the train by a door that
remained firmly locked throughout the
trip. There are on-board showers located
at the end of each sleeping coach.

The restaurant car (actually two coaches, one containing the kitchen and staff quarters, the other the seating area) provides good food, although the approach to service seems to be of the same vintage as the coaches. In addition, there is a very effective trolley service of drinks and snacks. The train crew, who were on duty for the entire journey, included an armed guard. This is not so much due to the high crime levels as to control drunken passengers.

The train first heads through the Cape Town suburbs and then into the Cape wine areas of Stellenbosch and Paarl. This area is characterized not only by the vineyards, but also by the famous white-painted, Dutch-style farmhouses. Of particular note is Huguenot Station in an area named after the early French settlers. This is built in the Cape Dutch style, but it has very British influences in the footbridge and signals. The Cape wine area is within the Cape Town electrified suburban rail network, which is served by brightly coloured suburban EMUs.

After initially travelling north, the train turns in a north-westerly direction,

● **ABOVE**
SAR coaches at Pretoria. The blue-and-grey Interpax coaches are of the type used on the Trans Karoo.

● **BOTTOM**
Typical Karoo scenery between Touwsrivier and Matjiesfontein.

● **BELOW**
An SAR electric locomotive of Class 7E on a freight train at Beaufort West. These 4,340 hp locomotives were built by UCW and the "50 Cycles Group" (a consortium of European electrical equipment manufacturers) in 1978–9. This class hauls the Trans Karoo between Beaufort West and De Aar.

which is the wrong way for Johannesburg, and it is this diversion to find a crossing-point in the coastal mountains that makes competition with road transport so difficult. After Herman, the line curves towards the mountains and follows a winding pass before descending into the Breede valley. This is an area of farmlands and orchards; a very English-looking landscape, except for the shapes of the distant hills.

After De Doorn, four hours out of Cape Town, a couple of very lengthy tunnels take the train to the start of the Karoo. One of the first things to notice is

Millsite, a few minutes before arrival at
Krugersdorp. Adjacent to the SAR
locomotive depot is the main store of
withdrawn and stored steam locomotives.

The morning run through the
Johannesburg suburbs showed a stark
contrast with Cape Town. Nearly every
house has high railings, usually with razor
wire, and several stations have guards
armed with shotguns.

The train proceeds from
Johannesburg, to end its journey at the
imposing Pretoria station. Opposite
stands the Victoria Hotel, now owned by
luxury train operator Rovos Rail. This is
a traditional colonial-style hotel, in
contrast to the buildings around it. Rovos
Rail also operates between Cape Town
and Johannesburg, but its service is even
more expensive than the Blue Train.

an ostrich farm complete with a rail-
connected loading dock. Another is the
sturdy shrubs covering the desert. These
have varied flower colours, and their
density thins out as the train gets farther
into the Karoo. The only "wildlife" visible
from the train are some very hardy sheep.
The other dominating features are the
interesting shapes of the hills, which tend
to be flat-topped and sheer-sided with a
surface of shattered rock and no
significant vegetation.

Two lasting memories of crossing the
desert are worth recording. After
travelling through a rare rain shower,
there was a magnificent rainbow against
the darkened sky and the strangely
shaped hills. Secondly, a stop at a passing
loop in the middle of the night. Not only
was the air very cold, but the author has
never seen a night sky so clear and starry,
and with no man-made light visible from
the horizons.

While the very necessary inclusion of
the heating van was unusual in October,
not everyone seemed aware of the
arrangement. The van was taken off the
train at Beaufort West. After this, the
train became exceedingly cold in the
desert night, not properly warming up
until the sun was well up.

The few trains that passed us on this
Sunday were all containerized freights. It

was clear that most sidings at local
stations were out of use, as road traffic
has taken over the local and short-haul
freight, leaving only the long-haul and
large-volume freight to the railways.
However, much of the route showed
signs of modernization, as curves and
gradients had been eased, and new
tunnels built to avoid difficult sections of
the route, indicating that the railway does
have a future.

The Johannesburg end of the journey
is dominated first by farm land, and then
by the mining industry, with many spoil
heaps visible until you are almost into the
city. One site worth looking out for is at

● BELOW
SAR suburban EMUs, including No. 13150, in
Cape Town carriage sidings, showing the old
and new liveries. The yellow livery is branded
"Metro". No. 13150, of Class 5M2A, was built
by UCW in the 1960s, one of a type that was
constructed by two builders between 1958
and 1985. The mountain in the background is
Devil's Peak, with Table Mountain behind
and to the right.

ISTANBUL TO BAGHDAD
THE TAURUS EXPRESS

Started in 1930, the Taurus Express
(Toros Ekspresi in Turkish) linked
London to Cairo and Berlin to Baghdad.
Only the English Channel and the
Bosporus needed ferries. With Germans
in charge of operations, it followed the
route of the Baghdad Railway, a Turkish
enterprise that had been funded with
money from the Deutsche Bank. Once
controlled by the French, the Baghdad
Railway was taken over in 1880 by the
British and in 1888 by Turkey.

From Istanbul the Ottoman Anatolian
Railway retained its French title, handing
over to the Baghdad Railway at Konya, an
Islamic centre famous for the Mevlevi

● **ABOVE RIGHT**
**The imposing walls of
the Citadel at Aleppo.**

Order of Whirling Dervishes. Like Rome
or Canterbury, the city has a holy
atmosphere.

In the south of Turkey, the railway ran
through the rich Cilician Plain that feeds
most of the otherwise rocky desert with
its patches of civilization. It was opened
from Adana to Mersin via Yenice in 1886,
but was taken over by the Deutsche Bank
in 1906.

The CFOA started originally as a
narrow-gauge line in 1873, along the
north coast of the Marmora Sea and
across the Ak Ova plain. After Arifiye,
36 m (118 ft) up, the line climbed
through the Baleban gorge, then across

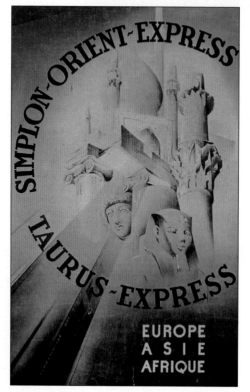

● **RIGHT**
**Poster of the Simplon-
Orient Express for the
inauguration of the
Taurus Express route
via Ankara in 1930.**

SIMPLON-ORIENT-EXPRESS

TAURUS-EXPRESS

EUROPE
ASIE
AFRIQUE

INFORMATION BOX	
THE TAURUS EXPRESS	
Termini	Istanbul and Baghdad
Countries	Turkey and Iraq
Distance	2,566 km (1,595 miles)
Date building commenced	
	1893

● **FAR LEFT**
The first Wagons-Lits sleepers in Asiatic Turkey, seen here on the Anatolia Express in 1927. These cars were put into service on the Taurus Express in 1930.

● **LEFT**
An SG type sleeping-car compartment, built in Birmingham, England, for the Taurus Express. A feature of the compartment are the holders for fob watches.

the smallish Akhisar plain where tobacco, corn and mulberries grew. It then ascends 294 m (965 ft) through a narrow gorge, whose walls are about 90 m (300 ft) above the railway, to Bilecik, a steam-lovers' paradise. Here worked western Turkey's last huge steam banking 2-10-2 tank-engines, which hauled trains 16 km (10 miles) up another 390 m (1,280 ft) at a 1:40 gradient to Eskesehir on the Central plateau.

From Eskesehir, where Turkey's main railway works is situated, a branch line turned east to Angora (famous for its wool), which was reached by rail in 1892. The city was renamed Ankara in 1921 by Attaturk, when he made it his nation's capital. The British ambassador, not wanting to relocate to Ankara, hired some sleeping cars and a diner from Wagons-Lits and lived in them during the week, returning to his palatial Istanbul Embassy at the weekends.

In 1927 Wagons-Lits created the Anatolia Express, which went as far as Ankara, the Russians not wanting German-influenced railways extending too far eastward. In 1895, influenced by Germany's *Drang nach Osten*, a railway to connect Konya and Baghdad was started simultaneously from both termini. By the time World War I broke out, the line had reached Samora (now in Iraq), 290 km (180 miles) south of Monsul and 121 km (75 miles) from Baghdad.

● **ABOVE**
Only two all-Wagons-Lits trains existed after the war: the Train Bleu in France and the Ankara Express in Turkey. The latter, hauled by a Henschel 2-8-2, is seen here arriving at Istanbul in 1957.

● **BELOW**
A view of the city of Aleppo, stretching out, taken from the walls of the Citadel.

● ABOVE
A visit to Egypt is not complete without a cruise. Here we see a cruise ship and a felluca on the Nile at Cairo.

From Konya the line crossed the 64 km (40 mile) long Konya plain, followed by the Karaman plain to Cakmak, where it climbed from 61 m (200 ft) to 366 m (1,201 ft) in 29 km (18 miles), mostly at 1:40. The summit was at Kardesgedigi, where the 1935-built line from Ankara was joined. Thereafter the Taurus Express ran by Ankara, and Konya was only a secondary route.

Now, as the train began its great drop through the Cilician Gates to Yenice, from 1,468 m (4,816 ft) to 34 m (112 ft) in 105 km (65 miles), the Taurus mountains were on all sides. Pozanti, the only town for miles around, is 32 km (20 miles) from the top. From Andna, the Germans decided that the flat line on the coastal plain through Antioch would be too close to the sea (fearing seizure by the British), so they took an inland route from the Cilician Plain. This climbed back up to 732 m (2,402 ft), where they built the 1,495 m (4,905 ft) long Amanus tunnel, which took the train to Fevsipasa. Here the Taurus Express turned south through Meydan Ekbez to Aleppo. From Aleppo the line ran on towards Tripoli, which was the main supply line to Palestine.

In 1927, Attaturk formed the Turkish State railways, which, in 1919, took over from the French from Pozanti to Favaipasa. The French formed two companies – the Cenup, or Turkish Southern, and the Syrian-Baghdad lines. Both were worked and run by the same management between Aleppo and Tel Kotchek, 76 km (47 miles) beyond the Syrian frontier at Nusaybin. Until 1939, travellers to Baghdad left the train at Tel Kotchek, now El Yaroubish, which had a Wagons-Lits rest house, and motored to Kirkuk, the terminus of the narrow-gauge line to Baghdad. The Baghdad Railway was extended to Sanora in 1940. After 1940 the Taurus Express became a through train with sleepers and a diner, for the 2,566 km (1,595 miles) from Istanbul to Baghdad. This service ended in 1966.

Before World War II the Taurus ran three days a week to Tel Kotchek and three days a week to Tripoli, with a connecting sleeper from Aleppo on the days when the train ran to Tel Kotchek. At Tripoli the passengers transferred to Model A Ford motor cars. To avoid the heat they drove to Beirut early in the morning and rested for about four hours before going on to Haifa, avoiding the mountain barrier by driving along the beach – there was no road.

At Haifa, Wagons-Lits ran a sleeping car to Kantara East in Egypt, crossing from Palestine at Rafa, after passing

● ABOVE LEFT
The impressive Sphinx at Giza, just outside Cairo.

● LEFT
The Istanbul to Ankara express near Kaysari.

Lydda Junction (for Jerusalem) and Gaza. The British-built Palestine Railways continued to run through to Kantara, where the pontoon bridge over the Suez Canal was removed for the benefit of larger liners. Passengers were ferried across to Kantara West, where Taurus passengers joined the last of the four daily trains of Egyptian State Railways, which had a Wagons-Lits Pullman running next to the dining car.

After Wagons-Lits withdrew in 1970, the Taurus Express continued to Baghdad, alternating with Haleb (Aleppo) or Gaziantep, where the dining car was removed.

The sleeping cars were accompanied by ordinary coaches, but today, because of the events of the Gulf War and continuing Kurdish troubles, the sleeping cars run only to Haleb or Gaziantep.

● RIGHT
One of the wonders of the ancient world, the pyramids at Giza are a romantic and evocative sign that the train is nearing Cairo, Egypt.

ISTANBUL TO KARS
THE DOGU EXPRESS

The Dogu Express, or Eastern Express in English, links Istanbul with Kars, the last town in Turkey before the Armenian frontier with Armenia.

Attaturk chose Ankara as his capital partly because it was the most easterly point of Turkey's railways when he came to power, and he immediately began extensions eastward. From Ankara, at an altitude of 876 m (2,874 ft), the line was continued for 300 km (186 miles) across the plateau before dropping 305 m (1,000 ft) at Pazali. There are a few tunnels to the Irmak River valley, a fertile area with poplar trees, maize, melons and sunflowers.

Running south-east, the line passes a munitions works before dividing at Bogazkopru, where the Taurus Express line to Adana turns south-west and the Dogu north-east. In 1935 the line reached Kayseri, some 378 km (235 miles) from Ankara.

The Dogu Express continues north-east to Sivas, 1,185 m (3,888 ft) above sea level, where the principal railway works for eastern Turkey are situated.

The line, completed in 1936, continues from a junction shortly before Sivas, to Samsun on the Black Sea coast, where Attaturk mounted his attack on the Ottoman Empire in 1918.

From Sivas, the Dogu Express continues at more or less the same level, turning south-east and climbing over the foothills to reach the Upper Euphrates valley at Cetinkaya. The next section through the narrow Atma Gorge, an area prone to earthquakes, was not completed until 1967–8.

The resultant railway is a masterpiece of Turkish engineering with 13 tunnels in 50 km (31 miles) on the line to the plain at Erzincan. Near Eric, a village with a few cultivated fields and meagre fruit trees in a small plain liable to flooding, where the inhabitants perch somehow in

● LEFT
This Turkish State Railways 2-8-0 was built by Humbolt of Paris in 1912.

● BELOW
Another Skyliner 2-10-0 hauls a freight train in the mountains of northern Turkey.

INFORMATION BOX	
THE DOGU EXPRESS	
Termini	Istanbul and Kars
Country	Turkey
Distance	1,944 km (1,208 miles)
Date of opening	1936

● BOTTOM
The Sultan Ahmet mosque in Istanbul.

primitive houses on the ledges on the gorge sides, there are 14 tunnels in 17 km (11 miles) of line.

In between the tunnels every kind of bridge is found crossing over the numerous clefts and tributaries that run into the Euphrates gorge. There are stone bridges, underslung-girder bridges, concrete and box-girder bridges – a *tour de force* as the precipices are so sheer as to be really frightening.

Finally the line drops down to Erzincan, 112 m (368 ft) above sea level. The Turks started building the line westward from Erzincan in 1937, but going east there are another 200 km (124 miles) across the plain to Erzerum, the capital of eastern Turkey, a line built in 1939. From here the train passes through more tunnels before emerging into the Araxes valley.

The Dogu follows the Araxes to Horasan before turning north, climbing to about 3,000 m (9,843 ft) and into the long Horasan tunnel.

The train then descends the fir-covered hills at a gradient of 1:40 to Sarikamis. The line from here to Kars was finished in Russian gauge in 1913 – just in time for World War I – and a narrow-gauge line was built from here to Erzerum in 1916. The Dogu ends its journey at Kars, usually arriving at the end of the day, in the gloomy dusk.

ISTANBUL TO TEHERAN
THE VAN GOLU EXPRESS

● BELOW
The eastbound Van Golu Express, east of
Malatya station.

The Van Golu (Lake Van) Express was
one of the last Turkish Railways routes to
link the west and east of Turkey. The lake,
97 km (60 miles) across and 1,719 m
(5,640 ft) above sea level, was far from
the railway until 1964. The Van Golu
takes the same route as the Dogu Express
between Istanbul and Cetinkaya, and
then follows the Euphrates to Malatya,
which was earlier reached from
Fevsipasa. In 1939 the line was extended
to Elazig with an altitude of 1,000 m
(3,280 ft). The difficult mountainous
route from Elazig was not started until
after World War II. It reached Genc in
1954 and Mus in 1955.

Ten years elapsed before the line was
continued to Tatvan on Lake Van's western
shore. The first part of the route follows
the River Ningrad, which turns south-east
and winds gently through the mountains
to join the Tigris. More mountains block
the way to Lake Van. The Van Golu
terminated here on Tatvan Pier, 1,884 km
(1,171 miles) from Istanbul. The Turkish
State railway (TCDD) operates a train
ferry that takes four hours to cross Lake

Van. From Van, a new railway was started
that ran another 160 km (100 miles) east
to Kapikoy, on the frontier, and over the
border to Razi in Iran.

The Iranians built this difficult line
through the rocky, harsh, undulating
desert, sending it a further 151 km (94
miles) to join, at Sharifkhansh, the line
from Djulfal (on the Armenian frontier)
to Tabriz and Teheran. One of the few
settlements on this stretch of the journey
is at Kotur, not very far from Lake
Urmia, which is almost as large as Lake

Van. This section was opened in 1971
when for some years an Iranian first-class
couchette car and TCDD first-class car
covered the 3,059 km (1,901 miles)
from Istanbul to Teheran in three days
and two nights. A diner was included on
the section Razi to Teheran.

Iran had no railways until World War
II, when British engineers built a line
from Nader Sharpur on the Persian Gulf,
via Teheran, to Bandar Shah on the Black
Sea. This was to be a means of moving
supplies to the Soviet Union an

INFORMATION BOX

THE VAN GOLU EXPRESS

Termini	Istanbul and Teheran
Countries	Turkey and Iran
Distance	3,059 km (1,901 miles)
Date of opening	1965

● LEFT
A former German war engine at the head of a
typical Turkish "mixed" train, which conveys
a combination of passenger-coaches and
freight-wagons.

alternative to the perilous North Sea/
Baltic Sea convoys. The line to Djulfa,
from where a Russian-gauge line ran to
Erevan and beyond, was completed later.

With the overthrow of the Shah in
1979 and the Kurdish uprising in Iran
and Turkey, the passenger service was

discontinued. There are just a few local
trains between Van and Kapikoy, but no
Iranian ones. The line is risky, if not
dangerous, and with growing road traffic,
freight seems to have ceased too. The
TCDD still operates the Van Golu from
Istanbul to Tatvan three days a week.

● **ABOVE**
One of Turkey's most common steam designs,
which was found at work all over the country,
with a former German Kriegslokomotive.
These were the war engines of which some
6,000 were built to a basic design to aid
Germany's war effort in World War II.

● **ABOVE**
The inauguration train of the Bandar Abbas
BAFGH Railway in Iran.

● **RIGHT**
A typical double-headed Turkish steam
train, with a German-built 4-8-0 piloting an
express passenger 2-8-2 Mikado built by
Henschel in 1937.

BASRA TO BAGHDAD

For all practical purposes, railways began in the land once called Mesopotamia during its Turkish Empire days, just as the Ottoman rule was coming to an end. However, it was the British Army, taking Mesopotamia early on in World War I, who laid most of the rail system, which operates to this day. Oil-rich Iraq embarked, together with Syria, on an expansion programme of its railways with faster trains linking Damascus with Baghdad on the historic line built by the Kaiser's Germany for the Ottoman Turks

● **LEFT**
Baghdad railway
station.

● **BELOW LEFT**
A Syrian Railways
2-8-0 built by Borsig
of Berlin in 1914
during that builder's
"British phase", in
operation south of
Damascus.

in the 1909–13 period. The line is of standard gauge and continues across the desert to Basra on the Gulf. Today rail services are sparse, with train speeds averaging scarcely 48 kph (30 mph) for "fast mails". The fastest trains run the 542 km (337 miles) between Basra and Baghdad in 11 hours.

INFORMATION BOX	
Termini	Basra and Baghdad
Country	Iraq
Length	542 km (337 miles)
Date of opening	1914

Passenger-trains on the Trans-Iranian line have their southern terminus at Khorramshah though the track goes through to Abadan, or Banda Khomeini, as it is now called. Technically an island, Abadan, seat of the great oil pipeline terminus and refinery, is a few miles further on. When it was demolished by the Turks at the beginning of the 19th century, on the grounds that Khorramshah's commercialism was detrimental to nearby Basra, the British and Russian governments stepped in to keep the peace by allocating territory to both sides. However, they reckoned without the Kuran River, a tributary of the Shatt-al-Arab, which promptly upped and changed its course, inserting a damp spanner into the works. As recent history has shown with a vengeance, nobody was

happy with the results. Basra, once in Iran, is now of course an Iraqi city, but the hate continues, and this was going great guns when I arrived in Khorramshah and wanted to reach Basra. I got there in the end by walking for miles across a no man's land of a desert, delayed lengthily and not very pleasantly by innumerable checkpoints and gun-toting soldiers.

A bevy of friendly Iraqis took charge of me in Basra, a city I found to be a hotchpotch of other people's developments: Carmathian, Mongol, Turk and European, with a thin veneer of Muslim. At the railway station I ran the station-master to ground, was invited to tea and finally – he learning of my inability to change my Barclays-issued traveller's cheque into local currency (Barclays being pronounced a "Lackey of Israel") – was given a first-class ticket valid for the air-conditioned deluxe overnight express to Baghdad.

From Basra to the Iraqi capital it is 611 km (380 miles), and the distance was covered in nine hours, which is a good rate of knots for a Middle Eastern train. For some way the route follows the Euphrates River and passes within two miles of Ur, of the Chaldees fame. We also flashed by a short platform

designated "Babylon Halt" which apparently even the little local trains pass with a derisive whistle.

My berth was almost up to European standards, and after weeks of rough living

and travelling on lesser trains and even lesser buses and lorries, it seemed like paradise. In the morning the train drew into West station, the Grand Central of the Iraqi capital.

● **ABOVE**
A Syrian-built 2-6-0 tank dating back to the 1890s heads away from Damascus with a Sunday excursion train.

● **LEFT**
After the day's intense sun the evening's mellow light brings relief to the border country between Syria and Lebanon as a Swiss-built 2-6-0 tank heads towards Damascus with an evening passenger-train.

DAMASCUS TO MEDINA

Every Muslim male is required to visit Muhammad's birthplace in Mecca at least once in his lifetime if he can. During the 19th century, the journey was hazardous in the extreme. The Arabs were reluctantly under Ottoman rule, and bands of vulnerable Turkish pilgrims were murdered as they journeyed through the desert. Eventually the Sultan of Turkey authorized the building of a railway between Damascus and Mecca to carry pilgrims in safety. Construction began in 1901, and seven laborious years later Medina, where Muhammad is buried, was reached 1,302 km (809 miles) to the south. This line, the Hedjaz, takes its name from the area alongside the Red Sea in Arabia where the holy city lies.

Trouble dogged every mile; marauding Arabs attacked the workers; the heat was intolerable, and violent sandstorms frequently caused work to be stopped. The Arabs, frantic that their holy city would be defiled, refused to allow the

railway past Medina. In wild fervour they invaded the railway construction camp and massacred the work-force. The line was destined to go no further, and pilgrims had to continue on foot over the remaining 370 km (230 miles) to Mecca.

The railway only carried pilgrims for seven seasons until the outbreak of World War I. The Turks allied with Germany, and Arab nationalists, supported by the British under Colonel Lawrence, partly succeeded in driving the Turks from the Hedjaz. To prevent enemy

reinforcements from getting through, Lawrence blew up large sections of the line. Indeed, so great was the damage that trains were forced to terminate at Ma'an in Southern Jordan. Today, almost 70 years later, not only does the southern section remain abandoned despite various attempts to reopen it, but many of the abandoned locomotives still lie half-buried in the sand.

The line now passes through three countries, and all would benefit by its reinstallation. In 1963 a consortium of

● **ABOVE**
A 2-8-2 crossing the desert, about 48 km (30 miles) from Amman. Although passenger traffic was ended by the Syrians in 1983, the line reopened for passenger traffic in 1987.

● **LEFT**
Nippon Pacific No. 82 storming up the bank out of Amman.

● **RIGHT**
A 2-8-2 pauses at
Mafraq near the
Syrian border. There
is a twice-weekly
service between the
two countries, both
for freight and
passengers.

British engineers began work. The task
was daunting. The section from Ma'an to
Medina is 845 km (525 miles) long and,
apart from being plagued by the elements
(and damage incurred by Lawrence),
48 km (30 miles) of embankment had
been washed away by the violent rains
that sweep over the Arabian desert every
five years. Half the route needed attention
with much of the track unserviceable.

Much work had been done by 1967,
when the Arab-Israeli War broke out and
Saudi officials ordered work to stop.
Work on the line was never resumed, and
the railway was again abandoned with
only the 467 km (290 mile) 3 ft 5¼ in
gauge line section from Damascus to
Ma'an remaining in operation.

● **LEFT**
A 2-8-2 crosses a
viaduct at a town
near Amman.

● **BELOW**
Nippon Pacific No.
82 on the viaduct on
the outskirts of
Amman.

INFORMATION BOX	
Termini	Damascus and Medina
Country	Jordan to Saudi Arabia
Distance	1,302 km (809 miles)
Date of opening	1908

MOSCOW TO VLADIVOSTOK
THE TRANS-SIBERIAN EXPRESS

It was in 1858 that proposals were first made for a Trans-Siberian Railway that would connect Moscow and European Russia to the Pacific. Owing to the Crimean War, however, it was not until 1875 that an official plan was put forward. During the ensuing years other plans were proposed until, in 1891, the Russian Government finally gave its official approval, and Crown Prince Nicholas cut the first sod in Vladivostok. The railway, one of the world's greatest engineering achievements, was seen by the Russian Government as a means of consolidating the Russian hold on Siberia and the Pacific provinces by both developing the Eastern economy and exerting a political influence on China.

● **LEFT**
Yaroslav station, Konsomol Square, Moscow. Built by the architect Franz Shekhiel in 1906, this is the western terminus of the Trans-Siberian Railway.

● **BELOW**
The Kremlin and the River Moskva in Moscow.

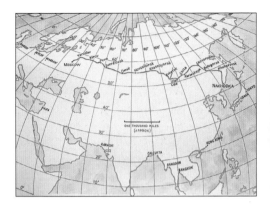

● **FAR LEFT**
Map showing the
route of the Trans-
Siberian Railway.

● **LEFT**
People queuing at a
food and drink
kiosk at Gorky Park,
Moscow.

● **BELOW LEFT**
The Rossia waits at
Khabarovsk.

Although work began in 1891, through rail communication was only established in 1903. This did, however, include the train ferry over Lake Baikal – the deepest lake in the world. In the winter, when the ice became too thick for ice breaking, rails were laid on the ice itself and the train was run over the lake. The line round the southern shore of the lake was not blasted out of the solid rock until 1905. Such was the terrain of this 68 km (42 mile) section that no fewer than 38 tunnels had to be bored. In places, the shore of the lake is almost vertical and up to 1,200 m (4,000 ft) high. The toughest gradient is just east of Ulan Ude, where a sharp incline of 1:57.5 is encountered.

At first, part of the route was laid across Manchuria (and known as the Chinese Eastern Railway) direct from Chita via Harbin to Vladivostok. This section over Chinese soil was necessary because the comparatively flat land of Manchuria made the line both cheaper and shorter. However, after the Russo-Japanese War, which strained the line to capacity by carrying large numbers of troops and supplies from European Russia to the Far East, a connection was built from Chita via the Amar valley and Khabarovsk. Although considerably longer than the direct route across Manchuria, it did ensure that the whole route was over Russian territory.

Although the line, which begins at Moscow, goes through Omsk, Irkutsk (on the shores of Lake Baikal) and Khabarovsk before terminating at Vladivostok, was originally built as single track, by 1913 most of it had been

● **RIGHT**
The Trans-Siberian
Express, one of the
world's greatest
engineering
achievements, and a
railway legend.

converted to double track. It was not
until the 1950s, however, that the whole
route was double-tracked. By the mid-
1970s, three-quarters of the line (from
the European end) had been electrified.

One of the most interesting features
of the line is the number of bridges. On
the western portion of the line alone
there are eight bridges of over 305 m
(1,000 ft) in length, including those over

the Irtish, the Ob and the Yenisei, all of
which are over 610 m (2,000 ft), while at
Khabarovsk, on the North Manchurian
frontier, there is another exceptionally
long bridge across the River Amur.

Between the two world wars, the
through passenger service was provided
by the Trans-Siberian Express, which had
a special sleeping car and dining facilities.
There was also the Blue Express, which

included ordinary "hard" and "soft"
accommodation as well as a sleeping car.
These trains, which were relatively light,
with only eight or nine carriages, took
just under ten days to complete the
9,611 km (5,973 mile) journey from
Moscow to Vladivostok, at an average
speed of only 40 kph (25 mph).

In 1913, an English traveller called
Pearson wrote a detailed account of the

journey, which began at Moscow's Yaroslav station. His train, headed by a highly polished Pacific locomotive, was composed of long green-and-gold carriages. The corridors were carpeted, and the dining car was decorated with an impressive ivory-white ceiling, large plate-glass windows and panelling. In those days the train also included a travelling bathroom, a chemist's shop and reading and games rooms.

Nine days on a train might not be everybody's ideal trip. Yet there are rail enthusiasts who say they dream of riding the Trans-Siberian Express. The author's experience of it when the country was still the Soviet Union, was not entirely the stuff of dreams. Although the four-bunk soft-class (Westerners were forbidden to travel hard-class) compartments were spacious and clean, there was a radio loudspeaker, which exuded the sort of thing expected from Stalinist Russia. The quality of everything, from coat-hangers to reading matter, was extremely poor. Moreover, the electric locomotive was Czech, and

● **ABOVE**
Travellers at the railway station, Moscow.

● **LEFT**
The "Rossia" Trans-Siberian Express (left) in company with the Peking Express. Both trains had been halted by an accident on the line, just west of Irkutsk.

● **BELOW LEFT**
A traditional Russian wooden house.

the silvery coaches were East German. Indeed, it would not be too far wrong to say that it was only the tea, served in the carriages from an old-fashioned samovar, that was genuinely Russian.

INFORMATION BOX THE TRANS-SIBERIAN EXPRESS	
Termini	Moscow and Vladivostock
Country	Russia
Distance	9,611 km (5,972 miles)
Date of opening	1903

BRUSSELS TO HONG KONG

There is no such animal as a Trans-Siberian Express listed in the Russian Railway timetables or, for that matter, in any issue of the *Thomas Cook Overseas Timetable*. What you will see, however, is a Train No. Two, which travels between Moscow's Yaroslav station and Vladivostok's Main station. There are also other numbered trains with names like Zabaikal, Rossia and Tomich, which cover major sections of the 9,297 km (5,777 mile) line.

All these could be termed "Trans-Siberian Expresses", though to cover the route of the so-called Red Arrow Express – a collection of different trains running between Brussels and Hong Kong – the Zabaikal, linking Moscow to Irkutsk, was used on this section of the journey.

● LEFT
The Irkutsk to Moscow coach nameplate on the Zabaikal Express.

● BELOW
The train speeds through the Polish countryside.

To attain Moscow from Brussels, the Ost West Express is the most convenient vehicle. This train leaves the Midi Station at 15.55 and arrives at Moscow Smolenskaya at 22.05 two nights later. It is now considerably faster and more

comfortable than it used to be during the Communist era, when gruelling checks by border guards in the then German Democratic Republic, Poland and the then Soviet Union held up progress for hours – in addition to the still continuing

● **RIGHT**
Berlin's Frauen
Kirche has been left
as it was after being
bombed in the
Second World War
as a reminder of the
horrors of war.

INFORMATION BOX

Termini	Brussels and Kowloon
Countries	Belgium to Hong Kong
Distance	21,384 km (13,290 miles)
Date link completed	1949

Siberia is autumn, when the seemingly endless landscape of birch trees turns to the colour of burnished gold. Crossing great rivers, such as the Ob and the Yenisei, on immense bridges makes for the most emotive sights.

Four days out, by which time the fare in the restaurant car has been reduced to mainly bortsch, macaroni and Russian champagne, the express reaches Irkutsk, capital of Siberia, and a not unattractive city with some timber houses of the Chekhov era still surviving. Here the

chore of bogey-changing that is effected at Brest to adapt the train to the wider Russian gauge.

On the Trans-Siberian line, the long-distance expresses are reasonably comfortable, with soft- and hard-class berths that can be used as beds. Tea is always on tap from coach samovars and is brought to compartments by the attendants. The best time to traverse

● **LEFT**
A Russian train
approaches a
country station.

● RIGHT
An interior coach view of the Ulan Bator to
Peking express.

● BOTTOM
A view from the train window of the
countryside of Outer Mongolia.

through coaches bound for Ulan Bator,
the Mongolian capital, or – once weekly
– right through to Beijing, are
transferred to what was termed the
Irkutsk-Ulan Bator Express. Maybe
things have changed for the better, but
the train used to be as dirty as the
blankets issued for sleeping. From Ulan
Ude, on the Russian-Mongolian border,
the train was headed by a rust-pink –
more rust than pink – diesel unit of
Mongolian Railways to deflect
southwards from the shores of Lake
Baikal, snaking into the low hills and
across rolling plains, the habitat of wild
camels, wild horses and the Gobi bear.
Occasional wind-swept villages of
hexagonal *yurts* draw the eye. The line
here is non-electric.

Ulan Bator's most attractive building
is its small and well-kept station. The city
itself is a dull one, centred on the
standardized Soviet-style parade-ground
square bordered by grim government
buildings but enlivened in recent years by
a pink stock-exchange. Though there is
only one through train a week to Beijing,
there are two a week from Ulan Bator to
the Chinese capital.

The author's onward journey towards
China was made in Chinese rolling stock.
This was a step up in the comfort stakes,
with shaded table lamps, jasmine-
flavoured tea in flasks, dainty seat
coverlets and chintzy curtains.

At Erlan, 36 hours later, the train
bogeys have to be changed back to fit
China's standard gauge, an operation that
can be watched by passengers so inclined.
Then, powered by a new and electric
locomotive, the train enters the Chinese
province of Inner Mongolia.

Railway construction in China has
been considerable in recent years. By the
time of the so-called liberation in 1949,
only 11,000 km (6,835 miles) of rail
track were still open to traffic, the
remainder having been destroyed by
many years of internal conflict. The total
rail system now exceeds 55,000 km

● LEFT
A train speeds through the old East Germany.

● BOTTOM
The Ulan Bator Express passing through the
wooded hill country of Outer Mongolia.

Beijing, is not the largest city in the
country – that accolade goes to Shanghai
– but the trappings of capitalship lie
firmly upon the city's shoulders. The
main station is a surprisingly modest
establishment, constantly overcrowded.
From Beijing southwards the train is
electric powered, and for another 36
hours one can enjoy eminently
comfortable living quarters and often
delicious scenery to match. The 2,400
km (1,500 mile) route lies through
sprawling cities and over prodigious
rivers, such as the Yangtse, where trains
clatter endlessly across great bridges.

Before Canton, round-topped peaks
give the lie to the idea that Chinese
landscape paintings are figments of
Chinese imagination, and provide an
intensely beautiful finale to the journey.
Here the line cuts through the gorges of
the Pei Kiang and a water-logged
territory of rice paddies peopled by half-
submerged peasants and water buffalo.

The ride from Canton to Hong Kong
is the smoothest of all. And there is
nothing like a three-week rail journey to
give the luxurious comforts of this unique
Anglo-Chinese city an added lustre.

(34,000 miles) and while, before 1949,
seven provinces had no railways at all,
now only Tibet is without rail
communication – though the line to
Lhasa has long been under construction.

Datong is a familiar name on account
of its huge factory that produced those
giant Chinese steam locomotives, but,
alas, it is no longer doing so. Visitors
were once lucky enough to be shown
around the works when these monsters
were in full production and, if they were
very lucky, even allowed to drive a newly
produced locomotive undergoing its
operational testing. China's capital,

QUETTA TO ZAHEIDAN
ACROSS THE BALUCHISTAN DESERT

● **BELOW LEFT**
The village of Skardu.

● **BOTTOM**
One of Pakistan's diesel-electrics,
which haul international services.

The lonely line that connects Quetta to the southern Iranian town of Zaheidan is known by some as the Nushki Extension Railway though it runs hundreds of kilometres past Nushki, across the border and 80 km (50 miles) into Iran. It leaves Quetta's main line at Spezand and continues parallel to the mountain ranges forming the frontier with Afghanistan. The line was laid during World War I, when the British and Russians "policed" the territory between the Caspian Sea and the Persian Gulf.

Between Dalbandin and Nok Kundi, a distance of 167 km (104 miles), the region is wholly without habitation, virtually devoid of vegetation and a hell upon earth. The line crosses long stretches of desert covered with sharp black stones broken only by patches of

coarse sand. For eight months of the year the heat is intense, and the "120-day wind" whips this sand into tight little whirlwinds that lacerate the skin. The whole desert is covered with sulphur dust, and water, when it is obtainable,

tastes like a concentrated mixture of common and Epsom salts. When there is any rain at all, the whole year's fall may occur within an hour. The river beds, bone dry for 90 days out of 100, then hurl the water, laced with quantities of stone, at the exposed railway. To overcome this disconcerting event, the engineers built Irish bridges, or "dips", and the drivers of the steam-hauled trains crossing them were expected to use their discretion as to whether they could pass through without water getting into their fireboxes and putting the fire out.

Then there are the *do-reg*, or marching sand-hills. These are crescent-shaped sand-hills formed by the wind and constantly on the move. Again the line is the target and, from time to time, diversionary track has to be laid to take

train halts for what seems to the weary passengers an interminable period while the crew is changed.

At Mirjaveh, on the Iranian border, there is a long passport check and general evacuation to the hut for the issue of Iranian railway tickets for the last 80 km (50 miles) to Zaheidan, which is reached – if there are no delays such as those mentioned above – some 30 hours after departure from Quetta.

the railway round the back of the *do-reg* to avoid several thousand tonnes of sand. The sand-hills move in parallel lines for many miles across the *dasht*. Their speed is 500–600 m (1,600–1,900 ft) per year, so the duplicated tracks are left in position and trains use whichever one happens to be clear of sand.

Sometimes the marching sand-hills cover the track, and then all the male passengers from the stranded train spend hours re-laying the track. Spare lengths of rail, shoes and sleepers lie alongside in readiness for just an emergency. These,

then, are just some of the vicissitudes of a trans-Baluchistan journey.

Hours behind schedule, the journey will be resumed across the terrible landscape. At a remote habitation, the

INFORMATIONBOX

Termini	Quetta and Zaheidan
Countries	Pakistan and Iran
Distance	650 km (404 miles)
Date of opening	1916

● **LEFT**
Young boys working in the fields at Tongul.

LINDI KOTAL TO PESHAWAR DOWN THE KHYBER

It is probably only the British who become charged with emotion at the mere mention of the Khyber Pass. Its fame is based on history rather than scenery, and the comparatively recent and universally known story of the Khyber is exclusively British – though the armies of Alexander the Great and the Mogul emperors Babur and Humayan also used its defiles.

The British-built line climbs to about 1,070 m (3,500 ft) on wide-gauge track without rack-and-pinion assistance, and even with two engines it is heavy going. From Lindi Kotal there was a once-weekly train to Peshawar run at no charge, simply as a gesture by Pakistan Railways to prove to the fiercely independent tribesmen that the line, in spite of them, was open and the Pakistan Government was the boss.

The old coaches were a morass of humanity intent upon going along for the free ride. With not an inch of space available, the author found a seat astride the right-hand front buffer of a steam locomotive made by the British Vulcan

● **LEFT**
Passengers stretch their legs in the heat of the afternoon.

● **BELOW LEFT**
Locomotive No. 2495 steams through a cutting in the red hills of western Pakistan.

● **BELOW RIGHT**
Tribal musicians meet travellers at the Khyber Pass.

INFORMATION BOX

Termini	Lindi Kotal and Peshawar
Country	Pakistan
Distance	64 km (40 miles)
Date of opening	1902

foundry in 1923. Two Pakistani passengers had already seated themselves on the other buffer, and a necklace of humanity encircled the boiler.

The 64 km (40 mile) ride that followed was a spectacular and unforgettable journey. The descent of the Khyber is the steepest non-rack stretch of track in the world. It is made in the form of a letter Z, the train changing

● **LEFT**
The train takes a
curve in this typical
western Pakistan
landscape.

● **BELOW LEFT**
The Pakistan/
Afghan border at
the Khyber Pass.

● **BELOW
RIGHT**
An armed guard
stands by the
regimental coats
of arms in the
Khyber Pass.

direction at each apex and, on the
steepest sections, safety track is installed
to divert runaway trains into the hills.
Until one became accustomed to the
motion, one felt extremely insecure
astride the metal seat. To maintain
balance, it was necessary to grip the
greasy ironwork with one's knees with
hands clamped to the buffer flanges like
limpet mines. The great hissing,
threatening boiler licked the passengers
with jets of steam, while one's
imagination worked overtime painting
mind pictures of what the relentless
wheels would do to anyone who had the
misfortune to fall off.

The train travelled at no great pace
through a series of short tunnels and
beneath empty forts, which gave a walnut
topping to every brown hill. The
Khyber's narrowest defile was
commanded by the oldest of these – Ali
Masjid – built high on a cliff, and near to
it was a showcase displaying regimental
badges, British, Pathan and Indian.

All around was an alien landscape,
burnt brown and exuding that air of
latent hostility so different from the
green meadows of England. Here was
magnificence for sure, but its
constituents were sharply formed crags
varying in shades of colour from deep

red to sandy yellow, punctuated by jagged
pinnacles of rock.

The plain below the pass was suddenly
upon the train, the brown and barren
hills abruptly deflated. Fortified villages,
their high mud walls blank apart from
firing slits, remained in evidence, their
unseen occupants presumably still ready
to repulse attack from wherever it might
come. At one point, where the line
doubled back on itself, one could see the
Khyber mountain looking impregnable to
man and train; not a gap or defile showed
anywhere. The train limped into
Peshawar, the once-in-a-lifetime
vice-regal ride at an end.

KALYAN TO HOWRAH
ACROSS INDIA BY TROOP TRAIN

One of the great experiences in life is to travel across a mighty land mass such as the Indian subcontinent, as it was known in 1945. This account is based on notes made at the time, but the expanded version was lost to the military censor because of the railway details it contained. Some things have changed dramatically since then, but the long history and traditions of the many peoples of that great land mass will ensure that much also remains the same.

It was not a journey made voluntarily, but as a soldier under orders, heading for the advance HQ of the Allied Land Forces in South-east Asia – wherever that might be. In the meantime, the railway and its surroundings were there to be enjoyed or endured as the case may be.

The author had landed at Bombay some weeks before and had travelled several times between there and Kalyan, using trains that were generally hauled by massive 2-C0-1 electric locomotives, built in 1925 by Metropolitan Vickers of the UK for the Great Indian Peninsular Railway standard (5 ft 6 in) gauge and operating on a line voltage of 1,500 d.c.

● **LEFT**
One of the large electric locomotives of the Great Indian Peninsular Railway easing a train from Kalyan into Victoria terminus, Bombay, in March 1945.

INFORMATION BOX

Termini	Kalyan and Howrah
Country	India
Distance	2,129 km (1,323 miles)
Date of travel	1945

● **BELOW LEFT**
A train load of cotton in a timeless scene.

● **BELOW RIGHT**
A train crosses a bridge while a young woman sits by the river with her water pot.

It was probably one such that was hauling the troop train, consisting of 14 coaches and two vans, a load of some 567 tonnes (560 tons) tare, which left Kalyan at 1100 hours on 8 March 1945.

The line was fairly level and straight as it passed through rather arid country, which allowed for speeds up to 113 kph (70 mph). Although I was travelling in third class, it was not overcrowded and the compartment was large. Windows that came right down and shutters to keep out the glare of the sun, coupled with the speed of the train, made things

● **BELOW**
A train crosses a river using one of the many
bridges on the Indian rail network.

● **BELOW**
A contemporary photograph of a scene that is
virtually unchanged since 1946.

● **BOTTOM**
A train steams through the Indian countryside.

reasonably comfortable, although the
well-shaped wooden seats encouraged
movement from time to time. There was
no through corridor connection, which
meant that lengthy stops were required
so that one could collect the meals
provided and wash personal utensils and
mess tins in the vats provided.

At the approach to the Western Ghats,
just beyond Khardi, hard climbing began,
with the line twisting and turning and
passing through several tunnels. It got
colder, and wonderful views opened up
of the plain below, followed by
spectacular engineering as the line clung
to steep valley sides.

At Igatpuri, electricity gave way to
steam haulage, and it is possible that
traction was put in the hands of a Class
XA1 4-6-2 built by Vulcan Foundry in
the UK in 1929. From here the line
undulated over a rather barren plain
dotted with villages until arrival at
Deolalih, a feared posting for army
troops, which gave its name to doolally, a
nickname for a form of madness.

Soon after departure from Deolalih,
the train began the long drag of some
80 km (50 miles) at gradients of 1:200 to
1:120 to the 914 m (2,999 ft) summit of
the line. At that time of the year, in the

dry season, the scene was forbiddingly
barren but enlivened by hawks circling
above looking for prey.

During the night, the train stopped
at Sonepur, at a station that proclaimed
that it had the longest platform in India,
and then at the major city of Nagpur,
where locomotives were changed, the
system from here on being the Bengal
Nagpur Railway.

By morning, the train was descending,
twisting and turning past sheer rock

faces. Toward the end of the day, the
countryside became more green until
jungle pressed upon the line. By night, it
can be very cold, but the temperature
soon rises with the sun and the hot,
steamy conditions were such as to
encourage us to sit with our feet over the
footsteps of the carriage, which provided
some interesting experiences when the
train crossed high bridges over rivers or
dried water-courses with an
unobstructed view of the ground below.

As night fell, flat country was again
encountered. In the night, the sight of
the enormous Tatanagar steel works left a
lasting impression. By morning, the train
was on double track some 80 km (50
miles) from Calcutta in low-lying, dank
and misty marshland, cold in the early
light. Lines proliferated, and we passed
local trains crammed with people with
others on the outsides and on the roofs
of carriages.

Howrah station, 2,129 km (1,323
miles) and 44 hours from Kalyan, was a
sea of people, with porters vying to carry
passengers' luggage to waiting rickshaws
and taxis. As the crossing of India came
to a close, one was left with wonderful
memories of a truly unique rail journey
set in unbelievable scenery.

DELHI TO COCHIN

Amid the chaos that characterizes all Indian railway stations, New Delhi's contains an air-conditioned haven that is the Foreigners' Booking Office, where comparative order is preserved. From here you can set out, armed perhaps with that open-sesame of Indian rail travel, the Ind-Rail Pass, on a journey south on the second longest rail route in the country.

The vehicle for much of the way is the Kerala Express. The train is not one of the "super expresses" that ply between Delhi and Bombay, but, while never generating great speed, its progress is reasonable enough. At intervals small flasks of tea and hot meals – ordered prior to delivery (vegetarian or "European") at ridiculously low cost – are served, and, come nightfall, the compartment seats are turned into bunks.

The route is not initially a spectacular one, the urban centres being Agra, Gwalior, Jhansi, Bhopol, Nagpur, Gudin, Coimatore and Cochin. The last of these is in the province of Kerala, its distinctive woods, lakes and coconut plantations making a sudden and picturesque change from the parched flatlands of central India. At Trivandrum, the Keralan capital,

● **ABOVE**
The station in New Delhi, India's capital city since 1931.

● **LEFT**
Panan bridge under construction.

● **BELOW LEFT**
A group of railway workers zip along the tracks near Cochin station, southern India

a bed may be acquired for the night in a dormitory of that British-inspired and now firmly Indian concept called a railway retiring room. The cost again is infinitesimal and, should one be averse to

the continual noises of snoring and hawking, private rooms are also available. Pillows, sheets and pillowcases are issued, and a lockable bedside cupboard is provided. A very welcome hot shower is also supplied.

From Cochin, a beautiful city of Portuguese ancestry overflowing on to a trio of islands, you can, if you choose, forgo the famed beaches of nearby

INFORMATION BOX	
Termini	Delhi and Cochin
Country	India
Distance	2,100 km (1,305 miles)
Commencement of building	
	1853

The bustling station at Rameswaram station, the ferry port for Sri Lanka.

Kovalam, take the short train ride to Cape Comerin, the extreme southern tip of India, where three oceans meet.

Another ride can be taken southward to Rameswaram on the Madras-Rameswaram Express, which can be joined at Coimbatore. Rameswaram, with its sacred shrine, is a ferry port for Sri Lanka, just across the Palk Strait. The town is approached by the gigantic, recently built Panan bridge, over which the train slowly trundles. The same train, a day later, will take the traveller back as far as Madurai, to view its massive temple, prior to joining a night train to the garden city of Bangalore.

From Bangalore, one travels on to Mysore and northwards to, eventually, Coa and Bombay on a variety of trains with varying characteristics and degrees of comfort. Prior to Bombay it is worth pausing at Pune – Poona of British Army fame – which is the site of another narrow-gauge mountain line, the Matheran Hill Railway.

The return to Delhi is on the crack Rajdhani Express, which, by the standards of the Indian railway system, is of sublime comfort and high speed. On it, attendants make the beds, and afternoon tea, dinner, early morning tea and breakfast are all included in the price of the ticket. However, after travelling for weeks on lesser trains, you might find this rather a dull one, lacking the charm of the true India.

DELHI TO JODHPUR
THE PALACE ON WHEELS

● **BELOW AND BENEATH**
The Fort of Jodhpur, one of the locomotives
that hauls the Palace on Wheels.

Though the Raj is no more, the romance of the train lives on in India – or at least it does for many foreign visitors, Britons predominating. To cater for these nostalgic longings, Indian Railways in conjunction with the Rajasthan Tourist Board produced a train to resurrect a glamorous past. They called it the Palace on Wheels. Alas, this palace of a train is no more, but another in the same vein has taken its place. The "Palace" was assembled from appropriate coaches unearthed from sources throughout the subcontinent, many rusting away in obscure sidings and some once owned by long-deposed maharajas. Restored to their former glory, they became the pride and joy of Indian Railways.

What set the final seal of authenticity were the two superb steam locomotives chosen to head them. To complement the image of the golden coaches, these giant monsters with their shining brass-work, glistening pistons and proud coat of arms at the front of the boiler were christened Desert Queen and Fort of Jodhpur. Crews were hand-picked from the cream

of drivers for this, the most prestigious train in all India.

On the inaugural journey, the coach, bearing the insignia of the Jaipur State Railway, was one which had once carried the Maharaja of Bikaner, while a more recent incumbent had been Mrs Gandhi, the late Indian Prime Minister. It was the most opulent and historic saloon of all, with pink upholstery, silver-embroidered curtains, teak wall panels and traditional carpeting. The suites consisted of a bedroom, amply proportioned, with a wide bed, a wardrobe and a bedside table, and a comfortable lounge, generously equipped with sofas and

INFORMATION BOX	
THE PALACE ON WHEELS	
Termini	Delhi and Jodhpur
Country	India
Distance	250 km (155 miles)
Date of first run	1982

● RIGHT
The Palace on
Wheels arriving at
Jaisalmer.

● BELOW
A driver's-eye view of the track ahead of the
Palace on Wheels.

armchairs. Two servants attired in turbans and smart Rajastani costumes were constantly at the guests' beck and call. Included in the train's make-up were a restaurant car serving gourmet dinners and fine wines, a lounge, observation car and library.

Rajasthan is a state made for such a train. Much of it is desert or semi-desert, but the towns of Jaipur, Udaipur, Jaisalmer, Jodhpur and Bharatpur are fairyland cities: pink-stoned, rock-pinnacled lakeside oases, dominated by fortresses and palaces, each flaunting an epic history engraved upon dramatically beautiful buildings.

Having rumbled through the night, the Palace would arrive at its destination where, after breakfast in bed, guests were invited to emerge on to the platform strewn with flowers, to be welcomed by a pipe band, elephants in regalia and troupes of dancing girls. Suitably garlanded, they would be whisked away for the tour of the day, broken by a superb lunch in a palace.

A none-too smooth metre-gauge track, emphatically not continuously welded, made sleep a little elusive for those not lulled by train travel, but this is to quibble. From the one-time centre of the Raj – Delhi – a traveller could begin a journey such as he or she was unlikely ever to experience again.

● OPPOSITE
BOTTOM
The Palace on
Wheels waiting at
Rajasthan station.

● RIGHT
The Desert Queen,
one of the
locomotives that
hauls the Palace on
Wheels.

SILIGURI TO DARJEELING

The railway that takes passengers from the heat of the Bengal plains to the blissful mountain balm of Darjeeling involves a climb of no less than 2,164 m (7,100 ft) in a distance of 88 km (54½ miles). Before the railway was built in 1879, exiles from the heat had to take the cart-road, which had been built by the Government at an astronomical cost.

The track is 2 ft gauge and, remarkably, while train loads have to be restricted, is worked wholly by adhesion. The steel rails, which weigh 41 lb per yard, are laid on wooden sleepers. Because the track has to be lifted so much in such a short distance, heavy gradients and sharp curves are unavoidable. On the journey there are banks ranging from 1:19 to 1:31 and curves of 15 m (50 ft) radius.

For the first 11 km (7 miles) to Sookna the going is easy, as the ascent is only 1:281. It is on this stretch that the

INFORMATION BOX

Termini	Siliguri and Darjeeling
Country	India
Length	88 km (55 miles)
Date construction commenced	
	1879

213 m (699 ft) long Mahanuddy bridge, comprising seven 30 m (100 ft) spans, is crossed. It is when the train leaves Sookna that the climb begins in earnest, for in the next 7.6 km (4¾ miles) the track ascends 265 m (869 ft). At the end of this section, the ascent was so sudden that originally the track had to describe a sharp loop through a deep cutting. However, in 1883 part of the

● **ABOVE** The train stops for a break and passengers take the opportunity to stretch their legs.

LEFT The little engine is inspected as it sits at the station.

OPPOSITE MIDDLE LEFT AND OPPOSITE MIDDLE RIGHT Various angles of the engine, which seems almost toy-like, that carries passengers from Siliguri to Darjeeling.

● **OPPOSITE BOTTOM** At an altitude of 2,258 m (7,408 ft), Ghoom is the second highest station in the world.

● **RIGHT**
The sign welcoming visitors to the town
of Darjeeling.

mountainside slipped into the cutting,
completely filling it, and the track had to
be realigned.

Between Rungtong, at 428 m
(1,404 ft), and Tindharia, at 860 m
(2,822 ft), a distance of just over 12 km
(7½ miles), the gradient stiffens to 1:29.
Just past Rungtong there is a sudden rise
of 42 m (138 ft), which is overcome by
what is practically a double loop that
involves sharp curvatures. Then, a little
further on, just before Tindharia, the
ingenuity of the builders is illustrated by
a "reverse". The line, climbing at a 1:28
gradient, enters a curve of 244 m
(800 ft) radius, where it reaches a dead
end at 754 m (2,474 ft). The train backs
up a second curve at 1:33, to another
dead end at 762 m (2,500 ft). After a
further climb at 1:28, the line reaches an
altitude of 773 m (2,536 ft).

The next section of the line, the
6.4 km (4 miles) between Tindharia and
Gybaree, encounters the heaviest average
gradient of the journey – 1:28. It is on
this section that "Agony Point" is
reached. Not only is the ascent steep but,

because of the tight squeeze for space on
the upper part of the loop, the train
virtually overhangs the hillside as it
negotiates a precipitous curve of 18 m
(59 ft) radius.

After this challenging stretch, the
route becomes less arduous, and once
Gybaree is reached the gradients become
slightly easier, a mere 1:32, for the 6.4
km (4 miles) to Mahanuddy, at 1,256 m
(4,120 ft) above sea level. After Sonada,
66 km (41 miles) into the journey, comes
one of the least exacting stretches of all –
the 1:36 climb to the summit at Ghoom,
2,258 m (7,408 ft) above sea level. From
here, the line descends to the city of
Darjeeling and journey's end.

KALKA TO SIMLA

● **OPPOSITE TOP**
The view, from the station, of Simla
and beyond.
● **BELOW**
The lovingly maintained rail station at Simla.

The Simla Mail does not go to Simla at all. To reach this one-time British hill station, one has to leave the main line at Kalka and transfer to the white-painted railcar for the five-hour haul up through the green hills. As the passengers take their seats in this undramatic little train, carriage attendants solicitously wrap rugs around their legs, as it is still only five o'clock in the morning.

For much of the way the line runs close to the road, their paths crossing at frequent intervals. To enable trains to climb the 1,524 m (5,000 ft) to Simla, 3 km (2 miles) of viaducts and 107 tunnels had to be constructed over a track length of 96 km (60 miles), such is the terrain. Two hours out, and the train halts at the

INFORMATION BOX	
Termini	Simla and Kalka
Country	India
Length	96 km (60 miles)
Date of opening	1903

little station of Barog, where the railcar waits while its passengers partake of a leisurely breakfast before setting off again into the tumbling clouds.

Occasionally the cloud and mist are rent by shafts of light to reveal a valley floor hundreds of metres below, ignored

by the busy little train, which has more important things than views on its mind as it hoots indignantly at buffalo and goats straying on to the track.

The Solan brewery halt is both a brewery and a station. The brewery came first, erected in the 19th century by a British company, which found good spring water here in the hills of Himachel Pradesh. In 1904, when the railway was built, the line cut right through the brewery, and passengers thereafter were treated to the rich aroma of malt and hops at the station approaches.

With each engaging of the gears, the little railcar gives a slight leap forward, reminiscent of the effects of "Kangaroo Petrol" when one is learning to drive a

car. In fact, the sight of this vehicle puts one in mind of a light blue Ford truck that has escaped from a museum. There are actually four such vehicles in service, built in 1927 and reconditioned in 1982.

The longest tunnel on the line is No. 33 at Barog, at a height of 1,144 m (3,753 ft) above sea level (at Kalka,) through which the train proceeds at the maximum permitted speed of 29 kph (18 mph). Including the viaducts, there are 869 bridges which gives an indication of the engineering problems faced during the construction of the line.

The car will halt at any station *en route* by request and – since there is no WC aboard – anywhere along the line for those passengers in urgent need.

However, above Solan station there is something called a "Relieving Lodge", which presumably caters for more onerous bodily functions. Simla station, presents such a magnificent view down

the mountains that the traveller feels amply rewarded for the 4½ hour ride.

● **BELOW**
The Kalka to Simla railcar standing at Kalka station.

PULGAON TO ARVI

The Pulgaon to Arvi line, originally a narrow-gauge branch from the Great Indian Peninsular Railway, will go down in history as the last genuine narrow-gauge line in India. It leaves the Bombay to Nagpur 5 ft 6 in broad-gauge main line at Pulgaon, where it has its own little station next to the main-line one, to meander through remote cotton-growing country to the town of Arvi some 33 km (20 miles) away. Immediately alongside Pulgaon station is a massive 19th-century British cotton factory, a truly "dark satanic mill", which is blessed with a fabulous steam hooter poignantly reminiscent of the industrial north of Victorian England. It is likely that the origin of the line lay in conveying cotton from the outlying areas to this mill. India's only other surviving narrow-gauge, 2 ft 6 in main lines are the tourist-operated Darjeeling Himalayan Railway and the famous tourist line in the south

INFORMATION BOX	
Termini	Pulgaon and Arvi
Country	India
Distance	33 km (20 miles)
Date of opening	1917

● **TOP**
The morning train, No. 643, leaves Pulgaon and passes a bullock-drawn cart of cotton bales heading for the factory next to the station.

● **ABOVE LEFT**
The ZP Pacific's driver in reflective mood at Arvi prior to working the evening train back to Pulgaon.

● **LEFT**
The afternoon train heads across the river at Kubgaon on the final leg of its journey to Arvi.

based on Ootacamun (known as the
"Ooty"). At one time the line had three
daily mixed trains each way, along with an
old Armstrong Whitworth diesel railcar of
1934. Today, with two daily trains each
way, the line is distinctive in being worked
by ZP Class Pacifics of traditional British
design but built by Nippon in Japan in
1954. These sprightly locomotives,
originally built for the Satpura lines but
transferred in 1976, are some of the last
Pacific locomotives in the world, certainly

the last in India with the exception of the
metre-gauge YP Class.

The appalling difficulties facing
maintenance engineers with the shortage
of spare parts means that only one
locomotive is in steam at any one time,
and the line has no crossing loops,
although formerly a loop did exist at
Rhona Town.

The line is a last vestige of a form of
transport that was once common in many
parts of the world and retains all the

characteristics of a classic country railway
of the late 19th century. Four trains a day
are scheduled to run: No. 643 leaves
Pulgaon at 08.00 and arrives in Arvi at
10.20; No. 644 leaves Arvi at 10.40 and
reaches Pulgaon at 12.25; No. 645 leaves
Pulgaon at 14.30 and reaches Arvi at
16.50; and No. 646 leaves Arvi at 17.30
and arrives in Pulgaon at 19.15.

There are nine stations on the route:
Pulgaon, Sorta, Virol, Rhona Town,
Dhanori, Pargothan, Pachegaon, Kubgaon

● **RIGHT**
Railway supremacy is
asserted at this level
crossing near Rhona
as ZP Class Pacific
No. 2 hustles its two
coach train over the
main road.

● **BELOW RIGHT**
The afternoon train
from Pulgaon to Arvi
overtakes a pair of
carts bringing cotton
in from the
surrounding fields.

● **BOTTOM LEFT**
Monkeys play around
the station name
board at Arvi.

● **BOTTOM
RIGHT**
The water pump
outside the station at
Pargothan attracts
women from the
surrounding villages.
Here they are busily
filling their urns as
the morning train to
Pulgaon prepares to
depart for Arvi.

crossings. This classic roadside tramway
is picturesque and rustic, travellers being
solely village people and mostly heavily
laden ones who use the train to carry
their bags of produce.

The trains consist of two bogie
coaches and on the outward journey
from Pulgaon the engines go tender first;
upon reaching Arvi the coaches are
shunted round to ensure that the brake
remains at the rear of the consist.

It is said that one tonne of coal is
burnt on the engine on each trip, which
seems excessive for such a small
locomotive so lightly laden. It is possible
that, as with so many rural Indian lines
that were worked by steam, coal is
thrown down at strategic points along
the track to favoured recipients in return
for rupees!

The quality of the coal is another
reason for sloth on the line, as much of it
turns to clinker and clogs up the firebox,
necessitating regular stops for "blow-
ups". If coal is unavailable, all trains are
cancelled. Likewise punctuality is treated
very liberally – lateness can be caused
either by mechanical problems or,

and Arvi. The line passes through remote
countryside, and many of the stations are
simple tin shacks in the middle of
nowhere, the villages they serve being
some some distance away. Rhona Town
serves a sizeable community which has a
large cotton mill, as does Kubgaon.

The line is paralleled throughout by a
road, which is generally well surfaced and
over which frequent buses ply their trade.
They provide serious competition for the
railway and prevent it from being
profitable. The only supremacy the
railway can claim lies in the many level

seemingly, the whims of the engine crew who have a frequent tendency of stopping for tea at Pargothan.

In today's world, the sheer joy of a railway such as this is always going to be under threat, and early in 1997 diesel servicing facilities were installed and ZDM4A No. 198 arrived from

Kurduwadi. There was no immediate question of the diesel taking over, as many spare parts had to be obtained, and ZP Pacific No. 2 continued as before. Fortunately, despite the line's incredible unprofitability, Indian Railways have extended the contract with the British owners to operate the line up to 2006.

● ABOVE
Travelling musicians entertaining passengers during the station stop at Sorta.

● BELOW
The picturesque rural nature and general remoteness of this country line can be gauged from this scene of the scrub and bush, which characterize much of the land.

COLOMBO TO KANDY

This picturesque, and often thrilling railway line was built between 1858 and 1868 to link Colombo, the present capital, with the former capital of what was then Ceylon, Kandy, in the mountains 488 m (1,601 ft) above sea level and 121 km (75 miles) distant. The system expanded to 1,530 km (951 miles) at the standard gauge of 5 ft 6 in and 138 km (86 miles) at the narrow gauge of 2 ft 6 in, the latter mainly up the valley of the Kelani River. Mileage has now been reduced to 1,390 km (864 miles) for the standard gauge and 63 km (39 miles) for the narrow gauge, which is being converted to mixed gauge. Another short narrow-gauge line, from Nanu Oya to Ragalla in the mountains, has closed.

However, in 1991, an extension of the broad gauge for 121 km (75 miles) from Matara to the pilgrim town of Kataragam on the south coast was begun, and there are proposals to extend this into the mountains to join up with Badulla, the railhead beyond Kandy and Nuwara Eliya. An 11 km (7 mile) branch from Anuadhapura to Mihintale in the north was due for completion in 1997.

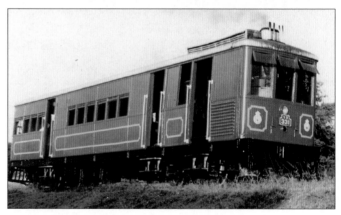

Steam traction was the mainstay of the railways until the 1970s. By then the high cost of imported coal had led to the early development of British-built diesel traction, both locomotives and DMUs, an attractively styled version of which worked the frequent local services along the pictureque coastline from Colombo to the resort of Mount Lavinia. Japanese-built DMUs bought in 1990 now operate the local services.

Colombo's main railway station is at Fort and is a "through" station. Five platforms served the broad gauge and there was one for the narrow gauge. It always was busy, but suburban traffic has

● **LEFT**
Another less technically advanced form of transport in rural Sri Lanka is the ox cart.

INFORMATION BOX

Termini	Colombo and Kandy
Country	Sri Lanka
Distance	121 km (75 miles)
Date of opening	1868

increased by 30 per cent since 1980. Just to the north of Fort lies the important station of Maradana, with no fewer than six platform faces for the broad gauge and three for the narrow. It is the junction where the narrow gauge heads off down the Kelani valley. About 1.2 km (³/₄ mile) further on, the large locomotive depot and repair shops at Dermatagoda at the right of the line provided eight long tracks for broad-gauge and two for narrow-gauge locomotives. This was by far the largest depot on the island and, for such a relatively small system, the

● **OPPOSITE TOP**
Colombo's House of Assembly, the seat of Sri Lanka's parliament.

● **OPPOSITE MIDDLE**
This railcar, No. 331 of Class V2, operated on the 2 ft 6 in gauge lines.

● **BELOW LEFT**
There were four batches of Class B8c dating back to 1922. Two of the batches were built by Hunslet Engine Co. of Leeds, England, and this machine was from the batch delivered in 1927. With an axle load of only 9.2 tonnes (9 tons), they were suitable for use on lightly laid track.

● **OPPOSITE BOTTOM**
The 2 ft 6 in gauge line from Colombo up the Kelani valley saw locomotives such as this neat J1 Class 2-6-2T No. 220.

● **RIGHT**
A familiar sight by the side of the line in Sri Lanka are the tea pickers working in the plantations.

the mainland of the Indian subcontinent.
It is also the end of the double-track
section, and the train for Kandy turns
away to the east, gently climbing to
Rambukkana, 11 km (7 miles) further on
at a height of 95 m (312 ft).

The 29 km (18 mile) section from
Rambukkana to Peradenya is one of the
most spectacular in Sri Lanka. Travellers
are advised to sit on the right-hand side
of the train to take advantage of the ever-
changing scene. A large 4-8-0 banking
locomotive of Class A1 is placed at the
rear of the train to assist on the 19 km
(12 mile) climb at 1:44, made more
difficult by numerous sharp curves down
to 201 m (660 ft) radius.

The route leaves the jungle floor and
climbs on ledges frequently cut from the
almost vertical rock faces. The expanding

number of different types of locomotive
that had to be maintained, ranging from
diminutive narrow-gauge 4-4-0T to
Beyer-Garratts, must have put a strain on
the skills and resources of the engineers.

The double-track main line generally
heads north-east through level
countryside with paddy fields, coconut
plantations and small villages with palm-
thatched huts. Areas of uncultivated land
are often ablaze with the blooms of wild
flowers, and brightly coloured birds
complete the scene. At Ragama, the
branch line along the west coast to
Puttalam goes off to the left.

By Ambepussa, 56 km (35 miles) from
Colombo, the train has begun to climb
away from the wide coastal plains through
coconut plantations until its arrival at
Polgahawela, 74 km (46 miles) from
Colombo at an altitude of 73 m (240 ft)
above sea level. This is the junction for
the main line northward, which finishes at
Kankesanturai, where there is a ferry to

● RIGHT
Class B1a 4-6-0 Sir
Thomas Maitland
was built in England
in 1927 by Beyer
Peacock and is seen
in a much more
colourful livery than
that used in 1945.

● RIGHT
Class B2c 4-6-0 No.
213 is one of several
engines delivered
from 1915 onward
and comes from a
batch manufactured
by Vulcan Foundry
in England in 1922.
It is essentially a
main-line
locomotive, and,
until the arrival of
Class B1, it was the
pride of the line.

views, first into the valley below and then into the far distance, are incomparable. "Sensation Curve" is rightly named for it is on a ledge with a 305 m (1,000 ft) sheer drop to the valley floor below. It is best seen from a train going toward Colombo, for it then appears that the line is going to take off into space.

Kadugannawa, 104 km (65 miles) from Colombo and 515 m (1,690 ft) above sea level, is where the banking locomotive is removed. The line then falls 41 m (136 ft) in the 9.6 km (6 miles) to Peradeniya Junction station, where the route to Newara Eliya and Badulla turns south while the other line turns north-east for the 6.4 km (4 miles) to Kandy. It is well worth pausing at New Peradeniya station to visit the nearby Botanical Gardens and wander through the extensive grounds.

The station at Kandy, 121 km (75 miles) from Colombo, had three terminal roads and one which continued through the station to Matale, 26 km (16 miles) distant and a centre for the cattle trade. Lightweight 4-6-0 steam locomotives were shedded here, together with two Sentinel Steam coaches, which worked local trains to Matale and Peradeniya.

● **BELOW**
Travellers will want to take time off in Kandy to visit the world-famous Temple of the Tooth. Here we see the temple across the lake of the same name.

● **ABOVE**
The Class B10 4-6-0 had the very light axle load of only 7.6 tonnes (7.5 tons) enabling it to work over lightly laid lines such as that to Matale. The class dates back to 1901.

TUMENJAN TO PYONGYANG

"What do you want to go *there* for?" exclaimed the Russian engine-driver in amazement. "Don't you know there are *Communists* there?" He made it sound as if Russia had never had anything to do with Communism itself.

I was ensconced in the cab of the leading heavy diesel unit of the two deemed necessary to haul one battered coach along the single-track line that runs southwards from Ussuriysk, the junction for Vladivostok, the city of which could be seen in the distance, to Pyongyang, the capital of North Korea. There were no more than half a dozen passengers on the train, and, beyond Ussuriysk and the eyes of authority, I was actually permitted to drive the train as far as Khazan, border town of the then USSR, China and North Korea. At this politically sensitive spot, it was deemed prudent for me to return to the carriage.

Tumenjan is the North Korean entry station on this remote line, and the red

banners and giant portraits of the "Great Leader" proclaimed entry into the hard-line Stalinist state where such propaganda drips from every village, town and city wall — even some of the mountain flanks.

INFORMATION BOX

Termini	Tumenjan and Pyongyang
Country	North Korea
Distance	*c.* 800 km (500 miles)
Date of opening	1899

Pyongyang's main station is a cross between a cathedral and an opera house in a city risen from the ashes of the 1950–53 Korean War to resemble a metropolis straight out of a Jules Verne fantasy (with a metro outshining even the architectural magnificence of Moscow's). Regretably, the marbled platforms of the station are closed to the rank and file who have to wait for their trains outside in the open.

Korea, as a whole, first opened its railway in 1899, and a 6,400 km (3,977 mile) network was developed during the Japanese annexation between 1910 and 1945. At partition in 1948, the network

One of the towns served by the
railway is Nampo, site of the 8 km
(5 mile) long West Sea Barrage, a major
engineering project of which North
Korea is justly proud. It was here that I
was allowed to ride in the cab of one of
the freight-yard's working steam
locomotives – the dirtiest I have seen for
quite a long time. While some of the
lines have been electrified in North
Korea, the majority of trains are still
diesel-hauled.

I left the country on the Pyongyang to
Beijing express, crossing the Yalu River
on the massive steel-lattice swing bridge
into China's Manchuria, with far less
rumpus than had one General Douglas
MacArthur in the early 1950s.

and stock were divided on a ratio of 2:1,
North Korea getting the greater share.
The war destroyed much of the network,
but this has now been rebuilt and
improved upon – particularly in South
Korea, which has outstripped in route-
length its fractious neighbour.

As in all one-time Communist states,
a permit is necessary for movement
beyond a certain radius. This means that
only those passengers engaged in labour
for the State can travel worthwhile
distances, which at least eliminates the
scourge of overcrowded trains. Besides
the line to Pyongyang from the Russian
border, the only other lines run from the
capital to the Chinese border at
Dandong and southwards to Haeju and
Kaesong, the town nearest the heavily
fortified demarcation zone centred upon
the village of Panmunjom (which, oddly,
Western visitors are permitted to visit,
albeit under guard, to stand just
centimetres away from the actual line of
demarcation separating the two halves of
the country).

SHENYANG TO HARBIN

The Chinese, in the midst of their modernization of the railways, are justifiably amused, not to say perplexed, that foreigners should want to travel thousands of miles to gape at their remaining steam-engines. Railway construction came late to Imperial China, forbidden (it is said) by successive emperors. By the 1880s, when the USA already possessed some 145,000 km (90,000 miles) of track, China had a mere 18,000 km (11,000 miles). However, once the ban was lifted the country took to railway construction with gusto. And no part of China is more rail-minded and enthusiastic about trains than Manchuria, a vast region, larger than France and Germany combined, that the Chinese call Dongbei.

Between 1876 and 1949, some 21,000 km (13,050 miles) of railway were built, though only half of it was operative following the civil war that led to the Communist take-over. Today's rail system exceeds 60,000 km (37,284 miles) with many single-track sections doubled.

It is in Manchuria, where there are huge deposits of brown coal, that steam

traction can still be observed. Life on the Manchurian railways is often hard – in winter, when temperatures fall as low as –25°C (–13°F), locomotives can freeze to the rails. Yet even at such times earnest train buffs descend on the yards to take pictures with frost-affected cameras and enter copious notes into their pocket notebooks. In fact so many such visitors now arrive that today the workers are less mystified by all the attention.

The capital of Manchuria's Liaoning Province – one of three provinces – is Shenyang, the former Mukden. This is the scene of the "Mukden Incident", which arose when an explosion on the railway line triggered the Japanese occupation. Sixty km (37 miles) away, on a branch of the main Shenyang-Harbin line, sits the smaller city of Fushan, site of the prison, still operational, that held Pi Yi, the "Last Emperor", whose cell is open for inspection.

● **TOP**
A view of Harbin's vast marshalling yards from Sankong Bridge, with the city of Harbin in the background.

● **ABOVE LEFT**
Harbin railway station.

● **LEFT**
A China Railways QJ Class 2-10-2 storms up Wang Gang Bank out of Harbin with a heavy freight bound for Changchun.

INFORMATION BOX

Termini	Shenyang and Harbin
Country	China
Distance	*c.* 725 km (*c.* 450 miles)
Commencement of building	1876

For true rail buffs the Shenyang-Harbin line puts on a huge display of gigantic black steam locomotives, or at least it did in 1990. The route takes a full day to cover, and longer if one stops off to visit the sheds, where visitors are welcome.

The line was once the so-called Russian Manchurian Railway, and there is much in Harbin to remind one of the long gone Russian occupation. Between the small towns of Lungxiang and Lancha, about five hours' ride from Harbin, a narrow-gauge railway, using fussy little steam-engines, transports both visitors and timber between forest and town. On the main line the long-distance trains are adequate rather than luxurious, but at the railway towns *en route* the workers in the sidings and sheds are the friendliest imaginable, much heartened by the interest shown by visitors.

Harbin railway station is the third largest in China, with an average daily departure of over 200,000 passengers. With a floor space of 14,200 sq m (152,848 sq ft), it contains five waiting rooms, 28 booking offices, a restaurant, a department store, a left-luggage office and a hotel with over 300 beds.

● **ABOVE**
One of the magnificent Japanese-built streamlined Pacifics in the Railway Museum at Shenyang. During the 1930s these engines worked the Asia Express between Shenyang – then known as Mukden – and Harbin.

● **ABOVE**
The city of Anshan, China's iron and steel capital, shows a wonderful diversity of architectures combined with the landscaped parks in which China excels.

● **LEFT**
A QJ Class 2-10-2 races down Wang Gang Bank and into Harbin on a frozen afternoon.

● **LEFT**
In China public transport is practised to a fine art as the private motor car barely exists. The back-up for China's excellent public transport system is the humble bicycle, and bike jams are a regular feature of rush-hour travel.

ULAN BATOR TO DATONG
ACROSS THE GOBI DESERT

The train out of Ulan Bator, made up of
seven coaches plus a baggage car, is
normally in pristine condition. Before
departure, all the coaches are given a final
clean by smartly dressed attendants.
Inside the four-berth coaches, the upper
berths make up as beds, while there is
plenty of room to sit on the lower seats,
each covered by an attractive clean cloth.

On leaving Ulan Bator, the views are
at first rather uninspiring. There is a
confusing mixture of austere housing,
steam-draped heavy industry and *yurts*
(tents) against a backdrop of low hills.
Items of railway interest include an
ancient working 2.8.0 steam locomotive,
a preserved industrial or narrow-gauge
engine and some 20 diesels. Once having
left the capital behind, the train winds
through a sparse landscape, with almost
bare hills to the left and occasional
clumps of forest on the right.

About half an hour into the journey,
the train loops around a set of three
aerials as it climbs on to a flat plateau. An
hour or so later it encounters an almost
volcanic outcropping, before curving left
and accelerating down a gentle
downgrade. The train now traverses a

INFORMATION BOX

Termini	Ulan Bator and Datong
Countries	Mongolia and China
Distance	1045 km (655 miles)
Date of opening	1929

● BELOW
A QJ Class 2-10-2 and a JS Class 2-8-2 are
subjects of interest at an intermediate station.

seemingly endless hot flat plain until it
reaches Choyr, where the landscape falls
away gently to the right.

There are subtle changes in the terrain
over the next couple of hours. A jagged
rocky ridge in the left middle distance
glows purple in the sunlight while the
plain becomes gently undulating with
dried grass and light soil on either side.
The sinuous nature of the route, despite
the level landscape, allows frequent views
of the twin diesels, which haul the train,
relatively slowly, through almost
mesmeric terrain.

On the border, the Mongolian officials
are all very smart and correct. A number
of soldiers stand to attention along the
platform. Formalities last between 23.40
and 01.00, and then the train is on the
move once again, this time entering
China or, to be pedantic, Chinese-
dominated Inner Mongolia.

The welcome at the first Chinese
station is very different from the arrivals
experienced in the once-Soviet sphere of
influence. The station is festooned with
coloured lights, and cheerful music is
relayed from loud-speakers, all in marked

Impressive public buildings and lesser structures
stretch towards the foothills beyond Ulan Bator.

● BELOW RIGHT
A carving of Buddha in the Yungang gorge.

contrast to both the desert and other
more drab administrations encountered
previously. The formalities can still be
lengthy, nevertheless, and some
passengers may miss the experience of
seeing the train being converted to run
on the Chinese gauge.

The line from Ulan Bator to Datong
was built by the Soviets to their broader
gauge of 5 ft but, following the cooling of
relations between them and China, the
Chinese re-laid their portion of the route
to the local (standard) gauge, viz. 1,435 4
ft 8¹/₂ in. This need to change gauge gives
the traveller the first opportunity to travel
behind steam. The locomotive hauls the
train about 1. 6 km (1 mile) to the shed
equipped to change bogies.

Apart from the engine crew, nearly all
the workers engaged in the operation are
female. The locomotive positioned, each
coach opposite a pair of jacks,
preparations are made to the bogies and
the brake gear. Then the coach is jacked
up, the bogies are rolled away, to be
replaced by a new set by overhead crane.
Finally the coach is lowered and fine
adjustments, if necessary, are made to the
position of the new bogies. Regular
practice has, however, made the initial
positioning of both coach and wheelsets
remarkably accurate. Once everything is
correctly positioned, and the requisite
connections have been made, the whole
process is repeated for the next coach.

During breakfast on the second day
the views of isolated forts and ruined
walls on the passing heights – remnants
of the defences of the Great Wall –
remind travellers that they are entering
China proper. The train follows a
winding river valley, as doubtless earlier
invaders would have done. They,
however, would not have encountered
increasing signs of industrialization as the

● BELOW
The train sweeps round a sun-baked village,
the passengers probably oblivious to the harsh
life of its inhabitants.

train approaches Datong. Pollution
control is still a relatively foreign
concept, and the fumes from the various
factories, mingled with the smell of
night-soil in the more rural areas, make
for a potent mixture.

A succession of passing steam-hauled
freights provides evidence not only of
industry but also of how effective the
distribution system of the Chinese is
compared with that of the Russians.
Water melons, pears, apples, plums,
grapes, cabbages, peppers, beetroot,
swede, carrots and chillies are all visible
on the trains and for sale in these
northern regions in contrast to the
former Soviet Union. A journey across
the Gobi Desert in many ways remains
one in time as well as kilometres.

FUJI TO KOFU

A pleasant one-day jaunt from Tokyo is to ride on the metre-gauge Minobu line, which runs from the city of Fuji, near the base of the famous Mount Fuji, to Kofu. A circlular trip from Tokyo via Fuji and Kofu is easily accomplished with a little planning. Fuji is served by both the Tokyo-Osaka-Hakata Shinkansen high-speed line (also known as the Tokaido-San-Yo Shinkansen) and the metre-gauge Tokaido line of Japanese Railways (JR). Trains operating on the Minobu line use the same station as the Tokaido line, and passengers can make a cross-the-platform transfer here. The Shinkansen Shin-Fuji station is several blocks distant from the metre-gauge station, making transfer between trains more difficult.

The northern end of the Minobu line joins JR's busy metre-gauge Chou Line a mile east of the main station in Kofu, where another cross-the-platform transfer takes place. There is frequent

● LEFT
Interior of a JR EMU assigned to the Fujikawa express trains. This train was the Fujikawa No. 5, heading to Kofu from Fuji.

and direct service to Tokyo on this incredibly scenic main line, and a number of interesting streamlined trains run this way, including the Super Azusa and the Boso View – which despite its name is not a circus train!

Fuji is an industrial city on Suruga Bay and warrants a considerable volume of freight service on the Tokaido line in addition to frequent passenger service. While making a connection to the Minobu line, passengers may see one of many intermodal freights pass through the station or watch a diesel hydraulic-switch engine shunt cars in the nearby yard.

● ABOVE LEFT
After a five-minute stop at Minobu, a local train's conductor checks his watch before departing for Kofu. Most of the Minobu line is single track with passing sidings at key stations. Local trains are required to clear the way for Fujikawa expresses.

● LEFT
A Fujikawa express train races through Hadakajima on its way to Fuji. The Minobu line passes through fabulous mountainous terrain on its run between Fuji and Kofu.

● **LEFT**
A local train, bound for Fuji from Kofu, coasts
downgrade toward its station stop at
Hadakajima.

INFORMATION BOX	
Termini	Fuji and Kofu
Country	Japan
Distance	97 km (60 miles)
Date of opening	Information unavailable

There are both local and express
trains on the Minobu line. Local trains
are usually equipped with JR's Spartan
but very clean electric multiple units
(EMUs) of the sort found in commuter
service all around Japan. The seating is
not of the best sort for a long trip, but
the windows are clean. Express service is
provided by considerably more luxurious
multiple-unit trains, which run as the
Fujikawa. A JR Green Pass will entitle
foreign visitors to travel on these express
trains; otherwise first-class tickets can be
purchased from JR. The Fujikawa
operates on a significantly faster schedule
than the local trains; it attains a top speed
of 85 kph (53 mph), and stops much less
often, making the Fuji-Kofu run in just
under two hours. Local trains can take a
little more than three hours to cover the
same distance.

Leaving Fuji, the Minobu line follows
the Urui River and winds through
residential neighbourhoods and industrial
areas of the city. In addition to the local
through trains, commuter trains also
serve suburban Fuji on the lower end of
the line. On a clear day, Mount Fuji is
visible to the north of the tracks. Several
miles out of town, the railroad leaves the
Urui and follows the Fujikawa River, one
of the most important waterways in

Japan. On the way up the scenic Fujikawa
valley, the railroad passes through many
short tunnels and provincial towns. The
line is primarily single track, with short
passing sidings at most stations allowing
for well-timed meets between opposing
trains. Towards Kofu the railroad drops
down into a broad agricultural plain.

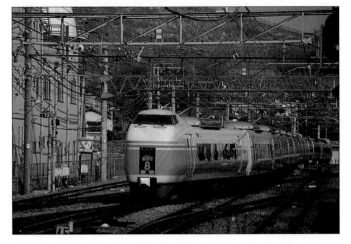

● **ABOVE**
The Minobu line features many tunnels,
including several long bores near Wariishi
Pass, located between Shimobe and Kofu.

● **LEFT**
A Super Azusa train departs the Kofu terminal
for Tokyo via the Chou line. Upon arriving at
Kofu from Fuji, passengers may continue on to
Tokyo on a number of interesting streamlined
electric trains, including the Super Azusa.

TOKYO'S YAMANOTE LINE

● BELOW
A Yamanote line train leaves Shinjuku.

The Yamanote line makes a 32 km (20 mile) loop through Tokyo, connecting the city's principal rail terminals at Shinjuku, Ueno and Tokyo stations. Other lines operate immediately parallel to this extremely busy metre-gauge electrified commuter line, including the busy Tokaido, Chou, and Seibu-Shinjuku lines, making the Yamanote Loop route one of the busiest railway lines in the world. In many places, the right of way has between six and twelve main-line tracks.

Many long-distance trains, including Japanese Railway's (JR's) overnight sleeping car trains, run alongside the Yamanote commuters. Riding the loop, one might even see one of the new streamlined silver and purple Super Azusa trains pacing your train on an adjacent track! Service on the Yamanote line itself is provided by JR EMU commuter train sets painted light green (all of the Tokyo area commuter train routes are colour-coded) that run around the loop continuously. The trains run every couple of minutes between 6 a.m. and midnight.

INFORMATION BOX

Termini	Shinjuku, Ueno and Tokyo
Country	Japan
Distance	32 km (20 miles)
Date of opening	Information unavailable

● FAR LEFT
At Shinjuku, on a platform adjacent to the Yamanote line, is one of JR's new Super Azusa train sets. Soon this metre-gauge streamliner will head out on the Chou line towards Kofu.

● OPPOSITE BOTTOM
A long Yamanote line train departs Habata station in the morning rush hour. These trains run on one- and two-minute headways at peak times, and are nearly always jam-packed right up to midnight.

● LEFT
The Shinjuku shopping district on a sunny
weekday morning is a primary destination of
many railway commuters. The Shinjuku region
of Tokyo is served by many railway lines
including the busy Yamanote line.

At Akihabara the Sobu line crosses the
Yamanote line on an exceptionally tall
elevated structure, with the Sobu line on
the upper level. Far below one can
observe the Shinkansen. Akihabara is
known as "Electric City", and the latest
electronic devices imaginable are
available here, from electric toilet seats
to singing alarm clocks!

Although the Yamanote line is run by
JR as part of the commuter rail network,
the level and quality of service resembles
a rapid transit line more than that of a
conventional commuter train line.

Most of the line is either elevated or
depressed through Tokyo, offering many
excellent views of the city. However, the
Yamanote line's principal attraction is the
astounding volume of rail traffic along
this route. Shinjuku station on the west
side of Tokyo presently ranks as the
world's busiest railroad station, including
two interurban electric terminals
adjacent to it. At rush hour, on any week
day, traffic through this terminal is
virtually continuous.

At Ueno, a 12-track flying junction
separates metre-gauge routes on to two
levels. (The Shinkansen is below ground
at this point.) It is not uncommon to find
six trains moving in different directions
through Ueno all at one time! Ueno
station serves Ueno Park, the location of
several museums and the Tokyo Zoo. The
Tokyo Science Museum is only a block
from Ueno station and features a
preserved JR 2-8-2 Mikado-type steam
locomotive and a semaphore signal.

The Shinkansen runs alongside the
Yamanote Loop at several places on the
east side of Tokyo. At traffic peaks these
high-speed trains operate every five or six
minutes, yet traffic on the parallel metre-
gauge line is even more frequent.

● RIGHT
Ueno station in
Tokyo, one of
several large
busy stations
connected on the
Yamanote line.

TOKYO TO NIKKO
BY TRAIN TO THE SHRINES

It is a cliché to state that Japan is a land of contrasts, but anyone visiting the country cannot help but come to that conclusion. A visit by train to Nikko is one of the many ways of experiencing this. Nikko is one of the major Japanese temple and shrine areas and, at approximately 150 km (93 miles) from Tokyo, is the nearest to the capital. The contrast is not only between the city noise and the calm of the temples, but also between the express train on the Tobu Railway, the Japanese Railways (JR) semi-rural branch line and a trip on the "Bullet train" (Shinkansen).

The round trip starts at Asakusa station in Tokyo. The area around the station, close to the Sumida River, is itself worth visiting, with its large number of craft goods shops and the large Sensoji Temple. This elevated station, integrated into the second floor of the Matsuya department store and at the end of a

bridge over the river, is the terminus of the Tobu Railway. The site is very cramped, and many of their trains now run through to the Eidan Hibiya metro line from a junction around 10 km (6 miles) out of town. There are only three six-coach platforms, and plans for a total rebuild are under discussion, not least to allow the Tobu's standard ten-coach

● ABOVE
Tokyo has two metro systems, a "private" company, TRTA, and the city authority's TOEI group. This is TRTA metro 05014 at Nakano, on the Tozai line. Asakusa station is served by the TRTA Ginza line.

● LEFT
Tobu Railway Spacia EMU departing Asakusa station, Tokyo, in December 1995. Note the curved approach to the station from the river bridge, on the right of the photograph.

trains to use the station.

Nikko can be reached on the
suburban trains, but the quicker and
definitely more comfortable way is to
travel on one of the Tobu's "Limited
Express Spacia" trains, which are formed
of streamlined EMUs. There are six
through trains in the morning, taking an
hour and 40 minutes, followed by a half-
hourly service for most of the day,
requiring one change at Shimo Imaichi.
The Spacia trains come complete with
hostess and drinks service, and the seats
are a pleasant contrast to the longitudinal
seats on the suburban trains.

The Asakusa ticket-office can be
confusing to those who do not speak
Japanese, but a little observation will
identify the special queue for these trains.
Seat reservation is compulsory, but can
be bought on the day, and there should
not be too many problems getting a place

INFORMATION BOX	
Termini	Tokyo and Nikko
Country	Japan
Distance	150 km (93 miles)
Date of opening	Infomation unavailable

● **LEFT**
JR outer-suburban
EMU 115-422 and
JR freight electric
locomotive EF65
540 at Utsunomiya.
The Tohoku
Shinkansen
platforms are in
the structure above
the platform on
the left.

● **BELOW**
JR's Utsunomiya
station. On the left is
the Nikko branch
train formed of
EMU 106-7. On the
right is outer-
suburban EMU
115-122.

on the next departure. Sign language is adequate to buy a ticket!

The main line of the Tobu Railway was built in the first decade of this century, and Nikko was reached in 1929 at a time of electrification and expansion. The present Asakusa terminus was opened in 1931. Through running of Tobu trains to the Tokyo metro, starting in 1962, was the first of its kind in Tokyo. The Tobu Railway is one of the largest private railways in Japan and carried over 945 million passengers on 463 km (288 miles) of route during 1994, totalling over four billion passenger kilometres (2.5 billion miles). Unlike commuter railways in other countries, but like most in Japan, the Tobu Railway is profitable, despite its cheap fares.

The line proceeds through the ever-expanding suburban sprawl of Tokyo for some time but eventually reaches the country area beyond. The landscape is attractive rather than dramatic, with the low hills, woods and paddy fields interspersed with farm buildings and small towns. However, as the journey

progresses, mountains come into view. Whilst the railway does not reach them, the mountains form a backdrop to the area around Nikko, with three peaks over 2,000 m (6,500 ft) within 20 km (12 miles) of the town.

There are no great engineering features on the line caused by the terrain. However, in order to avoid frequent level

crossings and to expand capacity in its evolution from a local line into a four-track commuter railway, significant stretches of elevated line have been constructed, on ugly concrete structures.

The Tobu station in Nikko is the closest to the town centre, although the JR station is only 200 m (650 ft) further away. The shrines are about 2 km

● **RIGHT**
The Shinkyo bridge, Nikko, a 1907 reconstruction of a 17th-century original. This can be seen from the road between Nikko and the shrine area.

● **BELOW RIGHT**
The "three wise monkeys" carving on the sacred stables at the Toshogu Shrine.

(1¼ miles) from the railway stations, along a road lined with many shops aimed at the Japanese tourist market. The more adventurous could try some of the food shops, most of which make few compromises for the non-Japanese. There is also a bus service.

Around half-way along the road is the Nikko Information Centre, which is also the main outlet for the cheapest way to visit the temples: the two-shrines-one-temple ticket. The ticket offices at the sites will try to sell you individual entry tickets, a far more expensive combination. The attendant in the office seemed surprised that a foreigner had found his way there and knew about this ticket. However, the information is given in any good guidebook, which will also help you understand the history behind this religious site.

The area contains (despite the name of the ticket!) four main attractions: the Rinnoji Temple, the Daiyuin Shrine, the Futarasan Shrine and the Toshogu Shrine. The latter contains the original of the "hear no evil, see no evil, speak no evil"

carving and is the most visited. However, all four are recommended, and are listed in the suggested viewing order. The Toshogu Shrine, dating from 1617 and including a five-storey pagoda, is undoubtedly the most famous and, unfortunately, has the crowds to match. This contrasts with the Daiyuin Shrine, which few people seem to reach. All the buildings are set amongst a forest of tall trees, giving an appropriately serene atmosphere to a site with religious links going back to the 8th century.

The return journey starts with the JR branch line from Nikko to Utsunomiya, which opened in 1890. The service is frequent, if not entirely regular, and starts from a white, half-timbered building, which appears in style to be a cross between Japanese and English Victorian mock-Tudor architecture. The train usually consists of a suburban-style two-car EMU.

The first part of the 40-minute journey is through the countryside and small towns. The significant number of

● **LEFT**
The Senso-ji Temple
complex includes the
massive Hozomon
Gate, seen here from
the temple steps.

● **BELOW LEFT**
JR suburban EMU
approaching Ueno
Station, Tokyo. This
train is on the upper
level, the tracks
visible on a lower
level are used by
long distance trains.
The Shinkansen
from Utsonomiya
and the north is on a
third, underground
level at this station.

school students on my train showed that
the railway was not just run for the
visitors to Nikko. The scenery becomes
more urban as Utsunomiya, a large town,
is approached. Its station is in two
adjoining parts: the main JR station and
the elevated Shinkansen platforms. There
is also a Tobu Railway terminus in the
vicinity, also with services to Tokyo.

JR is now the poor relation on this
route – although journey times are
comparable, most people visiting Nikko
now tend to use the Tobu line. However,
JR did not give up without a fight, and
the 1950s were characterized by the two
companies vying to provide the best
service and best rolling stock to gain the
most passengers; by the mid-1960s,
however, the Tobu had won.

The Shinkansen journey is on the
Tohoku line, which runs between Tokyo
and Morioka, to the north. Trains run
from Utsunomiya to Tokyo approximately three times per hour and take
around 55 minutes for approximately
108 km (67 miles). This journey will be
taken using the unreserved seating on the
Shinkansen, unless there was enough
time to plan the schedule in detail a day
or so in advance. The unreserved seats
are only in specified coaches, and the
ticket will indicate which. It is
recommended to be near the front of the
queue, which will be at exactly the right
spot on the platform to be opposite the
door when the train stops.

The Tohoku line opened north from
the Tokyo suburban station of Omiya in
1982, 78 km (48 miles) from
Utsunomiya, and reached Ueno in 1985;
the final section into Tokyo being opened
in 1991. The run to Tokyo is elevated for
much of the way through largely built-up
areas as far as Ueno, the main station on
the north side of Tokyo. From here, the
line is in tunnel to Tokyo station where,
although meeting the Tokaido line
Shinkansen, there is no end-on junction

as the power supplies and automatic signalling systems are different. There is also a big contrast between this station and Asakusa, where the journey started. However, whilst Tokyo station seems vast and very busy, it is not the busiest station in Japan, a distinction belonging to Tokyo's Shinjuku station.

This round trip, which provides something for those culturally minded as well as those interested in the railways, can be done comfortably in a day from Tokyo The relative cheapness of rail fares in Japan means the strong yen does not make the cost overly expensive. It should be noted that this itinerary is not sold as one ticket and rebooking will be required in Nikko, but my total lack of knowledge of Japanese did not prove a barrier to a fascinating day out.

● **ABOVE**
JR Shinkansen 221-204 arriving at Utsunomiya. The two central tracks allow non-stopping trains to overtake, a quite frequent occurrence which requires strict adherence to the timetable to avoid delays.

● **BELOW LEFT**
Close by the Tobu Railway's Asakusa station is the Senso-ji Temple. One of the buildings in the complex is this five-storey pagoda.

● **BELOW**
JR Shinkansen 221-25 at Tokyo, in the low-level platforms used by the Tohoku line. The green livery is unique to the Shinkansen on this route.

TOKYO TO OSAKA

Just after World War II, the Japanese proposed to build a straight line between Tokyo and Osaka that would allow trains to travel at 201 kph (125 mph). However, with the massive rebuilding that had to take place after the war, it was not until 1958 that an aerial survey of the route was made. The following year, within a week of Parliament approving the project, the ceremonial ground-breaking took place. In 1965, just 65 months later, the first full service between the two cities began.

To permit such high speed, the line was constructed so that no curve had a radius of less than 2.4 km (1½ miles). To avoid urban congestion and to minimize noise, the line is carried on viaducts with high parapet walls some 6.4 m (21 ft) above towns. There are no level crossings on the track, and valleys and estuaries are crossed on long viaducts. Where mountains block the way, no fewer than 66 tunnels, 12 of them over 2 km (1¼ miles) long, have been driven through the rock. To make allowance for the aerodynamic effect of two trains passing at combined speeds of over 400 kph (250 mph), the distance between the nearest rails of opposing track in the

● **LEFT**
The interior of an older Shinkansen train set of the sort now used on local trains.

● **BOTTOM**
A Tokyo-bound express races through Shizuoka.

● **BELOW**
The fastest regularly scheduled train in the world is the 300 kph (186 mph) Nozomi 500, which makes one round trip from Osaka to Hakata daily. It is seen here stopping at Okayama on its eastbound run.

tunnels has been increased from the standard 1.83 m (6 ft) to between 2.74 m (9 ft) and 2.89 m (9 ft 6 in). Because of the high speed, care also had to be taken when building the embankments to ensure that there was an adequate degree of compactness in the piled-up earth.

From 06.00 to 21.00, a Hikari (Lightning) train leaves Tokyo every 15 minutes and covers the 518 km (322 miles) in three hours and ten minutes – stopping only twice, at Nagoya and Kyoto – at an average speed of over 160 kph (100 mph). Each train consists of 16 cars and carries an average of 1,000 passengers per train.

Because of the tunnels and the high windows in the coaches, travellers do not get a chance to see much of the beautiful scenery the train passes. It is only when the line crosses the broad river valleys that they can appreciate the Japanese countryside and the distant mountains, including Mount Fuji, of which there are magnificent views.

Today the Tokyo-Osaka Shinkansen is the busiest of several Shinkansen routes, with trains departing Tokyo as often as

● RIGHT
A Tokyo-bound Nozomi train nears its destination. The wedge-shaped train sets are usually assigned to either the Nozomi or Hikari trains running between Tokyo, Osaka and Hakata.

INFORMATION BOX	
Termini	Tokyo and Osaka
Country	Japan
Length	518 km (322 miles)
Date of opening	1965

every six minutes at peak travel times. West of Osaka, the Shinkansen extends to Kobe, Okayama, Hiroshima and, by way of an undersea tunnel, to Hakata in the island of Kyushu. (The extension to Okayama opened in 1972, and to Hakata in 1975.) North of Tokyo, the Shinkansen extends to Niigata, Yamagata, Sendai and Morioka on separate routes. (The Morioka line opened in 1982.) Tokyo is the terminal for all lines, and there are no through trains between the western and eastern Shinkansen lines. However, there are regular express trains from Tokyo all the way to Hakata on the Osaka line.

Service is provided by three classes of trains: Kodama local trains, which make freqent stops; Hikari limited-express trains; and Nozomi extra-fare super-express trains. On the Tokyo-Osaka segment, there are now three generations of equipment in service, the newest dating from the early 1990s. The latest equipment is used for the Nozomi service. In March 1997 the Nozomi 500 entered service between Osaka and Hakata. This unmistakable train regularly operates at speeds of up to 300 kph (186 mph) and is now the fastest regularly scheduled train in the world. North of Tokyo, there is a pot-pourri of new train styles in service, including the double-deck "Max" trains.

● LEFT
One of the older Shinkansen train sets pauses to pick up passengers at Shizuoka. Many of these traditional "Bullet Trains" are now used as locals – albeit high-speed ones – while the newer equipment handles more glamorous Hikari and Nozomi express duties.

● BELOW
On a rainy April evening, two express trains pass at speed, while a local makes a station stop at Shizuoka. Service on the Tokyo-Osaka line is fast and frequent.

SINGAPORE TO BANGKOK
THE EASTERN AND ORIENTAL EXPRESS

The Eastern and Oriental (E&O) Express links Singapore, Kuala Lumpur and Bangkok. This luxury train started in 1993 and was the creation of James B. Sherwood, the owner of the Venice Simplon-Orient Express.

It is the world's first sleeping car train with a private shower and toilet in every cabin. The train consists of six standard double-bunk sleepers, seven State twin-bed sleepers and one Presidential double-bed sleeper with dressing-room. The whole totals 132 beds and is air-conditioned throughout with three dining cars, two service cars, a generator car, a bar car and an open-end observation car from which one can smell the jungle and hear the birds and the croaking frogs. The 22 cars are 433 m (1,421 ft) long and weigh 844 tons.

Built in Japan for the New Zealand Railways, the train is wholly redesigned by Frenchman Gérard Gallet, whose

VSOE-type rounded brass handles protect sharp angles in the bar car, with its pale ash panelling, lotus motif décor and clever mirrors. Here the piano tinkles, two fortune tellers attend and the tireless, helpful Thai staff serve drinks late into the night.

In the cabins, the genuine welcome of the Thai personal staff, the elegant diamond-patterned parquetry, set off with antique brass fittings, all convey a

highly civilized atmosphere to the guests. On leaving Singapore, afternoon tea is served, British Straits Settlements style. The sumptuous dining cars offer innovative Eurasian menus with fine wines. The brass torch and Pullman table lamps set off the lacquered Chinese or rare veneer panels, sparkling French glasses and gleaming silverware.

After passing customs at Singapore's Kappel station, the E&O enters Malaysia

INFORMATION BOX

THE EASTERN AND ORIENTAL EXPRESS

Termini	Singapore and Bangkok
Countries	Malaysia and Thailand
Distance	1,943 km (1,207 miles)
Date built	1909–18

● **ABOVE LEFT**
The observation car of the Eastern and Oriental Express, where passengers can admire the outstanding scenery alongside the track.

● **LEFT**
The Eastern and Oriental Express near Kanchanaburi, Thailand.

● **RIGHT**
The Eastern and
Oriental Express at
Kuala Lumpur's
magnificent station.

● **FAR RIGHT**
The Eastern and
Oriental Express
crossing the 800 m
(2,624 ft) long
bridge over the
River Kwai. This
multi-span steel
girder bridge spans
on stone pillars
approximately
4.5 m (15 ft) above
the water.

● **BELOW
RIGHT**
The Eastern and
Oriental Express
crossing the South
East Asian
countryside.

over the 6 km (3¾ mile) long Johor
Bahru causeway. Thereafter, as many have
already experienced, the train makes a
leisurely, varied journey on narrow-gauge
tracks through the Malayan rubber
plantations and primitive jungle, and later
through Thailand's terraced farmlands,
dotted with Buddhist shrines.

The train reaches Kuala Lumpur,
394 km (245 miles) from Singapore –
and the world's most beautiful station –
one hour before midnight. From now on,
the line is on single track and the jungle
closes in. After luncheon on the second
day, the scene begins to change as Karst
Limestone mountains rise from the lush
plains near Padang Besar, where the
Keretapi Tanah Malayu Railways (KTM)
hand over to the State Railways of
Thailand (SRT). On a historical foot-
note, KTM first ran air-conditioned
sleeping cars from Butterworth to
Bangkok as early as 1936.

The next morning, after passing
through Thai terraced farmlands during
the night, the train stops on the east
coast at Hua Hin. It is here that the Thai
royal family spend their holidays, and the
station is magnificent, with its royal

waiting-room flanked by topiary in the
form of elephants. Fresh supplies are
brought aboard here. Later, near Nakhon
Pathom, the express diverts some 70 km
(43 miles) to visit the infamous bridge
over the River Kwai.

Forty-two hours after leaving
Singapore, having travelled 1,943 km
(1,207 miles), the train arrives at
Bangkok's Hualampong station. Most
passengers end their journey here, but it
is possible to spend a third night aboard
by continuing 751 km (467 miles) north
to Chiang Mai.

SINGAPORE TO PENANG

Although the description of this journey has been compiled from notes made on several runs in 1946 when overall timings were low, it is described as if made on one occasion. Fortunately, the whole journey is still possible today, and long may it remain so.

On the day of departure, the "Day Mail" to Kuala Lumpur left from Singapore station at 07.00, not long after dawn. The station at Tanjong Pagar, somewhat out of the centre of the city, was built in 1932 in the European style of the day. At the time of writing, it is still in use and has an impressive high-ceilinged entrance hall with three storeys of offices on one side and a restaurant and hotel on the other. Murals in painted tiles depict scenes on the railway.

The train comprised 12 coaches and two vans and was hauled by a Class 564 Pacific built in 1945. The author's coach

was built in 1935 and rode very well. After departing on time, and the fireman having collected the single-line token from the signalman, the train swung round past the locomotive and carriage sheds at the right. On a siding were small 0-4-0 tank locomotives belonging to the Singapore Harbour Board awaiting disposal. An 0-6-0T of the Federated Malayan States Railway (FMSR), which had been bought to replace them, was on shed together with a couple of MacArthur 2-8-2s, still bearing their

● **TOP**
A MacArthur Class WD10G4 drawing a train out of the carriage shed at Singapore in March 1946.

● **ABOVE LEFT**
The trolley bus was popular in Singapore and Penang. This one, built between the two world wars and pictured in December 1946, is on a service in Georgetown, capital of the island of Penang.

● **LEFT**
On the journey, the traveller passes many villages of which this is typical.

British War Department numbers, a
Japanese C58 2-6-2 and an ex-Javanese
C30 2-6-2T, as well as the resident
FMSR Class I 0-6-2T No. 173 built by
Kitson of Leeds in 1913.

To the left were the sidings serving
the large dock area. Then the train ran
through a mixture of settlements and
open country, now swallowed up by
concrete and steel. Soon the train
reached the famous causeway, 1,080 m
(3,543 ft) long. To the right could be
seen various naval vessels anchored at the
large base.

At Johore Bahru, seat of the Sultan of
Johore, the scene changes dramatically.
Some authors have implied that, because
the railway builders chose to keep the
ruling gradient at 1:100 and followed
contours and natural routes to avoid the
mountains in the interior, there was little
difficulty in construction – but this is not
so. As the land is situated near the
equator and is subject to torrential rains,
numerous watercourses cut across the
line of the railway. Because of the swamps
and tropical rain forest, there were few

INFORMATION BOX

Termini	Singapore and Penang
Country	Malaya
Distance	783 km (487 miles)
Date of travel	1946

established land routes to follow. The
railway had come before track and road,
as most trade went by sea and river.

Consequently, the line twists and
turns, crossing numerous steel bridges
and at times affording tantalizing
glimpses of settlements or sudden distant
views. In places, great rock walls rise
alongside the line and, whether riding in
the coach or taking advantage of the
restaurant/buffet car, an alert traveller
will find much of interest throughout
the journey.

Johore Bahru had a number of sidings
and a locomotive stabling point. Today it
is a frontier station with the usual

disruption to be expected at such places. Heading north, the line was fairly level and straight, passing through jungle alive with wildlife. The jungle had been cut back from the track by 50 m (164 ft) or more, as a security measure, but this was also useful in that it helped to keep natural debris off the line and improved the driver's line of vision. Where the jungle had been cleared, there was mile upon mile of rubber and palm tree plantations interspersed with villages. At Layang-Layang was a particularly extensive plantation with its own narrow-gauge railway system and exchange sidings with the FMSR.

Kluang, 113 km (70 miles) from Singapore, was a place of some importance to the railway and a passing-point. Here, two rail-mounted Jeeps (the famous, little, wartime, rough-country vehicles) lurked in the small, wooden, locomotive depot.

Gemas, 220 km (137 miles) from Singapore, was and is, the junction for the line that cuts across the country for 516 km (321 miles) to Kota Bharu on the east coast. In 1946, Gemas had two 296 m (971 ft) platforms, extensive sidings, a four-road locomotive depot with an 18.2 m (60 ft) turntable and a two-road carriage shed. Movement was controlled by two signal-boxes each with

60 levers, now replaced by a modern 80-lever frame. It was normal for locomotive crews to be changed here.

There is a short climb out of Gemas, and it is just 53 km (33 miles) to Tampin along the main line, which kept as closely as possible to the western side of the peninsula to avoid the central mountain range that rises in places to over 2,133 m (7,000 ft). Tampin was the junction for the 38 km (24 mile) branch to Malacca on the west coast, which was not re-laid after the war.

The next stretch was notable for tin mines and rubber plantations as well as paddy fields, a feature often to be found in areas cleared of jungle. At Seremban, some 61 km (38 miles) further north, was the junction for Port Dickson, which sees only freight traffic now.

In the 59 km (37 miles), to Kuala Lumpur, the whole nature of the scene changed. There were more signs of habitation, and the scars of tin mining became more evident, especially near Sungei Besi, which claimed to have the largest tin mine in the world.

At Salak South Junction a 30-lever signal-box controlled the entrance to the short Sultan Street and Ampang branches, the latter now used for oil traffic. Port Swettenham Junction, 4.8 km

(3 miles) further north, had a 40-lever signal-box covering the entrance to the 43 km (27 mile) long branch to the west coast harbour of Port Swettenham and the Brickfields branch, leading to Kuala Lumpur's large freight yards.

Kuala Lumpur's ornate main passenger station still exists, with four platform faces covered by an overall roof. In 1945, it housed the headquarters of

the FMSR, which now occupies a nearby office block. The two 80-lever signal-boxes have been replaced by a single 80-lever modern box.

Some 900 metres (2,953 ft) to the south of the station on the west side was situated the 28-stall roundhouse with its 18.2 m (60 ft) turntable, pre-heating water plant, mechanical coaler, ash-plant and a workshop. Three large carriage

sheds served by 13 tracks were adjacent to the roundhouse, together with a carriage-washing plant. Both these depots were severely damaged in attacks by the US airforce, and in 1946 the ash-plant and coaler were not functioning and the pre-heating plant was wrecked.

Sentul locomotive, carriage and wagon works was situated about a mile down the Batu Caves branch, which diverged

● **ABOVE LEFT**
A view of Singapore's Chinatown.

● **ABOVE RIGHT**
A Swiss-built funicular railway to Summit Road on Penang Island.

● **RIGHT**
The traveller will see many mosques from the train. One such is the Ubundian Mosque at Kuala Kangsar.

● BELOW
The craft in the foreground was one of the means of getting from the Malayan mainland to Penang Island. The ship in the background was a "prize of war" and renamed *Empire Rani*, 17 April 1947.

● BELOW
Seen in December 1946, No. 402.03, one of the powerful 4-6-4Ts of the FMSR, was used as a "banker" for trains travelling over the Taiping pass.

● BOTTOM
Famous throughout the world for its rubber, this is one of the many Malayan rubber plantations which will be seen from the train.

north-west about 1.6 km (1 mile) from Kuala Lumpur station. The works was divided into two sections by a 61 tonne (60 ton) electrically powered traverser. The section to the south was devoted to locomotive repairs, with iron and brass foundries, pattern shop, tin- and copper-smiths' shops, stores and an electrical sub-station. To the north were the C & W shops, electrical and train lighting repair shops, paint shop, saw mill, smithy and boiler shops.

A short distance north of Kuala Lumpur lies Kuang, the junction for a 23 km (14 mile) long branch to Batang Berjuntai on which, at the half-way point, was situated the coal mine at Batu Arang, which provided steam coal for the FMSR. From here to Tanjong Malim, the 61 km (38 miles) of line ran through open countryside but a depressing sight was the wastelands created by abandoned tin workings.

For the 124 km (77 miles) from Tanjong Malim to the important town of Ipoh, the line runs along the eastern edge of the wide coastal plain and below the foothills of the mountains. The 71 km (44 mile) section to Tapah Road, the junction for the 29 km (18 mile) branch to Telok Anson, a port on the Perak River, is largely through jungle. Tapah Road was also one of the nearest points of access to the mountain resorts in the cool and highly scenic Cameron Highlands to the west of the line.

A 24 km (15 mile) long branch heads off westward to Tromoh. At Falim, approximately 1.6 km (1 mile) down, lies the locomotive depot for Ipoh, a substantial six-road building with a workshop and an 18.2 m (60 ft) turntable. The two-storey station building was imposing, and the station boasted no fewer than five platforms.

For the author, the line from Ipoh to Prai provided the widest variety of scenery on the whole journey, for it includes the climb to the summit of the line through what was generally known as the Taiping pass. From Kuala Kangsa, the railway ascended gently through rubber plantations, but at Padang Rengas the serious climbing began. For all trains of more than 152 tonnes (150 tons), banking locomotives were provided,

usually Class C² 4-6-4T from Taiping
locomotive depot. For 1.6 km (1 mile)
the grade is 1:80, and the scenery
became spectacular as the train twisted
and turned, passing now and again
through tunnels, the longest of which was
345 m (1,132 ft). Emerging from one of
these tunnels, the line crossed a viaduct
providing a splendid view of Gunong
Bondok and the valley of the Perak River.
The line descended for 8.5 km (5¼
miles) from the summit at Bukit Gantang
at the same 1:80 gradient, including in
this section the sharpest main-line curve
of 12 chains (241 m or 792 ft) radius.
The maximum banked load over the pass
was 660 tonnes (650 tons) if the train
engine was a Class S 4-6-2, which had
not only the maximum tractive effort of
13,370 kg (29,477 lbs) but also the
heaviest axle load of 16.25 tonnes (16
tons). The O Class were allowed 559
tonnes (550 tons).

Taiping, in the middle of the Larut
plain, was the centre for the local rubber
plantations and the once extensive tin
mining industry first established there

some 100 years ago. It was the junction
for the 12 km (7½ mile) long Port Weld
branch and there were a number of
sidings. Passengers were served by a
sizeable station with three platform
faces. Not far north of Taiping, the line
passes through low hills, and then there
is an 8 km (5 mile) long stretch of
straight track.

The 69 km (43 miles) from Taiping to
Bukit Mertajam is mostly level, and much

of the terrain is marshy. From Bukit
Mertajam, 775 km (481 miles) from
Singapore, the line to the Siamese
frontier at Padang Besar heads north, but
my train took the short westward branch
to Prai. This was double track, but made
single by the Japanese. From Prai, I hired
a native craft to take me across to
Butterworth, from where the FMSR
ferry was then running to the main town
on Penang Island, Georgetown.

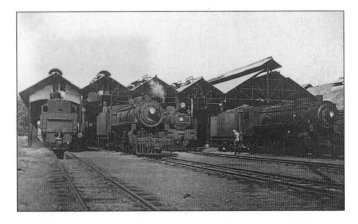

TANAHABANG TO RANGKASBITUNG

The account of this journey has been compiled from notes taken in August 1974. The journey is still possible today and is highly recommended.

Since the coaches were already packed with people, I decided to travel on the engine. There were 75 people already mounted on that locomotive – a modest 3 ft 6 in gauge secondary line diesel – of whom 23 were in the cab and the remainder on the front, sides and top. Undaunted I was hauled aboard.

Upon leaving the station, the train gingerly threaded its way through a maze of dwellings – colonization of the sidings and the disused rolling stock being considerable. One metre (3¼ ft) from the lines lay tightly packed dwellings, a mixture of tile, thatch and wood. We passed close to line-side stalls which, but for 7.6 cm (3 in), would have been collapsed by the engine.

INFORMATION BOX

Termini	Tanahabang and Rangkasbitung
Country	Indonesia
Distance	*c.* 70 km (43 miles)
Date of travel	August 1974

● **LEFT**
This scene at Kediri shows the "sandman", whose job it is to sit on the front of the locomotive and spray the tracks with sand to prevent slipping during the frequent tropical storms.

But this colourful scene, which stretched over a considerable distance, was tinged on this occasion with another pleasure, for the simple, delightful Indonesian state flag – the upper half red, the lower white – fluttered gaily and riotously from every building, wagon and stall. It was 18 August – Independence Day. During the week of celebrations even the locomotives bear flags, attached to special mounts incorporated on to the smokebox tops.

The journey was excruciatingly bad. The diesel crawled indolently along and stops were frequent. We had scarcely covered 16 km (10 miles) before even the locals were beginning to look drowsy. The driver was wedged up in a far corner of the cab from which he could see a little of the track ahead – presumably some agreement existed with the horde on the buffer beams that, should an

● **LEFT**
A typical sugar plantation scene on Java, showing the temporary track beds, which bring the wagons of loaded cane to the main-line railway. The locomotive, which patiently waits in the background, was built in Leeds, England.

Indonesian
Independence Day
celebrations on 18
August 1974, and
the state flag flutters
gaily on the smoke-
box top of Class B51
No. 39, a two-
cylinder 4-4-0 built
by Werkspoor of
Amsterdam. This
scene at the
locomotive shed at
Rangkasbitung
features a C27 4-6-
4T in the back-
ground, an engine
also built by
Werkspoor and
dating back to 1919.

● BELOW
A typical Javan sugar plantation worker
suitably attired for protection from the razor-
sharp leaves and stems of the sugar cane.

emergency arise, they must bang on the
engine's sides. Such conditions underline
part of the malaise of the Perusahaan
Negara Kereta Api (Indonesian State
Railways), in that the only passengers
who ever pay on a PNKA line are those
unfortunate individuals who dutifully
remain in the compartment or are unable
to escape the ticket-collector either by
climbing out on to the coach roof or
by obtaining another, equally precarious
place on the train by any of 20 or more
hazardous methods.

The engine, of course, is the driver's
preserve; few ticket-collectors ever
infiltrate that domain. My compassion for
the driver on this trip was put sharply
into perspective when the hat came
round. This was the driver's collection –
half the price of the normal fare, no
tickets issued and no questions asked.
Had I really thought the engine crew
would suffer such discomfort for
nothing? Honour among thieves was

never better epitomized than by the way
in which the hat finally did the round of
the engine compartment and was
dutifully returned to the driver full of the
passengers' rupiahs.

A plume of rich brown smoke erupted
from the loop ahead. We were crossing
with an eastbound steam train. Despite
the barrage of flags, I detected the

familiar outline of a Class 27 4-6-4T,
built by Armstrong Whitworth of
Newcastle upon Tyne in 1922, hauling an
unbelievably well patronized six-coach
Independence Day Special. Nearly five
hours after leaving Tanahabang, the
journey over the Javan paddy fields was
over as the train crawled into the small
town of Rangkasbitung.

● LEFT
A Class C12 06, seen
against one of Java's
famous sunsets,
following the
Independence Day
celebrations.

RANGKASBITUNG TO LABUAN

The unintended journey started with my inspection of a Werkspoor engine of 1909, a B51, which was standing idle in a siding at Rangkasbitung. Utterly fascinated, I entered the vacant cab. However, the Javan crew soon arrived and with an incomprehensible acknowledgement of my presence proceeded to back down on to a rake of decrepit rolling stock lying in the station. Suddenly the engine moved forward, and the unexpected journey began.

I had no idea where I was going and, although the crew were friendly enough, the language barrier made communication impossible. The epic way in which B5138 stormed out of Rangkasbitung that evening did justice to her Prussian lineage as, with trilling

● **BELOW**
The constant flurry of sparks that emanate from the chimneys of Java's steam locomotives is epitomized in this scene of a Class B50 2-4-0 built by Sharp Stewart of Manchester in 1885.

● **BOTTOM**
A typically decrepit Javan passenger-train, consisting of wooden-bodied four-wheeled coaches and hauled by B50 2-4-0 No. 14.

whistle, she charged through the suburbs and out of town.

Although the B51 burned a mixture of coal, wood and oil, during the journey's early stages the fireman was principally using coal. Dusk was rapidly advancing and soon our engine was pumping black exhaust into an azure sky, a pungently smelling frothy smoke, which continually swept round the cab and down the train. Our speed was greater than I had thought possible as the engine ferociously headed through the darkening landscape. The veteran's violent lurching over the rough track beds was stimulating enough, though on the few occasions when she was eased a pleasant aroma of coal smoke wafted back through the fire-hole door and into the cab.

INFORMATION BOX

Termini	Rangkasbitung and Labuan
Country	Indonesia
Distance	*c.* 55 km (34 miles)
Date of travel	August 1974

Darkness had fallen by the time we reached the first station – a wayside halt, which only merited our presence for a matter of seconds.

Soon the drama returned in all its affray. A hiss of steam escaping from the front end became audible and made an exciting foil to the throbbing rasps of exhaust. Speed mounted terrifyingly, and the engine became a mass of churning, pulsating machinery. The whistle screamed and wailed in long eerie bursts as we sped past lonely villages and small ungated crossings, but remote as we were and dark as it was, a few ox carts could invariably be discerned momentarily lit up by the swirling incandescence of B5138's fire.

Without warning she hit a downgrade, and the engine was really opened out. The roar became hypnotic. It was impossible to estimate our speed, the darkness outside revealing nothing from which a bearing might be taken. The crew, bathed in a shimmering orange glow, clung tenaciously to the cab sides. The fire, white hot, lit up the black exhaust trail, which raced in a swirling slipstream above the cab roof. It certainly felt as if we could to all intents and purposes have been hitting one hundred miles per hour (160 kph)!

I had come to Indonesia to find a locomotive dinosaur and by perfect fortune had found one in triumphant full cry – the last of her breed, a Prussian phantom and a living ghost of the great 19th-century steam age. With many kilometres now behind us it seemed that the country was beginning to flatten out and fireflies could be seen over the rice fields. It was about this time that our coal supply ran out, and the logs that had hitherto been ignored came into their own. The B51 responded in a flurry of sparks, brilliantly cascading in the paths of the fireflies. Suddenly, as the train sped onwards through different terrain, the fireflies were left behind, and, like the eclipse of a fireworks display observed with the awe of childhood, the magic was gone.

Soon we slowed down and speckled lights could be seen ahead. We had reached our destination.

● **ABOVE**
An Indonesian State Railways Class B51 4-4-0 takes water at Rangkasbitung. The Prussian ancestry of this German-built veteran of 1902 is in full evidence.

● **LEFT**
A brace of Class B51 4-4-0s – including No. 38 on which the footplate journey took place – raise steam in the depot yard at Labuan.

PORT AUGUSTA TO ALICE SPRINGS
THE GHAN

The heart of Australia has seen little potential for development beyond minerals and cattle stations. To serve the few hardy settlers who ventured into this harsh country in the early days, Afghans brought in the supplies with their camel teams. As the need for transport grew, the South Australian government commenced the construction of a narrow-gauge railway from Port Augusta in South Australia, first to serve the anticipated wheat and wool traffic in the false belief that "rain would follow the plough", and then to tap the minerals and cattle from further north.

The line to Hergott Springs, now Marree, was opened for traffic in 1884. This was the end of the famous Birdsville Track and a meeting-point for several cattle-driving routes. Three mixed trains a week handled the traffic. Beyond there, the line was constructed as Unemployment Relief and in 1891 reached Oodnadatta, 769 km (478 miles)

● **LEFT**
Following World War II, the Commonwealth Railways imported luxurious air-conditioned cars from Wegmann in Germany for the transcontinental service between Port Augusta and Kalgoorlie. These included a rounded observation car, seen here at Port Augusta in 1964.

INFORMATION BOX

THE GHAN

Termini	Port Augusta and Alice Springs
Country	Australia
Distance	1,240 km (770 miles)
Date of opening	1891

from Port Augusta. At first, one mixed train a week handled this extension, but this was soon reduced to one a fortnight, with trains averaging 19 kph (12 mph). In 1911 the Commonwealth Government became owners of the line, but did not take control of operations until 1916. They continued building the line, supposed to continue on to Darwin on the northern coast, stopping construction at Alice Springs, 471 km (293 miles) further north. The mixed

● **LEFT**
Early settlers believed that rain would follow the plough and called this place Farina, hoping it would become the heart of the wheat belt of South Australia. But rain did not follow, and the fields had to be abandoned. Little remained when this enthusiast special Ghan travelled the standard gauge of the 1964 period. Today, even the rails are gone as a new standard-gauge route further west bypasses this area.

An NM Class steam locomotive of the
Commonwealth Railways, with a water gin,
heads a tour train through the scenic Pichi
Richi pass.

train that served this line became known
as "The Ghan" in honour of the previous
traders. This ran twice a week, while
another service known as the "slow"
travelled weekly.

Travelling on the Ghan was truly an
adventure. The first section of the line
through the Pichi Richi Pass was very
scenic; its magnificent river gum trees are
a notable feature of an area currently
exploited by rail enthusiasts running the
Pichi Richi Railway. The line continued
alongside and through the Flinders
Ranges, made famous by many painters
in Australia, and then through flat salt
bush country and on to Marree. Between
there and Alice Springs, the lightly
ballastered track was subject to sand
drifts and on occasions to sudden
downpours that caused washaways,
making the route impassable until repairs
could be effected. Passengers starting out
on what was supposed to be a three-day
journey could suddenly find themselves
marooned in the desert for up to several
weeks, with food drops from aircraft not
being uncommon.

As the narrow-gauge route through
the Pichi Richi pass and the Flinders
Ranges limited the loads hauled, a new
standard-gauge line was constructed to
join the old route near Brachina, beyond
which the line was standardized to
Marree. In view of the problems with the
line beyond Marree, it was decided in the
1970s to build a complete new standard-
gauge line from near Port Augusta on a
more direct route to Alice Springs
bypassing virtually all of the old route,
leaving everywhere beyond the Leigh
Creek coalfields to more or less disappear.

Today, with standard gauge reaching
Adelaide's suburbs, the only adventure on
this trip — weekly in summer and twice
weekly in the cooler months — is the taxi
journey out of town to the standard-
gauge terminal, no doubt put there to
discourage patronage. From there, you
ride a luxury air-conditioned train in
pampered comfort. The wonders of the
"Red Heart" of Australia are certainly
well worth seeing, but it is not
recommended in summer for those not
prepared for temperatures that can rise
as high as 50°C (122°F).

● ABOVE
The real railway adventure in Australia was "The Ghan", originally all
narrow gauge, running from Port Augusta in South Australia to Alice
Springs in the Northern Territory. The starting-point was the exchange
platform at Port Augusta.

● ABOVE
An early vehicle used in Government Railway days in the vicinity of the
Pichi Richi pass was a Kitson steam rail motor. Coffee Pot, as it is
affectionately known, has been restored and is again in periodic service
for tourist groups. Here it is undergoing servicing in the Quorn
workshops of the Pichi Richi Railway.

SYDNEY TO BRISBANE
THE BRISBANE EXPRESS

● **BELOW**
The express on the long and arduous ascent to
Toowoomba. The vehicle behind the second
locomotive is a water gin, which is used to
augment the supply in the engines' tenders.

In the 1960s, two trains running on
entirely different routes were both called
the Brisbane Express. For travellers in a
hurry, and with little interest in the
journey itself, there was the one using the
newer 1,035 km (643 mile) coastal route,
much of the journey being done in
darkness. This service was actually divided
into two, with the Brisbane Limited
Express doing the journey in 15½ hours
and the slower Brisbane Express following
in 17 hours and 50 minutes.

For the tourist, the older route had far
more to offer, and although it did include
a night section, enjoyable stretches of
scenic country were traversed in daylight.
By the 1965 timetable, an early
afternoon departure of 13.55 meant that
the descent of the Cowan Bank and the
crossing of the Hawkesbury River would
be done in good light, as would the run
along the shores of Brisbane Waters.
There was well inhabited country as far
as Wyong and then timbered hilly
country nearly to Broadmeadow, the
junction for trains to Newcastle. This was
coal mining country, and a considerable
amount of coal traffic would be seen on

the way to Maitland, where the shorter
coastal route branched off to the north.
The "Main" route continued westwards
through relatively flat dairy country to
Singleton, passing through there about
dusk. In the darkness, the line began a
gradual climb towards the foothills of the
Great Dividing Range via Murrurundi,
the depot town for push-up and assistant
engines used by heavy traffic crossing the
range from both directions. The ruling
gradient there was 1:40 on both sides,
and provided many a spectacle as
locomotives struggled up the 8 km
(5 miles) of steep bank to Ardglen tunnel.

To the west of the range, the line
dropped in easier stages to Tamworth
before climbing the Moonbi Range to the
Northern Tablelands. Daylight came in
the beautiful hilly country before
Tenterfield, the last major town before
the Queensland border. Less than 18 km
(11 miles) brought the train to the
border and the change-of-gauge station at
Wallangarra. Here the narrow-gauge
express to Brisbane waited to continue
the journey through more scenic hilly
country to some of the finest rural land

INFORMATION BOX

THE BRISBANE EXPRESS

Termini	Sydney and Brisbane
Country	Australia
Distance	1,150 km (715 miles)
Date of opening	1888

● **ABOVE**
The famous and familiar sight of Sydney Harbour Bridge.

● **OPPOSITE BOTTOM**
One of the world's best-known landmarks is Sydney Opera House.

● **BELOW LEFT**
The view from Sydney centre looking down William Street to King's Cross.

● **BELOW RIGHT**
Part of the climb facing the early Brisbane-Sydney expresses near Toowoomba in Queensland. The diesel-hauled goods train is carefully easing itself down the first part of the descent towards Brisbane, Toowoomba being just over the crest in the middle background.

in Australia, the Darling Downs. After 5½ hours, the train reached the beautiful city of Toowoomba, famous for the magnificent gardens created by the local inhabitants.

The descent of the mountains from Toowoomba was an immensely scenic but very time-consuming journey. Because of this, the Queensland Railways had a co-ordinated bus/rail service between Toowoomba and Helidon at the bottom of the range, and Brisbane-bound travellers could spend over an hour in Toowoomba, eating, sightseeing or

whatever. They could then catch the bus and rejoin the train at Heildon for the final run into Brisbane. This option, however, meant that they missed much of the beauty of that part of the journey. In the reverse direction, Toowoomba dwellers could get home an hour ahead of the train by using the bus. The arrival in Brisbane would be shortly after dusk at 18.26 – 28½ hours after leaving Sydney, a run of 1,150 km (715 miles). Today this journey is no more, as a considerable length of the line from Glen Innes to the Queensland border has been abandoned.

BROKEN HILL TO ADELAIDE
THE BROKEN HILL EXPRESS

For centuries, man has dreamed of the pot of gold at the end of the rainbow, and prospectors have trudged into the wilderness in search of their fortune.

Few areas could have been more dismal than the country near the South Australian-New South Wales border. However, as early as 1876, galena (lead sulphide) was found on the NSW side, and by 1883 the Silverton area was booming with mines and even smelters. In the same year, galena was discovered at Broken Hill. The South Australian Government, seeing the potential of the area, hastily built a narrow-gauge line from Peterborough (then Petersburg) to the border, reaching there in January 1887, but it was not permitted to cross the border by the NSW government. This led to the formation of the private Silverton Tramway Company, later known as Broken Hill's gold mine. By this time Silverton, a town with 36 hotels, was declining rapidly. However, Broken Hill, though now declining, has been a boom town for all this century.

Though in NSW, Broken Hill is included in the South Australian time zone, and most commercial business is

● **ABOVE**
Between Terowie and Adelaide, the broad-gauge Broken Hill Express could have been handled by a variety of locomotives, the most eye-catching being the streamlined 520 Class. For a short period, the 23 km (14 miles) between Terowie and the main junction town of Peterborough had a third trail added to eliminate a short journey on narrow gauge where the standard gauge reached Peterborough. Here No. 526 works a broad-gauge route to Adelaide, that spelt the end of this section, leaving the once important break-of-gauge town of Terowie to become a ghost town.

● **BELOW**
The Broken Hill Express travelled most of its journey in darkness. Enthusiasts wishing to re-create the journey in daylight arranged for South Australian Railway's Garratt No. 402 to haul the train, seen here passing the isolated Mannahill station heading north.

conducted with the closer capital city of Adelaide. To make this connection a regular train service connected the two cities, with the Broken Hill Express being one of the few passenger expresses in Australia hauled for many years by Garratt locomotives. The others were in Queensland. This was basically an overnight service, and the South Australian Railway (SAR) built up the tonnage with freight wagons, thereby making it a mixed train.

To the east of the border, the Silverton Tramway Company, with its 58 km (36 miles) of line, provided the locomotives and a percentage of the freight wagons. The original locomotives were Colonial Moguls, followed in 1912 by the A Class, very English-looking 4-6-0s. In 1951, the W Class 4-8-2 semi-streamlined locomotives, similar to those used in Western Australia, took over before being replaced by 673kW Co-Co diesel electrics from 1960 to 1970, when the standard gauge bypassed the private line.

Early traffic on the South Australian side was handled by Y or X Class Moguls, but with the growing traffic bigger locomotives were soon needed, with the Chief Mechanical Engineer designing the highly successful T Class 4-8-0s, 78 of which were built from 1903 onwards, with some remaining in service right to

● **ABOVE**
The Broken Hill
Express was worked
by the Silverton
Tramway Company
on the New South
Wales side of the
border and a South
Australian Garratt
on their side of the
fence. Here we see a
re-enactment of the
border change.

the end of the steam era. These brought
the train 225 km (140 miles) to Terowie,
where one changed to the broad gauge,
with an S Class 4-4-0 continuing the
225 km (140 mile) journey to Adelaide
until the arrival of larger engines of the
Webb era in the mid-1920s.

In 1953, the 400 Class Garratts
arrived and rapidly took over the Broken
Hill traffic. From 1959, the SAR began

● **ABOVE
RIGHT**
The Adelaide
skyline.

● **RIGHT**
This plant, called
Black Boy, is
common along the
route of the Broken
Hill Express.

acquiring 830 Class Co-Co diesel
electrics, which eventually replaced steam
on this semi-desert route. This
standardization rang the death knell for
the Broken Hill Express with the Indian
Pacific eventually taking over the
passenger traffic on the line and the
broad-gauge services being withdrawn
from Terowie.

According to a 1953 timetable, the
Broken Hill Express would depart
from Broken Hill at 19.48 behind a
Silverton W Class, covering what was
possibly the most scenic part of this
semi-desert journey in darkness to the
border, arriving at 21.21. Here a 400
Class Garratt took over for the run to
Peterborough, where passengers for Port
Pirie had to make an 03.58 change of
train. From there the train reversed, with
a new locomotive for the short run to
Terowie, where Adelaide passengers
changed to the broad gauge at 04.50.
After a 20-minute allowance for
refreshments, the broad-gauge train
headed for an 09.20 arrival in Adelaide.

BRISBANE TO CAIRNS
THE SUNSHINE RAIL EXPERIENCE

Probably more than the other Australian states, Queensland relied on coastal shipping to service the large number of ports on its long coastline. This resulted in railways being built, but not along the coast. They were built as isolated lines running inland from the various ports. As passengers began demanding quicker and more reliable services from Brisbane to the northern centres, the Government began constructing lines to connect the various isolated sections. It was, however, not until the end of 1924 that it was possible to travel all the way, 1,679 km (1,043 miles), to Cairns in the far north.

The lines were lightly built with low-level bridges not far above the river beds. To the Government's surprise, the railways gained a considerable amount of goods traffic, and rural industry, particularly sugar, expanded rapidly. In the beginning, a trip to the north took 52 hours, which included a 24-hour stay in Townsville along the way. Services were soon improved, with the 1950 Sunshine Express departing Brisbane at 20.00 and arriving at Cairns two days later at 16.00.

However, time brought great changes. First came dieselization, and then the gaining of massive coal contracts by mines inland from the coastal ports. Lines had to be upgraded and realigned in many areas, new bridges built and Centralized Traffic Control introduced. Steam trains could handle a reasonable depth of floodwater when there was no

● **ABOVE**
One of the attractions of Kuranda are the waterfalls.

● **ABOVE**
No trip to Cairns in the far north of Queensland is complete without the final excursion to Kuranda, battling up the cliff faces with magnificent views of the coast, cane fields, rain forest, waterfalls and finally the enchanting market village of Kuranda.

● **ABOVE**
When steam was king in Queensland, the expresses between Brisbane and Cairns would have been worked by these beautiful BB18 1/4 Class Pacifics with their comfortable wooden coaches. A tour train stands at Nambour, typifying an express of the period. Parochial rail fans from interstate would often sing "I'll Walk Beside You" whenever Queensland trains were mentioned – hardly fair, as they provided a very efficient and reasonably speedy service in steam days and are now probably the most modern in the country.

● LEFT
The dieselized air-conditioned Sunlander express rumbles through the cane fields near Feluga in North Queensland in 1971.

appreciable current. With one leading, and another locomotive at the rear to steady the train, they could run down into a river and work their way across. This was completely out of the question for a diesel electric, so new high-level bridges were a must.

In the late 1950s, Queensland's magnificent Garratts brought 406 tonnes (400 tons) of coal to the coast. In the 1980s, six diesel electric locomotives, three leading and three in the middle of the train with Locotrol radio control, were bringing in over 10,000 tonnes (10,160 tons) at a time.

Electrification was the answer for this heavy traffic, and coal lines were electrified together with the coastal line from Brisbane to Rockhampton in 1989. Now luxury express trains such as the Queenslander cover the distance to Cairns in only 32 hours and 5 minutes.

With the connection of the isolated systems, to build maintenance depots for the new locomotives and railcars all over the State would have been a costly exercise, so most major work was carried out near Brisbane. Some person capable of lateral thinking, realizing that returning rail motors from the branch lines for periodic overhaul over this great distance was a slow and costly exercise, came up with the idea of using the trips to carry tourists, with local sightseeing trips laid on as a feature during the driver's rest periods.

While the expresses race over the distance in less than one-and-a-half days three times a week, the rail motor

exchange has developed into an exciting weekly six-day train tour, now with a loco-hauled train. It includes accommodation in quality hotels overnight and numerous trips to points of special interest, such as a boat tour to the Barrier Reef.

Unlike most lengthy rail journeys in Australia, there is no let up to the magnificent scenery for the full length of the railway line, be it Mother Nature or the rural properties, which are seen at their best in early spring. For the rail fan, too, there is the heavy traffic to be seen *en route*, and during the cane season, from August to November, a multitude of 2 ft gauge trains are busy rushing cane to the mills and sugar to the ports. Indeed, the highlights of the journey are not over on reaching Cairns. Further exciting rail trips can be started from there, such as the magnificent climb to Kuranda, rising along the cliff face past waterfalls, or, with the help of buses, tours can reach the Mount Surprise line and the famous Croydon-Normanton line.

INFORMATION BOX

Termini	Brisbane and Cairns
Country	Australia
Distance	1,679 km (1,043 miles)
Date of opening	1924

● RIGHT
The train from Cairns approaches Kurunda.

PORT KEMBLA TO MOSS VALE
THE COCKATOO RUN

● LEFT
Several short
journeys can often
provide more
pleasure and
excitement than one
long journey lacking
in variety. A day trip
in NSW is the
Cockatoo Run from
Port Kembla to
Moss Vale and
return. A stop is
made at Summit
Tank for passengers
to experience the
magnificent view
over the coastline.

In a deal involving the establishment of a steelworks at Port Kembla in New South Wales, the Government agreed to construct a railway line up the steep mountainsides to connect the new industrial area with the Main Southern Railway at Moss Vale, thus providing a shorter and cheaper link to the interstate markets in the south. The new line, approximately 70 km (43 miles) in length, was opened in 1932 and has handled heavy goods traffic, mainly coal, limestone and steel products, ever since.

Passenger-traffic has been rather light, as much of the line is through a water catchment area where the entry of people, the worst polluters, is discouraged. This passenger-traffic was usually handled by rail motors or two- and three-car passenger-trains. Many of the travellers have been tourists, as this is the most scenic line in NSW, rivalled only by the now abandoned Dorrigo branch.

The line leaves the coastal Illawarra line at Unanderra and almost immediately starts on a 1:30 gradient with magnificent views of the coast. This steep gradient is almost continuous until Summit Tank, some 20 km (12½ miles) up the mountainside. While the coast cannot be seen from the line at Summit Tank, time has always been allowed for tourists to walk a few steps to a lookout on the cliff edge for a view of the coast.

As this relatively short section of track became congested during World War II, with heavy steam-hauled goods trains taking over an hour in the section, it became necessary to provide a crossing loop within the section. Due to the difficult terrain, the Dombarton crossing facility was unique in NSW. Trains ascended up the mountainside and branched off to the left into a level dead-end siding on a slight rise. This rise gave the train a start for rejoining the main line, on its left, on to another dead-end

● LEFT
As the Port Kembla-
Moss Vale line in
NSW competed for
first place as the
State's most scenic
line, fairly regular
triple-headed tours
were run over this
steep line. Here in
1966 at Ocean View,
approaching the
summit of the line,
three of the famous
P or C32 Class
locomotives struggle
up the grade
towards some
enthusiastic
photographers.

● **LEFT**
In the days of government operation of passenger services on the route of the Cockatoo Run, this traffic was usually handled by railmotors or short trains hauled by a tank-engine. Here a C-30 Class tank-engine bites into the 1:30 grade with a few light carriages, a short distance out of Port Kembla in 1967.

INFORMATION BOX	
Termini	Port Kembla and Moss Vale
Country	Australia
Distance	70 km (43 miles)
Date of opening	1932

siding parallel to that used by the ascending trains. When the line was clear, the train backed into the first dead-end siding used by the ascending trains before again proceeding downhill. This parallel siding for descending trains also gave some protection to the other train in the case of a runaway. The line is also subject to rock falls, and concrete shelters similar to snowsheds have been erected in the worst sections to protect it.

Summit Tank, at 579 m (1,900 ft) above sea level, is a normal crossing loop and has a turntable for turning the third locomotive used to assist heavy goods trains, and allow it to return to the coast. From here the grade eases, with even a few downward stretches and with nothing worse than 1:60 compensated for curvature to the highest point near St Anthony's. Beyond here, it is relatively flat all the way to Moss Vale.

Dieselization improved running times and increased train loads, but it also brought problems. The slow continuous grind up the mountainside, with no activity required from the driver and the

continuous rumble of the motor behind him, lulled drivers to sleep and resulted in two head-on smashes. This hastened the introduction of "vigilance controls" on locomotives, forcing drivers to react at quite short intervals, and thus keeping them alert. Today, the goods traffic continues, but passenger traffic is handled by an enthusiast group known as 3801 Limited who run trains four times a week. Steam haulage is used, except in the summer months when a diesel hydraulic locomotive substitutes.

● **ABOVE RIGHT**
Once off the train, there are some unique road signs to be seen.

● **RIGHT**
This journey passes some beautiful coastal scenery.

SYDNEY TO PERTH
FROM THE PACIFIC TO THE INDIAN OCEAN

Although railway construction in Australia proceeded in earnest from the 1850s, it was not until 1917 that it was possible to cross the continent from ocean to ocean, a distance then of 4,352 km (2,704 miles) by rail. When this journey became possible, Australia was caught up in a muddle of different railway gauges, making this trip quite an adventure for travellers who were rail enthusiasts, but something of a nightmare for those who were not. The current route is standard gauge and fairly direct, but in those days it was necessary to travel via Melbourne and Adelaide.

According to timetables published shortly after the opening of the transcontinental line, a traveller from Sydney would board his standard gauge train at 19.25 on, say, Sunday evening and travel throughout the night to the Victorian border at Albury, where at 07.23 he had 23 minutes to change to a broad-gauge train that would arrive at Melbourne at 12.51. Here there was another change, to a broad-gauge train

● **LEFT**
A triple restoration: the Great Zigzag on the western side of the Blue Mountains in NSW, with Queensland Railway's express passenger locomotive BB18 1/4 No. 1072 hauling a set of ex-South Australian narrow-gauge cars. The popularity of this restored feat of engineering has resulted in trains running daily through this spectacular countryside for the pleasure of tourists.

INFORMATION BOX	
Termini	Sydney and Perth
Country	Australia
Distance	3,961 km (2,461 miles) since 1970
Date of opening	1917

departing at 16.30 and again travelling overnight to arrive in Adelaide, South Australia, at 09.55 on Tuesday. Fifty minutes later, he would be on yet another broad-gauge train (no through carriages on any of these services) northwards to Terowie, where half an hour was allowed for refreshments and a change to a narrow-gauge train. This then worked its way by a circuitous route to Port Augusta,

● **LEFY**
An XPT Intercity express speeds along the deviation, including ten tunnels, that was used to bypass the old zigzag at Lithgow. The viaducts and old formation now carry tourists in 3 ft 6 in gauge regular services.

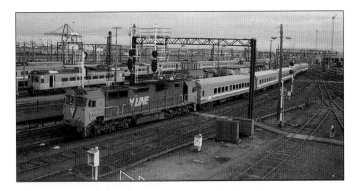

arriving at 22.05 on Tuesday for the next change – this time a standard-gauge train for the journey across the Nullarbor Plains.

Over a day and a half would now be spent crossing this semi-desert, with the longest straight in the world, 478 km (297 miles), to reach the gold-mining town of Kalgoorlie at 13.38 on Thursday. Here he had a lengthier stop, no doubt for a little tourist activity, as the narrow-gauge express to Perth did not leave until 17.15, with an 09.47 arrival at Perth on Friday morning. The whole journey had taken just over four-and-a-half days, allowing for the two-hour time difference between the two sides of the continent. For the period, the trains were suitably comfortable, but these stops and changes – and the scramble for food, supplied at stations and not on the train – must have been somewhat irritating.

It was not until 1969 that the route via Broken Hill to Perth was completely standardized, and in 1970 the Indian Pacific service was inaugurated, cutting the journey down to 3,961 km (2,461 miles) and a running time of just over two-and-a-half days. Since then, a standard-gauge line has been laid almost into Adelaide and, unlike European railway systems that would provide through cars, for use from Melbourne through Adelaide to Port Pirie to attach to the train, the Indian Pacific takes a lengthy and time-consuming side jaunt from near Crystal Brook to Keswick in the Adelaide suburbs and back. This must cause frustration to through passengers.

Today, after departing from the Sydney terminal at 14.55, the train is soon through Sydney's inner suburbs and at Blacktown is on the "speedway", a fairly straight and level run on which trains are known to attain their best speeds. After

crossing the Hawkesbury River beyond Penrith, the train begins the climb into the Blue Mountains. The current route is the third ascent of the mountains, the first having been a zigzag. This starts as a cut on the side of a cliff face with spectacular views. A 1:60 grade is fairly consistent as far as Valley Heights, where the real climb begins. Originally, this was continuous 1:30 with numerous 8 chain (20 m/66 ft) radius curves, but most of these curves have been improved to better than 11 chains and the grade to 1:33. Spectacular views continue to the western descent. Beautiful rolling agricultural country continues as far as Parkes, but by now the train is running in darkness. From there it is semi-desert almost all the way to Perth.

● **ABOVE**
Prior to the standardization of the east-west route across Australia, most travellers would have preferred the journey through Melbourne to the slow narrow-gauge journey from Broken Hill in NSW to Port Pirie in South Australia. Now, having lost this traffic, Melbourne is still a very busy railway centre, as seen in this view of the approaches to Spencer Street station.

● **BELOW**
As in many parts of the world, Australia has seen a decline in rail passenger traffic in recent years. Thirty years ago, many of the major expresses, especially at holiday time, had to be run in several divisions to cope with the loading. The Overland, making the connection between Melbourne and Adelaide on the east-west route, was one such train. The second division is seen here crossing the Murray River Bridge.

BROKEN HILL TO SULPHIDE JUNCTION

Although passenger expresses tend to dominate railway enthusiasts' records, there is one goods train that has achieved an equal fame. This was simply known as the W-44 block ore concentrate train from Broken Hill to Sulphide Junction.

Although the South Australian Railways had been reaping the revenue from silver, lead and zinc ore haulage from the rich Broken Hill mines since 1888, the New South Wales Railway did not enter competition until 1927. This was at the same time that the east coast was joined to the isolated Menindee to Broken Hill line. Sulphide Corporation had already established zinc smelters at Cockle Creek, near Newcastle, and had been taking the Broken Hill ore by train over 400 km (249 miles) to Port Pirie in South Australia. They then shipped it another 2,000 km (1,243 miles) by sea to Newcastle for further transfer to Cockle Creek. The new line made it possible to take the ore by train 1,252 km

(778 miles) direct to the smelter.

The first part of this journey to be affected was the semi-desert area between Broken Hill and Parkes, where steam haulage was rapidly replaced by 49 Class Co-Co units. These 875 hp units were specially pressurized to keep out the

dust on this 679 km (422 mile) first stretch over hot and dusty plains. The block train consisted of 16-bogie concentrate wagons and a brake van totalling 1,036 tonnes, (1,020 tons) with a typical departure from Broken Hill at 11.30 for arrival at Parkes 03.24 the next

● **ABOVE**
A New South Wales 3644 assists Garratt 6014 with a heavy Western goods at Borenore in 1966. Seventy-five of the 4-6-0 (C)36 Class, known affectionately as "Pigs", were built for express passenger-traffic from 1925 but ended their days on express goods. The 42 (AD)60 Class Garratts were the main goods power at the end of steam.

● **LEFT**
The journey takes the traveller through the Blue Mountains National Park.

INFORMATION BOX

Termini	Broken Hill and Sulphide Junction
Country	Australia
Distance	1,252 km (778 miles)
Date of opening	1927

morning. Here the story changes as the diesel was replaced by a Garratt steam locomotive assisted by a "Standard Goods" Consolidation or a 36 Class 4-6-0 express locomotive relegated from passenger services. The train now faced a ruling grade of 1:60 to travel the 86 km (53 miles) to Molong in 3 hours and 20 minutes, arriving at 10.00. Here there was another change, as the assistant engine came off and was replaced by a modified Garratt. These modified units had enlarged cylinders, while the addition of duplicate controls allowed the crew to face the direction of running when working in reverse.

This new Garratt was attached with the bunker leading to remove the smoke nuisance later in the journey when working hard through the Marangaroo tunnel. At 10.35 the two monsters thundered through clouds of automotive

dust towards the 1:40 grades *en route* to Orange East Folk. The modified Garratt then continued unaided to Bathers, received assistance up the Raglan Bank, and then went on alone again to Lithgow.

Lithgow is the beginning of the crossing of the Blue Mountains, and in earlier days the climb was started with a zigzag. This was replaced in 1911 by a double track through ten tunnels. Nevertheless, the start of the climb was 1:42 around an 8-chain (20 m/66 ft) curve, and prior to electrification heavy goods trains had two Standard Goods and NSW's most powerful non-articulated locomotive, the 57 Class Mountain,

leading, with a further Standard Goods pushing from the rear – a sight and sound never to be surpassed.

W-44 had two 49 Class electric locomotives over this stretch, with one coming off at Newnes Junction and the remaining unit continuing onwards. At Katoomba, at the top of the 1:33 descending grade, the train was stopped and grade-control valves set before a safe journey down the mountains could be started. These grade-control valves permitted only a very slow release of the Westinghouse Brakes, giving the locomotive time to recharge the air reservoirs between brake applications on the long descent. On joining the Main Northern Line, an additional 46 Class assisted to the then end of electrification at Gosford. At 01.24 a modified Garratt with Standard Goods assistance departed on the final leg of the journey, arriving at Sulphide Junction at 03.28.

● **ABOVE**
One of the many fine views of the Blue Mountains to be experienced on the journey to Sulphide Junction.

● **RIGHT**
The final leg of the journey for the block train was on the Main Northern Line, but this section was run in darkness. Here another goods service on the same route sees a 60 Class Garratt taking over from a 46 Class electric locomotive just north of Gosford yard.

FERNTREE GULLY TO GEMBROOK
PUFFING BILLY

The main routes radiating from the Victorian capital, Melbourne, were broad gauge. With the great depression of the 1890s, the Victorian government sought cheaper ways of handling the traffic in remoter parts of the State, with the result that four branch lines were built to 760 mm gauge for these areas. However, with the double handling of all freight and the coming of motor road vehicles, these lines soon became liabilities. Cutbacks and closures commenced in 1944, with services no longer running to Walhalla, and the final closure was that of the Beech Forest line in 1962.

The line from Upper Ferntree Gully to Gembrook was closest to Melbourne and became a popular tourist entry to

INFORMATION BOX

PUFFING BILLY

Termini	Ferntree Gully and Gembrook
Country	Australia
Distance	29 km (18 miles)
Date of opening	1900

the Dandenong Ranges. However, following several landslides about 10 km (6 miles) from Upper Ferntree Gully, railway services were abandoned from August 1953. The 29 km (18 mile) line had first been opened in December

● **RIGHT**
The Puffing Billy Preservation Society's 2-6-2T locomotive No. 7A crossing a curved wooden viaduct shortly after leaving Belgrave in Victoria, while hauling one of its regular tourist services into the Dandenong Ranges.

● **OPPOSITE BELOW**
There are many types of plants and flowers which can be seen from the train. One of these is the Olinda Rhododron.

● **OPPOSITE AND BELOW**
Animals can also be seen such as the koala and the kangaroo.

1900, and with a speed limit of 24 kph (15 mph) the journey took two-and-a-quarter hours.

However, in December 1954, a Melbourne newspaper sponsored trips between Upper Ferntree Gully and Belgrave, about 5 km (3 miles) away, and following public demand further trips were run. In Easter of the following year, the Puffing Billy Preservation Society was formed with the aim of ensuring the retention of the fan trips. These lasted until February 1958 when, with the expansion of the Melbourne Metropolitan area, the Government decided to widen the gauge to Belgare and electrify the line.

The volunteers of the PBPS again went into battle to attempt to restore and re-open the balance of the abandoned line. Through the work of the volunteers, aided by the 3rd Field Engineer Regiment of the Citizen Military Forces, scouts etc., a new station and locomotive depot was built at Belgrave and the line restored to Menzies Creek, about 5 km (3 miles) away. This included a 2-chain (20 m/66 ft) radius deviation around the landslide, which had caused the closure

of the line. Services recommenced in July 1962, and the society also established a museum at Menzies Creek.

Since then the society has grown in leaps and bounds, and work is in progress from both ends to complete the line once again to Gembrook. Passenger-traffic is heavy and growing, with most of it being handled by NA Class 2-6-2T locomotives, an 1898 American Baldwin design, although later engines of the same design were built locally. Also serviceable is a

former timber line Climax, but this is too slow for regular traffic. The society owns a Victorian Railways narrow-gauge Garratt, and a South African Garratt has recently been acquired for conversion to 760 mm gauge to handle the growing traffic. New carriages are currently being built, so there is certainly confidence in the future. A Taiwanese Shay has been acquired for the museum, as well as a large variety of narrow-gauge locomotives from over Australia, which makes a visit well worth while.

The route has a ruling grade of 1:30, limiting the load of the NA Class locomotives to 90 tonnes. Tight curves abound, and much of the country is heavily timbered. In places the suburban sprawl can be seen, and later a few farms. From Menzies Creek, the line descends to Clematis, once known as Paradise Valley, an area of rolling fields and stately homes, before the downhill run takes it to the banks of Emerald Lake and Lakeside, the current terminus for the tourist services. Unfortunately this part of Victoria has been subject to some disastrous bush fires, but the railway has survived and continues to progress.

ZEEHAN TO STRAHAN
A WEST COAST SAFARI

Though the smallest state of Australia, Tasmania probably has the greatest variety of scenery, and any traveller thinking of assessing the State in a few days has much to learn. The north-west coast has a very English atmosphere about it, but heading southwards along the west coast we find rain forest in rugged mountainous country cut by deep ravines. This wild country, however, has meant more to Tasmania's economy than the rest of the State, for the area is rich in minerals, possessing huge deposits of tin, lead, silver, gold, copper and iron ores. As it is difficult country for road construction, access to the deposits was generally achieved by tramways or railways.

In its day Mount Bischoff was the largest tin mine in the world, and the Van Diemens Land Company connected the

INFORMATION BOX	
Termini	Zeehan and Strahan
Country	Australia
Distance	46 km (28 miles)
Date of opening	1892

area to Burnie with a horse tramway in 1878. This was soon converted to a 1,067 mm gauge railway, the first 59 km (37 miles) now being the northern end of the private Emu Bay Railway.

Galena (lead sulphide) deposits were found at Zeehan, and transport for the silver was also needed. The Government was finally persuaded to construct a line to the coastal port of Strahan, and in 1892 this 46 km (28 mile) line with a ruling gauge of 1:40 was opened.

Meanwhile, huge copper ore deposits had been found at Mount Lyell, and by

● **ABOVE**
The Mt Lyell Mining & Railway Company's line connecting their copper mine in Tasmania with the coast was through lush rain forest. This is a passenger's view ahead shortly before the line closed in 1963.

● **BELOW LEFT**
Tourists inspect the push-up engine, while the lead engine fills its tanks at the summit at Rinadeena.

● **BELOW RIGHT**
From the left, a tourist bus waits on a flat wagon to be shunted on to the train; a hired Tasmanian Railways diesel–mechanical locomotive waits with a goods-train bound for Zeehan; No. 6, an immaculate Dübs 4-8-0, and an Australian Standard Garratt waits with a goods-train that will follow behind.

● **RIGHT**
One of the problems leading to the closure of the Mt Lyell railway in Tasmania was the cost of maintenance on the "quarter mile bridge" over the King River, seen here being crossed by a Drewry diesel locomotive.

1899 the Mt Lyell Mining and Railway Company had constructed a tortuous but very scenic 34 km (21 mile) line of which 7 km (4^1/$_2$ miles) was operated on 1:16 and 1:20 grades on the Abt rack principle to Regatta Point near Strahan, a journey of two hours' duration. The Emu Bay Railway, seeing business potential in this area, pushed their line southwards through dense forests and over various streams to reach Zeehan, 142 km (88 miles) from Burnie, in 1901.

As the Government had connected Strahan to Regatta Point in 1900, it was then possible to travel all the way from Burnie on the north-west coast to Mount Lyell, using three different carriers. Owing to the light track, speeds were seldom in excess of 16 kph (10 mph), but in 1912 when a fire, caused by arsonists, occurred in the Mount Lyell mine with 170 men underground, the train racing breathing apparatus, rescue equipment and personnel to the mine cut

five hours off the journey, resulting in the saving of many lives.

The copper and barytes from Mount Lyell was loaded on to shipping at Regatta Point, and the silver from Zeehan went on the Emu Bay railway, leaving the government line to decline rapidly, operated by one locomotive and a railcar. The line closed in 1960.

Tourism was growing on the west coast and the Mount Lyell Railway, probably the most scenic in Australia

with its rack line over mountainous rain forest country and the King River gorge alongside, soon attracted its share. Unfortunately the owners and the Government still decided to close the line in 1963. Today, eight diesel-hydraulic locomotives coupled together bring in Mount Lyell ore between Zeehan and Roseberry. Tour trains periodically travel the line, and a Dübs locomotive is currently under restoration with a view to recreating the "West Coaster" express.

● **RIGHT**
Just north of Rosebery on the Emu Bay Railway in Tasmania was the Pieman River bridge, here being crossed by a tourist special of Tasmanian Railway's coaches in their "blood and custard" colours being hauled by a 10 Class BBR diesel-hydraulic locomotive during Easter 1965. With the damming of the river for hydro-electric purposes, the line has since been deviated to higher ground and a new bridge built.

PACIFIC COAST MOTORAIL

Since surfing became fashionable, a section of over 30 km (19 miles) of the Australian coastline just north of the New South Wales border from Coolangatta to Southport has been developed into the major holiday destination in Australia. Known as the Gold Coast, it caters for almost all levels of society, the temperate climate allowing it to be a resort all the year round.

Queenslanders had had access by a narrow-gauge train for many years, but, owing to the slow service, buses soon won this traffic and the line closed. However, with the Brisbane suburban electrification, a new line is being opened along part of the length of the coast.

The big influx of tourists come from the south – New South Wales and Victoria – though direct transport has been slow in coming to feed this area. Prior to the mid-1920s, Sydneysiders had to travel north to Brisbane by the main northern line, which crossed to the west

of the Great Dividing Range. Then they continued to the Queensland border, well inland from the coast, where a change was made to the narrow gauge to cross the Great Divide again and descend to Brisbane, where another train was caught to the Gold Coast.

The Clarence River was the main obstacle to a coastal journey. An isolated section of railway had been built from Lismore via Byron Bay to Murwillumbah, about 32 km (20 miles) south of the

border on the coast, prior to the turn of the century, but it was not until 1924 that the two sections of coastal line faced each other across the Clarence River at Grafton and a train ferry service was introduced. Although the standard-gauge track reached Brisbane in September 1930, the ferry continued until May 1932, when a double-deck road-rail bridge was built over the river.

The Department of Railways, however, did not see an early need for

● **ABOVE**
Hauled by two 442 Class locomotives, the Pacific Coast Motorail heads north from Lismore. The locomotives and the sitting cars at the end of the train are in a short-lived "candy" colour scheme, while the power car and sleeping cars are of stainless steel.

● **LEFT**
With the elimination of almost all locomotive hauled passenger-trains in NSW, the Pacific Coast Motorail was superseded by the XPTs. Here an XPT charges through regrowth timber country near Bonville in northern New South Wales.

● **RIGHT**
The 1990s saw the
introduction of XPT
inter-city services,
speeding up the
timetable
considerably. Not
only was the speed
limit raised to 160
kph (100 mph) but
also many of the
smaller stopping-
places were closed.
Here we see a
southbound XPT
crossing Boambee
Creek between the
coastal resorts of
Coffs Harbour
and Sawtell.

● **BELOW**
The southbound
Pacific Coast
Motorail
approaching
Lismore.

more direct traffic to the Gold Coast, and
intending travellers had to catch the
Brisbane Express and change trains at the
crack of dawn for a branch-line service to
Murwillumbah, where a bus would
complete the journey. Eventually the
traffic potential of the holiday seekers
was realized, and in the early 1970s a
through service to Murwillumbah was
introduced, which included car carriers
for those wishing to travel around the
extensive holiday area. This was known as
the Gold Coast Motorail.

Whether owing to interstate jealousies
or a desire to promote the northern coast
of New South Wales, in the 1980s the
train also unloaded cars *en route* at Casino
and was renamed the Pacific Coast

Motorail. Today, with the almost
complete elimination of locomotive-
hauled passenger-trains, this service has
gone. Now an XPT service runs the route,
with a bus connection at Murwillumbah.

The Motorail service, with sleeping
cars, departed Sydney at 06.25 with the

INFORMATION BOX

Termini	Sydney and Murwillumbah
Country	Australia
Length	935 km (581 miles)
Date of opening	1932

first light of dawn creeping over at
somewhere near Coffs Harbour. Here the
mountains come almost to the coast, and
the huge banana plantations, which cover
the hillsides, could be seen from the train
between the various tunnels.

The train turned inland and ran
through hilly and well-timbered country
northwards to reach South Grafton, a
former meal-stop, where it crossed the
river and continued north through
undulating timber country to the town of
Casino. Then came Byron Bay, the
easternmost point of Australia. Further
north, sugar cane country was entered,
before the train finally descended to the
Tweed River at Murwillumbah, where it
arrived at 13.05.

CHRISTCHURCH TO GREYMOUTH
THE TRANSALPINE ROUTE

New Zealand is not well known for its railways. This is a shame, as some of the scenery traversed is the equal of anywhere else. The 233 km (145 mile) long Midland line is probably the most scenic route in New Zealand. Construction, by the English-financed New Zealand Midland Railway Company, commenced in 1885.

Unfortunately progress was slow and after ten years, with only about 60 km (37 miles) in service, the Government took possession of the line and continued its construction. In those days, with limited engineering equipment available, the most difficult task was the boring of the tunnel section from Arthur's Pass to Otira. After much consideration of alternative ways of crossing the mountain range this 8.6 km (5^1/$_2$ mile) long tunnel, with a descent at 1:33 from Arthur's Pass to Otira, was started in August 1908, but was only opened almost 15 years to the day later on 4 August 1923.

It had been a very difficult bore, with World War I adding to the problems that nature imposed. At the time of its

● LEFT
Between Otira and Arthur's Pass on the Transalpine route is an 8.6 km (5^1/$_2$ mile) long tunnel on a 1:33 grade. To assist trains through the tunnel, three Toshiba Bo-Bo electric locomotives working in multiple are used through the tunnel. At Arthur's Pass the threesome prepare for the next journey.

opening, this tunnel was claimed to be the seventh longest in the world. With such a steep grade in such a long tunnel, working heavy trains through by steam was most uncomfortable, not to say dangerous, and so the tunnel was electrified at 1,500 volts d.c., and five Bo-Bo locomotives were imported from the English Electric Company.

This tunnel, however, was not the only one along the route. Another 16 tunnels occur in a very short section near Staircase along the scenic gorge of the

Waimakiri River, as do many spectacular viaducts and bridges, and a further two tunnels at the western end of the line.

Commencing a journey from Christchurch, a little over the first hour of the trip is spent travelling over the Canterbury Plains *en route* to Springfield, 71 km (44 miles) away. From here the Alps come into view and the line follows the Waimakariri River in its spectacular gorge. Four large viaducts and 16 tunnels are features of the next section to Avoca, 97 km (60 miles) from Christchurch. Soon mountain ranges become visible, and the line parts company with the Waimakariri River a little before Cora Lynn, 125 km (78 miles) from the start of the journey.

From here the train enters Arthur's Pass National Park, a popular tourist destination throughout the year. Arthur's

● LEFT
In 1923, to make more bearable the passage through the 8.6 km (5^1/$_2$ mile) long Otira tunnel, with its 1:33 grade, New Zealand Railways electrified the tunnel. With the original electric locomotives worn out, five replacement Bo-Bo units of 1286 hp were obtained from Toshiba in Japan. Normally these locomotives worked in threes, one being spare and one in the workshops for servicing. Here they are seen at the Arthur's Pass end of the tunnel.

● LEFT
The Transalpine route across the South Island
follows the Waimakariri River for a
considerable portion of the journey. This view
is taken from the train.

INFORMATION BOX	
Termini	Christchurch and Greymouth
Country	New Zealand
Distance	233 km (145 miles)
Date of opening	1923

Pass station, at an elevation of 737 m
(2,418 ft), is the highest station in the
South Island of New Zealand. Once
through the Otira tunnel, rivers and lakes
are a feature of the continuing scenery.
Coral mining activity is evident near the
west coast, as the gold rush that sparked
interest in the west coast never really
happened. At Greymouth, on the west
coast, the present-day journey ends
some 4 hours and 25 minutes after
leaving Christchurch.

From 1939, in steam days, much of

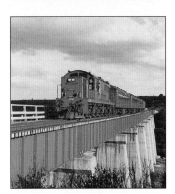

the traffic was handled by New Zealand's
most powerful non-articulated
locomotives, the Kb Class. Through the
Otira tunnel the trains were hauled,
generally triple-headed, by electric Eo
Class locomotives. These old electrics
were replaced in 1968 by five new
Toshiba units, which are also worked
with three coupled together. Steam had
now been replaced by Mitsubishi diesel-
electrics with a Bo-Bo-Bo wheel
arrangement. These units are powered by
Caterpillar diesels and are rated at 670kV.

● ABOVE
RIGHT
Diesel electric
locomotive Dj-1218
crossing the Kowai
viaduct. This is the
first viaduct on the
Transalpine route,
just before the
railway enters the
Waimakariri gorge.

● RIGHT
Dj 1218 hauls a
tourist train across
the Broken River
viaduct on the
Transalpine route.
The view on one side
of the train is
unfortunately
blocked out by the
windshield needed
to prevent trains
being blown off
the bridge in
bad weather.

CHRISTCHURCH TO WELLINGTON –
THE COASTAL PACIFIC EXPRESS

The route from Christchurch to
Wellington travels through spectacular
scenery which is the equal of anywhere
else in the world. In 1991, there were
only long-distance passenger services
operating over five routes, and only one
of these, Wellington to Auckland, had
more than one train each way per day. In
addition, Auckland and Wellington have
commuter railways, the latter electrified.
Subsequently, New Zealand Railways
(NZR) has been taken over by Wisconsin
Rail of the USA (who have also taken
over most of the UK freight operation
under the name English, Welsh &
Scottish Railways).

This train journey is from
Christchurch to Wellington by the
Coastal Pacific Express. More accurately,
it goes to Picton, from where the railway-
owned inter-island ferry must be taken
to reach Wellington. This journey
exemplifies the problem facing long-haul
services in New Zealand, for it takes
nine-and-a-half hours by rail and boat,
but only one hour by air. There is only

● **ABOVE**
The old "colonial" style is nicely represented
in this street in Christchurch.

● **BELOW**
The sea reflects the blue of the sky in this
placid scene near Christchurch.

limited consolation in the fact that the
roads are not much quicker.

The journey starts from Christchurch
station, a big 1960s building on a large
site, both echoing the past rather than
the drastically reduced present. Two of
NZR's other passenger services also start
from here, the Trans-Alpine Express
going over Arthur's Pass in the New
Zealand Alps to Greymouth and the
Southerner Express to Dunedin and
Invercargill.

Christchurch was home to one of the
four areas of electrified railways in New
Zealand, the short and now dieselized
route through the tunnel to the nearest
port at Lyttelton. The other electrified
sections, all remaining, are the summit
tunnel at Arthur's Pass, the central
section of the Wellington to Auckland
main line (the North Island Trunk) and
the Wellington suburban network.

The Coastal Pacific follows the South
Island Trunk, as it hugs the eastern side
of the South Island. This line took a long
time to build, as it was affected not only
by the difficult terrain to be crossed, but

● **RIGHT**
Diesel locomotive DF 6162 at the head of the
Coastal Pacific Express at Kaikoura. Thirty
1,230 kW locomotives was delivered by
General Motors Canada in 1979–80.

also by various communities each
preferring different routes. The current
general route was decided upon in 1883,
although the first section along this route
had been opened in 1872. The final
detail of the route was revised several
times until the late 1930s. The through
route was only completed in December
1945, when the section between
Parnassus and Wharanui was opened.
The further delays had been brought
about by two world wars and economic
depressions, both local and global. The
track is laid to 3 ft 6 in Cape Gauge,
although some early sections had been
laid initially with a gauge of 5 ft 3 in.
Although only around 100 km (60 miles)
of the 348 km (216 miles) is by the sea,
it is visions of the rugged scenery on this
section that remain in the mind of the
rail traveller.

The railborne part of the journey
takes 5 hours and 20 minutes to reach
Picton, where there is a 50-minute
connection into the "Interislander" ferry.

● **ABOVE**
South-east of Blenheim there are views from
the train of Cook Strait, with the North Island
visible in the distance. The railway curves
around to pass through the cutting in the
centre of the picture.

● **LEFT**
A view of coastline from the train south of
Kaikoura. The route of the railway and coastal
road can be seen hugging the coastline around
the promontory.

INFORMATION BOX

Termini	Christchurch and Wellington
Country	New Zealand
Distance	348 km (216 miles)
Date of opening	1945

of the line and various sites to be seen
from the train. Cream teas are available
as part of the food service, along with
cold snacks and a bar service. This
innovation obviated the need for the
trains to make long stops at certain
stations to allow passengers to visit the
refreshment rooms, a practice that had
continued right up until introduction of
the Coastal Pacific.

Leaving Christchurch, the route
crosses flat farmland before entering the
rolling hill country of North Canterbury.

The train consists of three coaches and a
baggage van hauled by a DF Class diesel
locomotive. The coaches are a batch of
vehicles modernized for what amount to
tourist services introduced in September
1988 by enlarging the windows, covering
the seats with lambswool, installing a
public address system etc. They were
painted in the long-distance passenger-
coach livery of blue with red-and-white
stripes. There is a hostess aboard the
train, giving a commentary on the history

● RIGHT
Gorse frequently
provides a startling
splash of colour on
the journey to
Christchurch.

● BELOW
The Cook Strait lives
up to its reputation
for rough seas.

The foothills of the central mountain
range are visible almost immediately.
Soon the traveller becomes aware of a
recurring feature of the journey, the
crossing of the estuaries of rivers flowing
down from the Southern Alps into the
Pacific Ocean. Some of these estuaries
are very wide and require long viaducts
to take the railway across. The Ashley
River, 35 km (22 miles) from
Christchurch and the second river
crossing, is one of the longest at 549 m
(1,801 ft). After around 80 km (50
miles), the train reaches the highest point
on the line, 135 m (443 ft) above sea
level, at Spye. Just before Parnassus, the
706 m (2,316 ft) bridge crossing the
Waiau River is the longest on this route.

The Pacific coastal section, between Claverley and Wharanui is very attractive, hugging the rocky shore and including 20 tunnels in its 100 km (60 miles). The statistics for this stretch of line (plus the stretch to Parnassus) give some idea of the work involved – there are 43 bridges totalling 3.2 km (2 miles) in length; 2.9 million cubic metres (102 million cubic feet) of rock and spoil had to be excavated; and between Goose Bay and Kowhai the road had to be extended over the beach to make way for the railway. Hawkeswood cutting, just north of Parnassus, is, at over one kilometre ($\frac{2}{3}$ mile) long and up to 19 m (62 ft) deep, the largest in New Zealand. It is near here that the train passes from Canterbury into Marlborough on crossing the Conway River.

After leaving the coast, the railway crosses the salt lakes of Lake Grasmere on a causeway. The section on to Blenheim includes a double-deck viaduct

near Seddon to cross the Awatere River,
where the railway track takes the top
deck, and the road takes the lower.

After Blenheim the line passes into
one of New Zealand's major wine-
producing areas. A little way north of
Blenheim is the 293 m (961 ft) bridge
across the Wairau River. The stretch
through hills to Picton crosses the 129 m
(423 ft) Waitohi viaduct, once the largest
timber trestle bridge in the country, but
now a concrete bridge. Picton, a small
town that has flourished as a result of
being the port for the inter-island ferry,
is approached on a 1:37 gradient, the
steepest on the route. This gradient is a
result of the town's picturesque setting,
surrounded by large hills, which form a
major barrier for the railway.

Most stations no longer have freight
facilities as a result of transport
deregulation in the 1980s, and rail
business is now dominated by container
traffic. The increasing power available
from newer locomotives is allowing an
increase in train weights and a reduction

in the number of services.

The inter-island roll-on, roll-off
ferries were introduced in 1962, with
management passing to NZR in 1971.
This service is marketed as the
"Interislander". The four crossings each
way per day carry road and rail vehicles
and form an integral part of the New

Zealand railways freight network.

The port of Picton is a fair way from
the open sea, on a side fjord off the
Queen Charlotte Sound. While this does
not have the towering mountainsides that
the name suggests – for that one should
visit Milford Sound on the south-west
corner of the South Island – the hilly

country around the watercourse is attractive. Nearer the sea, seals can often be seen sunning themselves on the rocks.

The boat journey across the Cook Strait takes 3 hours and 20 minutes for the 52 nautical miles (96 km). One of the ferries used is the *Aratika*, originally built in France in 1974 as a train ferry but converted in 1976 to carry cars and passengers along with rail wagons.

While the approach to Wellington is by no means as scenic as the departure from Picton, it gives a different view of the city, the central area of which is steep enough to warrant a (Swiss-built) funicular. Foot passengers are met on the quay at Wellington by the "Interislander" shuttle bus and taken to the bus station outside Wellington railway station.

Anyone visiting New Zealand should try to make time to travel the Coastal Pacific Express. The scenery alone is worth the time; the glimpses of the "real" New Zealand, away from the tourist areas, are a bonus.

● **ABOVE**
The impressive rocky coastline at Castle Point near Wellington is a popular spot for visitors.

● **BELOW**
The attractive coastline near Wellington is further embellished by a geyser.

PICTON TO CHRISTCHURCH
THE COASTAL PACIFIC EXPRESS

● **BELOW LEFT**
Centre cab shunters exchange wagons
between ship and shore.

Historically, the important commercial
centre of Wellington, on New Zealand's
North Island, has been linked to the city
of Christchurch – seat of provincial
government and gateway to the vast
agricultural hinterland of Canterbury –
on the South Island, by a network of
coastal steamers.

  The first proposal for a rail line to join
the two was mooted in 1861. A broad-
gauge line was commenced northwards
under the auspices of the Provincial
Government in 1872. It was later
converted to 3 ft 6 in gauge in 1877. A
line southwards from Picton was opened
in 1875. Further construction followed
as resources and political decisiveness
permitted, but, even by 1916, the
northern line had reached only so far as
Wharanui, 90 km (56 miles) from
Picton, while the southern section
penetrated as far as Parnassus, 133 km
(83 miles) from Christchurch. It was to
be another 20 years before meaningful

INFORMATION BOX	
THE COASTAL PACIFIC EXPRESS	
Termini	Picton and Christchurch
Country	New Zealand
Distance	rail 348 km (216 miles); sea crossing 80 km (50 miles)
Date of opening	1945

progress was made in closing the gap,
through the fearsome mountainous
terrain around Kaikoura. The line
opened throughout officially on
15 December 1945.

  In 1954, a rail roll-on, roll-off ferry
altered the connecting sea crossing and,
in 1988, the service was transformed by
the introduction of rebuilt rolling stock.
The trip provides four main features of

● **LEFT**
No. 6110 at the head
of the southbound
Coastal Pacific
Express at Picton.
The locomotive is a
DF Class Co-Co
built by General
Motors, Canada, in
1979 and is rated at
1250 kW.

interest. After the sea crossing, memorable in itself, comes the ride through the hills of Marlborough, followed by the exhilarating passage through the harsher mountains around Kaikoura with the Pacific Ocean as an intimate companion, and finally the gentler landscape leading towards Canterbury Plain.

After the passage across the exposed waters of the Cook Strait, one enters the comparatively sheltered area of the Marlborough Sound. Here there is a multitude of islands and islets, some little more than wave-washed rocks, others massive crags or verdant mounds. Wildlife is abundant.

The final passage to the port in its sheltered setting is almost serene after the earlier bluster. The community of Picton, with its jetty, rail and freight yards and low-rise housing, is dominated by the surrounding ridges and peaks, not unlike a port serving the Western Isles of Scotland.

One can watch the unloading and loading of railway traffic from the ferry if one wishes or, perhaps more prudently,

retrieve one's baggage from the somewhat unsupervised free-for-all below. Once rightful ownership is secured, there is time to survey the train that will provide the rest of the journey.

The concept of a "luxury" service on the route had followed the successful introduction of a similar service between Christchurch and Greymouth through the alpine scenery of South Island. Several existing coaches were converted, receiving large (2 m x 1 m; 6 ft 6 in x 1 ft 4 in) panoramic windows, separated by narrow pillars, that provide excellent visibility. The seats, which face each other in pairs across a large snack table either side of the central aisle, have high backs and are sumptuously furnished in sheepskin. Wall to wall carpeting, large ventilators, curtains and an effective public address system furnish an attractive environment. Internal colours are pink and grey, while the external livery is mid-blue relieved by white-and-red bands. A buffet car provides both snacks and a full bar service. Uniformed attendants and a well-informed

● LEFT
Road and rail share the narrow coastal strip between Pacific breakers and mountains, which proved such an obstacle to the construction of the line.

conductor making sensible use of the PA all add to the ambience of the journey.

Once everyone is aboard, the train winds out of Picton and commences a steep 1:37 climb, and rumbles across the sweeping 129 m (423 ft) Waitohi viaduct. The town, itself originally known as Waitohi, is overshadowed by tumbling tree-clad foothills, jumbled peaks and the waters of the sound. By Elevation, 4 km (2¹/₂ miles) from Picton, the mountains take on an Italianate or Austrian alpine air, with strands of conifer and dusty logging tracks, but the pastures below with their scattered specimen trees owe more to English parkland, albeit with trees unfamiliar to visitors.

Before Blenheim, the train passes the blue waters and gravel banks of the Wairau on a long low bridge. Blenheim itself serves as the gateway to the increasingly well-known wine growing regions of Marlborough. Beyond Blenheim, the train commences yet another long ascent, this time towards the bleaker regions of Dashwood Pass, the 8 km (5 mile) 1:53 climb being presaged by a sweeping horseshoe curve. The mountains here are softened by the effects of the elements into smooth folds rather than pronounced peaks, the more sheltered pockets offering a refuge for isolated clumps of low trees.

Another grade takes the train to the unusual bridge over the Awatere River. This is a combination bridge with the railway carried on an upper deck and the road below. The next point of note on the trip is Blind River, the site of the worst crash on the line in 1948 when six people were killed. The train then crosses over a long causeway, the vast salt lakes on the approach to Lake Grasmere.

Near Wharanui, the long stretch of coastal running begins. From here the traveller can enjoy some one-and-a-half hours of superb scenery before the stop at Kaikoura. For much of the way, railway and road are squeezed into a narrow strip between beach and mountain. In the approximately 100 km (62 miles) of line to Oaro there are 20 tunnels, numerous embankments and steep cuttings, sharp curves and lonely bridges, of which there are more than 40 along the central section of line. One stretch of track, known as the "Blue Slip", is notorious for the highly unstable nature of the ground through which it passes in cutting: the local rock of blue pug absorbs water easily, and the whole hillside is heading slowly for the sea.

As gullies come down to the sea and the train speeds on, there are glimpses of remote valleys, sheltering between flowing hills and rising gently to more majestic and mysterious mountains. The sinuous course of the line, which follows the indentations of the sea, is interrupted

as Kaikoura – its name is said to be from
the Maori *kai* (food) and *koura* (crayfish)
– is approached. This fishing centre and
former whaling community lies on a
peninsula about half-way between Picton
and Christchurch.

　　Here the train pauses long enough for
passengers to alight from the train and
stretch their legs, a reminder of when it
needed to stop for refreshments.
Onboard buffet facilities now make such
an extended halt redundant, but the old
building is still there and retains much of
its former charm.

　　Leaving the town on another curving
viaduct, there is a further period of
spectacular coastal running with a stretch
of line with nine tunnels in as many
kilometres. Beyond Oaro, at sea level
again, the train climbs steeply and
encounters the almost kilometre ($^2/_3$
mile) long tunnel at Amuri Bluff and the
adjacent Okarahia viaduct. Soon the
suburbs of Christchurch come into view
and this spectacular journey is sadly over.

● ABOVE
RIGHT
Canterbury has seen
many architectural
styles, and as yet
traffic has not
reached the urban
levels found
elsewhere.

● OPPOSITE
Clumps of low trees
find sheltered
pockets in the
windswept hills
beyond Blenheim.

● RIGHT
The ferry port of
Picton on South
Island nestles in the
lee of mountains at
the head of
Marlborough
Sound.

ACKNOWLEDGEMENTS AND CONTRIBUTORS

The Publishers would like to thank the following contributors for pieces written in this book.

George Beherand
Europe: Paris to Istanbul; Calais to Istanbul. Egypt: Cairo to Aswan. Turkey: Istanbul to Baghdad. The Middle East: Istanbul to Kars; Istanbul to Teheran; Malaysia and Thailand: Singapore to Bangkok.

Gary Buchanan
South Africa: Cape Town to Victoria Falls.

Tom Ferris
Ireland: Dublin to Cork; Cavan to Leitrim; Dromod to Belturbet. Northern Ireland: Londonderry to Burtonport.

Colin Garratt
India: Pulgaon to Arui. Indonesia: Tanahabang to Rangkasbitung; Rangkasbitung to Labuan.

Alex Grunbach
Australia: Port Augusta to Alice Springs; Sydney to Brisbane; Broken Hill to Adelaide; Brisbane to Cairns; Port Kembla to Moss Vale; Sydney to Perth; Broken Hill to Sulphide Junction; Ferntree Gully to Gembrook; Zeehan to Strahan; Pacific Coast Motorail. New Zealand: Christchurch to Greymouth.

Frank Hornby
Europe: Across Europe by MEDLOC.

Alan Pike
UK: Edinburgh to Wick/Thurso. Europe: London to Cologne. Switzerland: Cornergrat to St Moritz; Pilatus. Europe: London Waterloo to Bern. Hungary: Budapest to Lake Balaton. India: Kalyan to Howrah. Malaysia and Thailand: Singapore to Penang.

Graham Pike
Portugal: Tunes to Lisbon. China: Ulan Bator to Datong. New Zealand: Picton to Christchurch.

Christopher Portway
Canada: White Horse to Skagway. Peru: Juliaca to Cuzco. Ecuador: Gauyaquil to Quito. Albania: Fier to Vlore, Shkoder to Durres. North Africa: Casablanca to Gabes; Nairobi to Kampala. Iraq: Basra to Baghdad. USSR: Red Arrow Express. Pakistan: Quetta to Zaheidan; Lindi Kotal to Peshawar. India: Delhi to Cochin; Delhi to Jodhpur; Kalka to Simla. Europe/Asia: Brussels to Hong Kong. North Korea: Tumenjan to Pyongyang.

Brian Solomon
USA: The San Francisco Muni; St Albans, Vermont to Washington DC; Boston to Chicago; Chicago to Oakland; Seattle to Los Angeles; Bellows Falls to Chester, Vermont; Chicago Metra; Milwaukee to East Troy; Boone Scenic Railway. Japan: Fuji to Kofu; Tokyo's Yamamite Line.

Max Wade-Matthews
Introduction; Chile: Santa Rosa de Los Andes to Las Cuevas. Paraguay: Asunción to Encarnación. UK: Leicester to Loughborough; Fort William to Mallaig; Settle to Carlisle; London Euston to Glasgow; London King's Cross to Edinburgh; London Paddington to Swansea; London Euston to Holyhead; London Paddington to Penzance; London Victoria to Dover; Bedford to Bletchley. South Africa: Cape Town to Pretoria. Jordan: Damascus to Medina. USSR: Moscow to Vladivostok. India: Siliguri to Darjeeling. China: Shenyang to Harbin. Japan: Tokyo to Osaka.

Kenneth Westcott-Jones
Canada: Toronto to Vancouver; Sault Sainte Marie to Hearst. USA: Chicago to Seattle; Pueblo to Durango; Manitou Springs to Pike's Peak. Mexico: Los Mochis to Chihuahua. Brazil: Santos to São Paulo.

Neil Wheelwright
Canada: Vancouver to Squamish; Norway: Norway to Flåm. South Africa: Cape Town to Pretoria. Japan: Tokyo to Nikko. New Zealand: Christchurch to Wellington.

- **ABOVE**
The Glacier Express, on one of the world's most spectacular scenic railway journeys, Gornergrat to St Moritz, Switzerland.

Picture Acknowledgements
The majority of the pictures in this book were provided by Milepost 92 ½. The Publishers would also like to thank the following people and organizations for additional pictures:

Howard Ande: p9. Adrian Baker/Photobank: pp231M, 231B, 234B, 234T. Jeanetta Baker/Photobank: pp188T, 189T, 189BR, 191TL, 213T, 215B, 217T, 236T, 237B. Peter Baker/Photobank: pp134T, 134B, 135B, 190T, 191BL, 212B, 214T, 215TL, 216B, 236B. Paul Barney/Travel Ink: p227B. Nick Battersby/Travel Ink: pp150T, 151B. George Behrend: pp90, 91T, 92, 94, 96B, 97, 151M, 151TL, 152B, 153T, 154T, 156T, 157BL, 158T. Beyer Peacock & Co. Ltd: p144T. W G Boyden/F Hornby: p123ML. Gary Buchanan: pp140BL, 140M, 140BR, 141, 142T, 143T, 145B. Brian Burchell: pp5, 77T. Carlos Reyes-Manzo – Andes Press Agency: pp48B, 49M. Trevor Creighton/Travel Ink: pp224B, 225T, 225BL. A E Durrant: pp52, 53BR, 142T, 145T. The Eastern and Oriental Express Press Office: pp130, 210T, 211TR, 211B. Abbie Enock/Travel Ink: pp152T, 152M, 153B, 154BL, 155B, 173. Tom Ferris: pp56-7, 58T, 59-61. Alex Grunbach: pp 222M 224T, 225BR, 226, 227T, 228TR, 228L, 229T, 230, 231T, 232-3, 234T, 235B, 237T, 238-43. Allan Hartley/Travel Ink: pp170T, 171. Frank Hornby: pp86M, 87T, 88T, 89T, 122, 123MR, 124T, 125. G Holland: pp228L, 229B. T Hudson: pp23TL, 48T. Brian Lovell: pp208B. Office National des Chemins de Fer, Rabat: pp132-3. Ontario Government Tourism: pp13TL. A W Mace: pp65T, 82T. Gavin Morrison: pp50, 51TL, 51BL, 54M, 54B, 143TR, 143B, 144B, 160-1. David Patterson: pp10T, 11TR. Jeremy Phillips: p227M. Alan Pike: pp67, 86B, 87B, 87M, 88B, 89M, 89B, 98-103, 104, 105, 106, 109, 110, 111, 112, 113, 114, 115, 212T, 212M, 213M, 213B, 214B, 215TR, 216T, 217B, 254. Graham Pike: pp11M, 118B, 119TR, 120B, 121, 196-7, 244, 246M, 246B, 247B, 248-53. Christopher Portway: pp10B, 19B, 53T, 53BL, 54T, 64TR, 116, 117, 163B, 165M, 166T, 168, 169B, 176-81, 192B, 193T. Seaco Picture Library: pp82B, 83T, 91B, 95T. William Sharman: pp64B, 65B, 68, 69B. Gordon Smith/Photobank: p236B. Brian Solomon: pp1, 4, 20, 21, 23TR, 23B, 24, 25, 28-43, 198-201, 208T, 208M, 209, 255, 256. South American Pictures: pp46 (David Lorimer), 47 (Tony Morrison). SX Picture Desk: pp10M, 11M. Gordon Stemp: p58B. David Toase/Travel Ink: pp162B, 163TR, 164T, 165T, 165B. Max Wade-Matthews: pp62R, 134M, 167T. A M Wellington: p47. Kenneth Westcott-Jones: pp10TL, 22R, 26, 27, 44, 45, 136-7, 162T, 163M, 164B. Neil Wheelwright: pp14, 15, 16, 17, 126-9, 146-9, 201-7, 245, 246T, 247T. Thanks also to ianród éireann for supplying some of the pictures used for the journeys in Ireland.

INDEX

● ABOVE
**Boone & Scenic Valley's only active steam
locomotive is No. JS8419, a 1988 product of
China's Datong locomotive works.**

● ABOVE
A Fujikawa express train at Shimobe. Shimobe
-Onsen is a principal station and most trains,
including the Fujikawa expresses, stop here.

NOTES

NOTES

NOTES

NOTES

NOTES

NOTES

NOTES

NOTES